OASIS JOURNAL

2014

Stories

Poems

Essays

by Writers Over Fifty

Edited by Leila Joiner

Copyright © 2014 by Leila Joiner

All rights reserved. No part of this book may be reproduced or transmitted in any form or by any means, electronic or mechanical, including photocopying, recording, or by any information storage and retrieval system, without permission in writing from the publisher.

Published in the United States of America by:

Imago Press
3710 East Edison
Tucson AZ 85716

www.oasisjournal.org

Names, characters, places, and incidents, unless otherwise specifically noted, are either the product of the author's imagination or are used fictitiously.

Cover Design and Book Design by Leila Joiner

ISBN 978-1-935437-90-1
ISBN 1-935437-90-9

Printed in the United States of America on Acid-Free Paper

In fond memory of Steven Snyder
and Rebecca Rouillard,
whose poetry has appeared often in
OASIS Journal.

ACKNOWLEDGMENTS

I want to thank the OASIS Institute, all the judges who have generously volunteered their time to select our contest winners and comment on the work of our authors, and all the writers over fifty who continue to contribute their work to *OASIS Journal* every year.

May we all have many successful years ahead of us.

LIST OF ILLUSTRATIONS

"Broken Mirror" © scol22i, p. xxii

"Steam boat" © Foto Factory, p. 34

"Two Gems," photograph courtesy of Fred Bridges p. 66

"Melting Time" images courtesy of John Barbee, p. 82

"Birthday Card" courtesy of Kenneth A. Yaros, p. 88

"Medieval Printing Press" © Juulijs, p. 114

"Single Tree in Donegal" © morrbyte, p. 160

"Camels," photograph © Plum Rote, p. 232

"American football player, silhouette" © Sveta Che, p. 292

"Semper Fi" image courtesy of Alan Dennis, p. 313

CONTENTS

EDITOR'S PREFACE	xvii

WINNER: BEST NON-FICTION CONTEST
    DISILLUSIONED
       Tabinda Bashir
	1

WAITING FOR THE RAIN *Anne Whitlock*	6
A PLACE AT THE TABLE *Jennifer Holliongshead*	7
WISHES *Anne Whitlock*	16
SPRING *Bella Hollingworth*	18
TWO EGGS, AN ORANGE, AND SIX BLACK OLIVES *Muriel Sandy*	19
FACE TO FACE *Nancy Sandweiss*	22
OUR FIRST VALENTINE'S DAY *Yasue Aoki Kidd*	23
MYRIAD FACES OF CHANGE *Ida Jean Smith*	25
GONE TOO SOON *Leona A. Jones*	32

FIRST RUNNER-UP: BEST NON-FICTION CONTEST
    MISSISSIPPI MEMOIRS
       Irene Thomas
	35

BIG DADDY PLAYS AND IS SWEPT INTO THE NIGHT *Fred Bridges*	38

THE PERFECT PITCH *Helen Muriel Ganapole*	39
AT THE AGE *Una Nichols Hynum*	41
TEDDY BEAR PICNIC *Bobbie Jean Bishop*	42
A BEARY, SCARY MOUNTAIN VISIT *Helen Jones-Shepherd*	43
WOMAN IN THE MOON *Claudia Poquoc*	47
THE DEER *Lois J. Godel*	48
BIG FLUFFY *Eleanor Whitney Nelson*	49
WHITE SANDS, N.M. 1953 *Betty Birkemark*	56
POWWOW *Florence Korzin*	57
BREAKFAST IN BED *Kathleen O'Brien*	58
DECEMBER BRUNCH *Jean Brier Lusk*	59
THE STRONGEST MAN *C. A. (Chuck) Peters*	61
WIELDING YOUR MACHETE *Diana Griggs*	65
TWO GEMS CAME OUT OF THE HILLS *Fred Bridges*	67
MARK'S CHAIR *William Killian*	68

WELSH CAKES *Diana Griggs*	70
MY DAD'S SAD STORY ABOUT THE WAR *Ruth Moon Kempher*	71
LITTLE STAR'S MIDNIGHT JOURNEY *Aleane Fitz-Carter*	77
A CHRISTMAS LESSON *Bonnie Papenfuss*	81
TIME IS…SLIP/SLIDING AWAY *Marilyn L. Kish Mason*	83
THE TWELVE DAYS OF CHRISTMAS *Leona A. Jones*	85
BIRTHDAY *Helen Benson*	87
IT'S THANKSGIVING: "DADDY'S" HERE! *Kenneth A. Yaros*	89
BECAUSE I AM HUMAN *Mark S. Fletcher*	95
THE HEALING *Joanne Johnson*	97
RECENT PAST *Bella Hollingworth*	101
RONDA, SPAIN *Dolores Greene Binder*	102
SECOND RUNNER-UP: BEST POETRY CONTEST BASTING THREADS *Ruth Moon Kempher*	104
MOVING ON *Helen Moriarty*	105

COOKIE MACHINE WITH DAD 111
    David P. Cresap

YARD SALE 112
    Norma Glickman

THAT SUNDAY 113
    Rosa Needleman

MEMORIES OF MY FATHER 115
    Laverne Gephart

SMOKE RINGS 118
    Marilyn L. Kish Mason

MY FATHER USED TO… 119
    M. C. Little

ARM IN ARM 120
    Claudia Poquoc

YOU DON'T HAVE TO LOOK TOO FAR 121
    Nancy J. Alauzen

"DON'T STOP TALKING ON MY ACCOUNT" 122
    Sabine Ramage

SIGNALS 123
    Marie Thérèse Gass

A DANCE WITH YOUR DEAD FATHER 128
    Seretta Martin

BONSAI LESSONS 129
    Sandra Shaw Homer

HONORABLE MENTION: POETRY
    THE PRUNING 135
        Lynda Riese

ATTIC ROOM 136
    Rita K. Ries

MOVING 137
    Barbara Scheiber

MINOTAUR 140
    Anita Curran Guenin

FOOD FOR THOUGHT 141
    Buck Dopp

GARGLE 144
    Margaret Golden

ONION EGGS 145
    Phillis J. Seltzer

MODERN MYTH: EQUALITY OF THE SEXES 148
    Irene Thomas

SECOND RUNNER-UP: BEST FICTION CONTEST 149
    HIGH NOON IN THE GARDEN OF GOOD AND EVIL
    Judith O'Neill

HOW MANY? 153
    Jeffrey Widen

HOW MANY 155
    Ila Winslow

SWAN 156
    Sarah Traister Moskovitz

A SPECIAL PLACE IN OUR HEARTS 157
    Ruth Featherstone

NEXT 161
    Keven Bellows

THE ISLAND OF MY CHOICE 163
    Carole Kaliher

GOLDEN TIES 170
    Margaret S. McKerrow

REMEMBERING KITTY 171
Anna Mae Loebig

THE GENERAL 173
Betty Birkemark

SYNCHRONICITY 176
David Ray

WINNER: BEST FICTION CONTEST 177
THE LAST ACT
Andrew J. Hogan

SOUVENIR OF MIAMI 191
Shelly Lynn Fletcher

QUEEN GUINEVERE 195
Jean Brier Lusk

WILDERNESS RETREAT 196
Janet Kreitz

ALMOND EYES 197
Richard Lampl

FIRST RUNNER-UP: BEST POETRY CONTEST 206
APRON SONG
Bobbie Jean Bishop

FIRST RUNNER-UP: BEST FICTION CONTEST 207
ED'S HALLEY
Wynn Melton

FACELESS BRIDE 212
M. C. Little

IT TAKES TWO TO TANGO 213
Aris DeNigris

MY SHADOW DANCES 218
Terrie Jacks

GUTTER BALL *Barbara Ostrem*	219
IN THE BEGINNING, THE WORD *Nancy Sandweiss*	220
WHAT'S LUCK GOT TO DO WITH IT? *Elisa Drachenberg*	221
CHANGES IN COVE, UTAH *Kathleen Elliott Gilroy*	233
EMPTY *Steven Snyder*	234
ODE TO A WINTER NIGHT *Wilfred E. Mossman*	235
FALLS *Joan T. Doran*	236
WINNER: BEST POETRY CONTEST DYAD *Lynda Riese*	237
LEAVING *Linda Klein*	238
A SACK OF POTATOES *Mary R. Durfee*	239
I WILL BE THERE *Bob Schurr*	242
SECOND RUNNER-UP: BEST NON-FICTION CONTEST CALVIN *Jean Brier Lusk*	243
THE ROSE TREE *Albert Russo*	244
THE GARDEN *Sherry Stoneback*	245

HONORABLE MENTION: NON-FICTION OVER THE RIDGE FROM PARADISE Susan Cummins Miller	247
NEVERMORE Maurice Hirsch	260
THIS LITTLE PIGGY Mitzie Skrbin	261
MESSAGES IN THE SAND Dorothy Parcel	263
SOMEONE ELSE'S SHOES Shirley Shatsky	266
RITUAL Bonnie Papenfuss	268
STOLEN Tilya Gallay Helfield	269
FRIENDS FROM THE SENIOR CENTER Anita Curran Guenin	271
BODY MEMORY Carol Christian	272
THE ADVENTURES OF FLIGHT ATTENDANTS Mary Margaret Baker	273
HONORABLE MENTION: POETRY A STUDY OF SMALL DAYS Bernadette Blue	276
MOVEABLE FEAST Phylis Warady	277
STILL LIFE Bill Alewyn	279
OF POLITICS AND PINS Joan E. Zekas	285

A LONER'S PLEA *Jean Marie Purcell*	287
IN HIGH GEAR *Kathleen O'Brien*	288
THROWN ROD *Mo Weathers*	289
GOING HOME TO KILL *William Killian*	291
I WOULD HAVE BEEN A HERO IF… *Michael B. Mossman*	293
THE KICK IS UP AND IT'S GOOD *Barbara Nuxall Isom*	295
SOPHOMORE YEAR *Una Nichols Hynum*	298
HONORABLE MENTION: NON-FICTION MY UNIBROW: POST-TRAUMATIC TWEEZER DISORDER *Teresa Civello*	299
THE BAT *Robert Puoriea*	303
A LIFE IMAGINED *Alan Dennis*	305
LIST OF MATERIALS CONTAINED *John Barbee*	320
A LESSON LEARNED *Rosemary Bennett*	322
QUESTIONS FOR JUAN GONZALES *Maurice Hirsch*	323
HONORABLE MENTION: POETRY	324

ODE TO A KEROSENE LAMP
Una Nichols Hynum

CHILI-PEPPER HOT   325
David Braun

FOLKLORE AT ITS BEST   329
Jack Campbell

NOT WHAT THEY SEEM   332
Maurice Hirsch

MOXON'S MASTERPIECE: AN ALTERNATE HISTORY   333
Neal Wilgus

HONORABLE MENTION: POETRY   345
OUTSMARTING THE TECHNOLOGY
Judy Ray

THE PERKS   346
Carol Christian

POWER   347
Sarah Traister Moskovitz

LOSING SOMEONE CLOSE   349
Keith Trammell

GIVE ME A NEWSPAPER   351
William Killian

CONTRIBUTORS' NOTES   353

ORDER INFORMATION   375

EDITOR'S PREFACE

This thirteenth annual edition of *OASIS Journal* contains the work of 106 writers over fifty from the U.S., Canada, France, and Costa Rica.

Many anthologies and magazines choose a theme for each issue. I never select a theme in advance, but am constantly surprised to find that our contributors unknowingly group themselves around specific themes. Is this proof of Jung's "collective consciousness," I wonder? This year's theme appears to be "home," and everything contained in that concept: moving to new homes, missing the old homes, returning home, leaving home, finding a home. Maybe, in spite of Thomas Wolfe, we *can* all go home again for, to quote Robert Frost, "Home is the place where, when you have to go there, they have to take you in." Looks like we're in good company when we speak about what home means to us.

Contest winners are noted below, along with information about our judges and their comments.

L. J.

FICTION: JUDGE, REBECCA CRAMER, writer, anthropologist, and educator, the author of three novels in the Linda Bluenight Mystery Series: *Mission to Sonora*, *The View from Frog Mountain*, and *High Stakes at San Xavier*.

WINNER: "Last Act" by Andrew J. Hogan

"Last Act" meets all the tests of a solid short story. The writing is clear and engaging. There's an emotional quality to it that lends even more suspense to the story, and there's plenty to begin with. The end is quite riveting.

FIRST RUNNER-UP: "Ed's Halley" by Wynn Melton

"Ed's Halley" is a good old-fashioned western yarn with a touch of whimsy and humor. Its short length is actually an asset to the story. Using 19th century western lingo isn't that easy but the writer does it well.

SECOND RUNNER-UP: "High Noon in the Garden of Good and Evil" by Judith O'Neill

"High Noon in the Garden of Good and Evil" could be read by adults and children alike. It captures the times and puts the reader behind the child who is its subject. It would have been nice to see a bit more description of the colorful settings in both these short pieces.

NON-FICTION: JUDGE, SUSAN COLLINET, three-time editor of *SandScript Literary Magazine*, entering her seventh season as House Manager and Volunteer Coordinator of *The Rogue Theater* in Tucson, Arizona.

WINNER: "Disillusioned" by Tabinda Bashir

The opening paragraph builds a strong foundation for this story, which continues to pull the reader in. The story of a displaced doctor in a foreign country, who cannot find normalcy and/or contentment living in the US, is strongly connected throughout, with well placed dichotomies like the "Hollywood USA" vs the narrator's reality of USA life; her intimate relationship with nature vs her tainted impression of surrounding humanity. The point of the story is driven by the opening paragraph and never gets lost in the narrative. The unfortunate event during her walk in the park has sealed her disillusionment and frustration with her life in America and the narrator expresses this with absolute honesty and perhaps a misplaced self-respect. The final paragraph is stunning. I applaud this writer.

FIRST RUNNER-UP: "Mississippi Memoirs" by Irene Thomas

The song Ol' Man River is the perfect backdrop for this story. I appreciate the way the author presents the reader with two simple observations written with the delicacy of a ten year old and in so doing, describes the essence of the Great Depression without bias or regret. The gaiety of the boat party with "some of the wealthier people of St. Louis" was thrilling to a child whose biggest problem was blisters from her new shoes. The fancy food, white tablecloths and silverware were far from what she observed with her Father a few weeks later. The families living in cardboard boxes, the folks lining up for food, the sick children, "remnants of humanity." Her Father stepping up to help a disabled old woman get food, the ten year old feeling embarrassment for her. These are all successful images in this story with powerful connections to Ol' Man River, He jes keeps rolling along.

SECOND RUNNER-UP: "Calvin" by Jean Brier Lusk

The winning element in this brief story is its surprising and unexpected ending. It is so well written that the reader is unprepared for what is to come.

It's also a very informative piece to those who may seek alternative assistance in managing Diabetes, and even includes the tender imaging of Calvin's methods: "lick the inside of her elbow, sit on her chest and purr loudly," etc.

HONORABLE MENTIONS:
"Over the Ridge from Paradise" by Susan Cummins Miller (good journalistic quality writing)
"My Unibrow: Post-Traumatic Tweezer Disorder" by Teresa Civello (well written humor)

POETRY: JUDGE, DAN GILMORE, author of *A Howl for Mayflower* (a novel), *Season Tickets* (a collection of poetry and short stories), and two collections of poetry, *Love Takes a Bow* and *Panning for Gold*. His poems have appeared in *Atlanta Review, San Diego Reader, Aethlon, Blue Collar Review, The Carolina Review, Sharing House Journal,* and *Loft and Range*.

WINNER: "Dyad" by Lynda Riese
So beautifully and easily made, from child to child-husband, very moving details, just the right amount. The sibilant "s" hissing as steam clouds the bathroom mirror, the round vowel in "sorry" is as close to perfect as you can get. Oh my, "his pale sex that floats aimlessly." So perfect. And the last line brings tears to my eyes. Fantastic, very powerful.

FIRST RUNNER-UP: "Apron Song" by Bobbie Jean Bishop
First three words—great. The turn to Saint Myrtle's second skin, very atmospheric; "trickle down genes" and the last three lines blow me away—especially "blood-red threads transfusing yesterday." Very smart, well crafted and moving poem.

SECOND RUNNER-UP: "Basting Threads" by Ruth Moon Kempher
I like the atmosphere established in the first three stanzas, the stakes that are revealed in the fourth, love the "roast's rind," "the gored bristle." And I'm very moved by the last three lines. Finely crafted poem.

HONORABLE MENTIONS:
"The Pruning" by Lynda Riese
"A Study of Small Days" by Bernadette Blue
"Ode to a Kerosene Lamp" by Una Nichols Hynum
"Outsmarting Technology" by Judy Ray

OASIS JOURNAL
2014

Stories

Poems

Essays

Winner: Best Non-fiction Contest

Disillusioned

Tabinda Bashir

When you leave everything behind, something terrible happens to your life. It snaps. Like a crack in the window pane. Never to be joined again.

When you find yourself in a setup quite the opposite of what you had, your brain, in a way, stops functioning. It hibernates. Of course, the mundane activities of life go on willy-nilly. But you seek orientation; you want to know where you are at. Neither your past nor your present seem to be able to guide you through your predicament. Gradually, your previous values and experiences grow fuzzy.

The day-to-day routine of life brings you into contact with people and places, and, with the wonderment of a newborn, you begin to look at your surroundings and the world afresh. New standards, so different from the old, begin to take hold. The past gets overshadowed and muddled; it becomes difficult to recall bygone memories and events. You go through a period of confusion until, over time, you begin to register the creeping new realities that slowly push back the old ones. You begin to absorb and adjust—but not quite. Surprises pop up where you least expect them. They lurk in the most unforeseen places and times. Faced with the futility of reliving or redeeming the past, you just give up and decide to go with the flow of events.

Something similar happened to me about thirteen years ago, when I immigrated following my retirement as a practicing doctor. Before that, I had been visiting the United States every few years for vacations. Like anyone coming from a developing country and having been fed on a Hollywood image of the U.S., I thought things looked beautiful, perfect, Utopian. This country seemed to be the place where no one suffered; everyone you talked to was happy and healthy. The colors, the scenes, the shows, the plentiful food bedazzled me, and I fancied being here to share the bliss.

When time and circumstances dictated, I came.

Getting settled, though, presented a different picture. Store clerks and businessmen displayed the same old qualities of trickery prevalent all over the world. At first I brushed it aside as a quirk of human nature, but small incidents kept piling up. I told myself, "Well, accept it." I looked around for activities suitable to my age and health and discovered some writing and reading groups where I could participate. Life started limping along.

Then came 9/11. I was horrified to see the upsurge of hatred and bias that finally crumbled my Hollywood image. Americans were, after all, the same as everyone else, even more so because of the force they could exert. Never mind, I said to myself. My life must go on. And I continued with my writing groups, lunches with group members, my walks, and my daily activities as best I could.

Near where I live, as in many other residential areas, there is a park. It has a small lake with a fountain in the middle, a path around it, and lots of geese. Beautiful flowering trees surround the path and are spaced across the vast lawns. The main parking lot to the north is at the back of a nearby shopping mall. A creek flows east toward a housing estate. On the west are lawns with playgrounds and a small baseball court, with a children's school at the far end. To the south, the paths join a main road.

I try to finish all my activities during the day and be home by evening, just as I have been taught since my school days. Whenever I get time, I go to the park and spend about an hour walking around the lake. The path slopes slightly towards the lake, so, because of my arthritic feet, I like to walk on the outer left edge, which is more level. I change sides for people coming from the opposite direction.

These walks give me a much needed respite from the present jumble of daily demands and memories of the past. Some geese swim in the water without causing a ripple, while others preen themselves or just sit on the grass. Watching them puts a soothing balm on my fidgety mind. As I walk around, I look at the peaceful trees and bushes, always standing in their places, filling the atmosphere with beauty and perfume when in bloom. I tend to lose myself in this abundance of splendor. The birds, the trees, and I become one.

I talk to the geese, and they seem to understand. When they are standing right in the middle of the path, deep in a wordless discussion, I tell them to move in my own language, and they give way reluctantly. A goose once stood on the side of the path, trying to gauge if she should cross or let me go first. Then she thought better of it and hurried on to the water, just as I would do in front of an oncoming car.

My interaction with the trees also goes on. I know all their branches by now. I admire the appearance of new buds and applaud when they change into flowers. Leaves change color and shed at the exact time appropriated by nature. Yellow, red, maroon, brown, and sometimes black, they cover the ground like a carpet that rolls gently with the wind. The grass takes a rest. At times I discover a branch of a tree that has been cut. Its white wound goes through color changes until the scar becomes a permanent dark brown reminder of what was.

My connection with plants and animals reminds me of the universality of nature.

People, however, are a different story. They are bound by their history, culture, and law. I am already used to the indifference and occasional rudeness of the cashier or the person behind the desk. After all, most are immigrants themselves and must be having problems of their own. My encounters with the other walkers in the park are sometimes funny and sometimes downright shocking.

Most people come with their dogs. I don't feel comfortable with dogs because they are rather unpredictable. So I stick to the side of the path, look straight ahead, and pray for the best. Sometimes a dog is so friendly he pulls on the leash and wants to lick me. I shudder when he wants to smell me from head to foot. The owner, usually an elderly woman, sees me shrinking and says to her dog, "No, no, no. Leave the good lady alone. Good girl, good girl."

I give her a big smile and say, "Lovely dog. What's his name?"

She gives me a bigger smile and says, "She's a girl. Her name is Sally."

"Oh, what a lovely name," I say and rush on.

At other times it is just the opposite. The dog is ferocious and wants to tear me to pieces. I step back. The owner pulls at the leash and says to me, "Please don't mind him. He's so playful."

Really? We go through the same polite conversation, and the owner apologizes as if for a spoilt child.

I get a big scare when the dog is not on a leash. At such moments I just freeze in my spot until the dog has decided which way it wants to go.

A strange incident took place the other day. I was walking in the park at about 4 p.m. As usual, my thoughts roamed around the trees, the geese, and how bright the sun was. I tried to cover my head and neck with my scarf to avoid sunburn.

Then I saw a man coming toward me with a dog and no leash. *Oh, God,* I thought. *Here comes trouble.*

The man himself did not look quite right. Although he was still some distance away, I could see that he had bowed legs, and he was wobbling. I wondered what could lead to such a staggering gait. Since I am a doctor, a number of diseases came to my mind. I crossed over to the right side and walked straight in an effort not to provoke the dog. The dog went along peacefully. Then the man came nearer and just as he passed me, I heard a thick, low, trembling, "Hmmm."

I was already concerned about his health. I looked back. His face was red, his breathing labored, his chest wall thumping, and he had both his hands extended towards me. He looked ill. I thought he wanted support. So I advanced and held his hands, thinking that I would lead him to the nearest bench. Like any doctor, I began calculating about how to manage the patient.

He pulled my hands and caught me in a tight hug. I got the strongest whiff of a stinking body odor. I pushed him back and asked, "What is the matter? Can you speak? Are you not well?"

He did not let go of my hands. I had to wrench them out of his grip. He still said not a word. Instead he pointed towards me, then himself and gestured, "Let's go."

I pushed him back hard. Again I asked, "Can't you speak?"

He pulled at his shirt, then pointed at me and gestured obscenely, "No?"

I shouted, "No, you—" I wanted to say bastard, but did not. I pushed him hard and went on my way.

Strangely, the dog was quiet throughout. Quite possibly he had witnessed many scenes like that. For all I know, the person may have been plain drunk. In the country I come from, we have little or no experience with alcohol-related problems.

That man had spoiled my walk. I was very angry and felt helpless. I did not know what to do, who to ask. I saw a car in the parking lot with someone sitting in it. He must have enjoyed the show. Other than that, the park was completely empty. I was not sure if I should have called 911. I did not know if blatantly hugging strangers in open spaces in broad daylight was an offence. I did not know if having a dog off a leash was an offence. My knowledge of the law and the police is mostly based on what I see on TV, and there the police do not come across as a very friendly institution.

I rushed to my car and drove home. Later, I thought that, if this event had taken place in the dark, there could have been serious consequences. I am advised by friends that I should have called 911.

I hope there is no next time like this. All the same, I think I should buy a pepper spray. But just getting the pepper spray is not enough. Life has to be learned by living it, and that takes years. Such opportunity may not be available to a person who has spent most of her time on earth elsewhere. Those who emigrate at a younger age find it easier to adapt. Their minds assimilate information quickly.

At times, this vast country feels claustrophobic. One has to devise activities to break the clutches of solitude. Telephoning and e-mailing friends and relatives left far behind helps but a little. Listening to old songs is the same. Then one just sits by the window, looking at people going about their lives, wondering what, if any, mishaps they have had. What hidden problems trouble them in their outwardly normal lives? The inability to just go and ask is a torture in itself.

Writing and tearing up the pages is how my frustration gets expressed. Again, one goes back to the usual day-to-day activities and thinks of going out for a walk—a diversion that is always available, but at what cost?

The glass pane is cracked. The crack runs from one end to the other. Smaller cracks around the corners hurt even more. I have to keep this glass intact. I shall use cello tape to keep the fragments in place. The strips should be arranged strategically so the glass looks whole—not so much for others to see, but for my own contentment. I was a normal self-respecting person before I came here.

Waiting for the Rain

Anne Whitlock

They were nomads in a land
with no temperate zone,
moving from place to place
like itinerant workers.
The stars pulled them
like magnets, but they couldn't
move faster than the sun,
for they were sun signs
totally unsuited:

My father a slow burning fire
extinguished by the rain
and an unknown number
of Irish whiskeys
on a side-winding road
out of Riverside.
My mother a hot desert wind
pushing relentlessly on.

We were squatters on my aunt's
doorstep fifteen miles from the sea
in a house with pink hydrangeas.
We were squatters in my
grandfather's apartments
and my mother never bought
her way out of indenture.

They were not writers—my parents,
nor their parents before them
and their stories lie buried
in layers of limestone and
slate under desert sands
where the ocean receded.

I am a water sign, but they
brought me here to the desert,
and I have grown old
waiting for the rain.

A Place at the Table

Jennifer Hollingshead

It was a day not long after my fourteenth birthday, and my mother was crouching in front of me with a mouthful of pins. I edged the hemline of my skirt upward, hoping she wouldn't notice.

She shook her head and spat out the pins.

"It isn't decent, Jenny," she said, tugging the hem back down.

"Wendy always wears her skirts at least that short," I argued as she stuck in a pin. My mother always had the pins, which gave her an advantage. I pulled the skirt as low on my hips as it would go, so it would appear longer.

"It's going to fall right off," my mother warned.

"It's hipster, Mom; it's mod."

It was 1967 and hemlines were up—way up—while waistbands were down—way down—to the hips. To achieve the mod look, the skirt I was wearing needed to be no wider than about 12 inches. To complicate matters, my family and I were living in Nairobi. The global marketplace didn't exist back then, and ready-made imports were hard to find in Kenya, even in the capital city. So my mother and I spent long unhappy hours at the sewing machine, nearly always culminating in a hemline war like the one we were engaged in.

On that day I finally compromised, but only because I remembered that the fabric nearly always shrank. My mom finished pinning, handed me needle and thread and escaped. I sat down to sew.

It was a pleasant place to work. Scent from the jacaranda wafted through the open window protected by an iron grill. Other houses were close but, following British tradition, tall hedges separated each property, so we never saw our neighbors.

The white ones, that is.

We had other neighbors who were called "squatters." They lived in the cornfield that started where our lawn ended and stretched down to the creek that flowed past the bottom of the hill. Their house had mud walls and a straw-thatched roof and it blended perfectly with the surroundings; an entire family lived there, almost invisibly. Once, my father, homesick for his farm in the U.S., tried planting some sugar corn in our back yard. He dug up a small plot next to the carefully tilled field of our African neighbors. To the immense delight of our Kenyan help, my father's corn never got past knee-high. By contrast, the squatters' field grew up lush and tall. Our "house boy," Gichuki, along with James, our gardener, and the Kenyan farmer would stand out by our patch of stalks that was dwarfed by the crop next to it, and they would exchange jokes in Kikuyu about the corn. At least, I think it was about the corn because they would point, say something, and then break into laughter. So much for the superiority of the bwana in the big house.

But on that day I was not thinking about corn because my mother and I were deeply involved in hemline wars. "It's not decent, Jenny," my mother protested as I edged the hemline upward. I pulled the skirt as low on my hips as it would go so it would appear longer.

My mother, not noted for her patience, sighed and pinned the hem where I wanted it. I'm not very patient either, and I sewed with long, looping stitches to get finished as quickly as possible. I was rewarded when I met Wendy downtown at the Jacaranda cafe. I was wearing the skirt, a ribbed high-necked sweater we called a skinny, a wide belt, and my new chunky-toed shoes.

"Far out," she said.

When I look back on that time, I'm amazed at how my friends and I were able to absorb pop culture. Satellites, computers, and the Internet were years in the future. Overseas editions of magazines and imported clothing from Europe were rare in Nairobi. You could scour the length of Bazaar Street without finding a single mini-skirt or pair of bell-bottoms. Instead, it was easy to find lengths of beautifully embroidered silk for saris for sale by the mostly Asian businesses, while the central market was filled with bright Kanga cloth and—in those unenlightened days—zebra-skin purses, wallets, and shoes. Once I sighted a pair of red suede sling-backs among them and nabbed them instantly. I knew they were the latest thing, but how? I didn't see a single copy of a fashion magazine for the entire two years I lived in Nairobi. We absorbed information strictly by word of mouth, some of it incomplete and strange. When my friend, Wendy, arrived from Britain, we crowded around her like prisoners hungry for news from the outside world.

Wendy told us about Carnaby Street, Twiggy, mods and rockers. She had a wardrobe filled with micro minis, wide shiny plastic belts, and pale textured stockings—pantyhose had yet to be invented—and she had buttons reading "Far Out" and "Britain Swings Like a Pendulum Do." She brought the Beatles' latest album to our end-of-term party: *Sergeant Pepper's Lonely Hearts' Club Band*. She bravely shortened the skirt of her school uniform to mid-thigh. It didn't last long. Our headmistress, Miss Eugenia Hill, insisted on the one-inch-below-the-knee rule.

I showed Wendy a button someone had given me from the United States. It read HOBBIT. I had puzzled over this word for a long time and hoped Wendy could explain it. She couldn't, but she quickly made something up. It stood for House Of Bloody Bitches In Training, she told me, and was the name of Miss Harthoorn's alma mater. We all hated Miss Harthoorn. She was a thin-lipped, unrealistically red-haired teacher of 30 years' experience, whose British accent cut like a knife.

"REALLY, gulls," she would drawl after asking a question and receiving silence in return. "You ought to know that. It's general knowledge."

One unhappy day, Nicolette, who was from Holland, raised her hand and asked: "Who's General Knowledge?"

The U.S. government—unlike its Dutch counterpart—had provided the families it was sending to Kenya with a two-week orientation to that country. I had learned many things. I could count to 10 in Swahili, ask for tea, and sing a rather charming love song called "Malaika." I was also introduced to a few of the Briticisms that I was likely to come across in a country where third generation ex-patriots still spoke of going "home" to England. But certain critical information was left out. My government failed to inform me, for example, of the various colloquialisms designating bodily functions. Wendy's mom once asked me if I wanted to "spend a penny?" When I looked mystified, she clarified with, "Go to the loo?" I finally got it when she said "the W.C." Oh right, the bathroom.

But I entered more difficult terrain with my introduction to menstruation. In those repressed days, one did not speak openly of such things, particularly, as they said, in mixed company. However, while at home I had been an avid reader of *American Girl* magazine, which had kindly provided me and my fellow "preteens" with several articles designed to ease our way through this transition to womanhood. One article told me that all

I ever needed to do, should the unthinkable happen and I got my period unexpectedly, was to whisper to another woman, "My friend has arrived." Any woman, the writer cheerfully assured me, will understand. On the face of it, this seemed wonderful: a secret code, bonding all women together. Unfortunately, this author had never visited East Africa and certainly had never met Miss Miller, gym teacher at Delamere Girls School. Thus it came about that at our weekly swimming class, held at the local YMCA pool, I was sitting fully dressed while the rest of the class had changed into swimsuits, my friend having put in an appearance that morning and swimming being a forbidden activity, according to my guides at *American Girl*. Miss Miller was taking role in her notebook, and she stopped and stared at me.

"Why aren't you in your swimsuit?"

"I can't go swimming," I said.

"Why not?"

I still thank the embarrassment protection gods that I didn't say, "Because my friend has arrived."

"I just can't," I said.

"Why? Pee? Is it pee?"

"Well, no," I said, hesitantly. "Not pee exactly."

"Then what is it?"

"I have my period," I blurted out, one eye on a neighboring group of boys. If they heard that, I'd die.

"Right," said Miss Miller, whose title of games mistress seemed well earned. "You have P. Next time just say so."

She jotted something next to my name in her little black notebook. I felt like Hester Prynne. Except my scarlet letter was P.

Later, after I left the country, Delamere Girls School would be renamed State House Road School for Girls. I'm glad they changed the name—only Miss Harthoorn knew who Lord Delamere was—but the new name sounds like a reform school. I'm surprised they didn't name it for the country's long-time president, Mzee Jomo Kenyatta. Kenyans celebrate two holidays a year in honor of Kenyatta: one for his release from a British prison, where he served time for his work in the Mau Mau rebellion prior to independence in 1963; and another for his birthday, although exactly when he was born is a mystery—dates vary from 1886 to 1890.

My class was invited to State House one day when Princess Margaret of England paid a visit to the president. It was a short walk up State House

Road to the grounds of the president's residence, and I was trudging beside Tirza under the flickering shadows of the Jacaranda trees. I didn't want to walk beside Tirza. I wanted to walk with Wendy, but she had skipped ahead with Gillian, and I was staring at their backs, puzzled and resentful.

"We're putting Jenny in Coventry," Wendy said to Gillian, without looking at me. "For telling on Nicolette."

"What's Coventry?" I asked, feeling a familiar flicker of anxiety. Was Wendy going to turn on me? She was my best friend.

"No one speaks to you," Wendy said, glancing back. "You told Miss Rook that Nicolette wrote in your copy book."

"She did," I said.

But Wendy and Gillian smiled at each other and walked ahead. I fell back, beside Tirza, who was a large, brainy girl from Israel.

"What's Coventry?" I whispered. "How long does it last?"

I looked up at Tirza's calm face. Maybe she wouldn't speak to me either. But Tirza, as usual, was kind and patient, although for once she was as ignorant as I was.

"Oh, Jenny," was all she said, her voice heavy with resignation.

So I trudged unhappily toward my first and only live view of President Jomo Kenyatta. We entered through the North gate and filed onto the lawn, an apron of emerald green in front of the imposing State House. The arched windows and columned verandas of the sprawling white building gave it an Old South look, which seemed at odds with what little I knew of Kenyatta's policies.

We never learned anything about Kenyatta in school, but I had heard of "Kenyanization." Asian business people were leaving the country in droves as the government pressed for African ownership of both businesses and land. The road to the airport was frequently clogged with long lines of cars packed with emigrating Asian families. They weren't going to India or Pakistan, however. They were heading "home" to England.

We stood on the lawn behind a string of fluttering pennants. I could see Kenyatta in the grandstand in front of us, a white-suited figure holding his signature cow-tail flyswatter. He was a large man with a calm, bearded face. Next to him was the princess in a big hat and a flower-print dress that I imagined was suitable attire for a garden party. We arrived, all of form 2A, which consisted mainly of girls called "European," although we were from North America, Australia, and Israel, as well as Europe. There was a lone Kenyan, Anne, and one Asian, Sateh. I wonder now what Kenyatta thought as we lined up in front of him, a group of mostly white-skinned school girls wearing uniforms in the best British imperial tradition: green skirts, white shirts, stiffly knotted striped ties, gray blazers emblazoned with the school motto, "Live to Learn." We even possessed straw hats called boaters that we wore each day while traveling to and from school. There we stood under the hot blue African sky on a lawn blazing with scarlet and fuchsia bougainvillea and sang an old English folksong: "Down by the Sally Gardens."

"My love and I did meet; down by the Sally Gardens, she laid her snow white feet," we trilled.

I thought about Gichuki's feet, earth-hardened, their deep color turned gray and cracked at the soles. He walked barefoot outside, immune to the stony red gravel of our own garden pathways. Even Wendy's feet, I reflected, were far from "snow white."

I don't know, of course, but I imagine Kenyatta was thinking something like, "We have a long way to go."

In that time, 35 years ago, I inhabited a privileged island of white culture surrounded by the seething mystery of Africa, which I glimpsed from a distance, even though I lived there.

"Visited our friend Grace's samba," I report in my diary from 1967. "Her father has six wives and 38 kids. Wow!"

We were not there to criticize. My father's work at University College was to train mathematics teachers; his larger role was to assist Kenyans in their quest to take control of their own country. Nevertheless, we were of the colonizers, and we knew it. My parents had hired a so-called houseboy, Gichuki, just like every other white family in Nairobi.

Gichuki scrubbed the clothes by hand in the bathtub and lived in a garage-like building on our property; it had two stalls with a cold water shower and a toilet. Gichucki had to walk outside to get to them. My parents insisted we address him as "Mr. Gichucki," although it was impossible to tell how old he was. He had deeply creased skin and red-rimmed eyes, but no gray hair. Inside he wore soft canvas shoes; his feet made shh-shh-shh on the polished parquet floors as he shuffled from room to room.

But colonizers or not, my parents were also liberal, enlightened Quakers who believed in equality. They insisted that the "houseboy" sit with us at the table for dinner.

"After all," my mother said, "he cooked the food, so he ought to be able to sit down and eat it."

It was good logic and left no place for my own adolescent agonizing. It wasn't long before I understood that having "the boy" eat dinner with the family was unheard of. None of my friends' families did that. Their houseboys were silent and obsequious; the families they worked for, outwardly polite and privately cutting.

"Thanks very much," Wendy said when the houseboy placed her obligatory early morning tea by her bedside when I was staying at her house for the weekend. "Bloody wag hasn't boiled the kettle properly," she whispered as he left.

Wag? I was shocked. Wasn't that as bad as saying "nigger?" What if he heard her say it? I almost choked on my tea. But for me to say anything to Wendy was unthinkable. Her friendship was essential to my well-being, or so I thought, and I took care of her the way you would a prize filly. I remember her that morning, sitting up in bed, her pale blue eyes looking at me over her teacup. Her blonde hair was so fair that the threads were like filaments of nylon, and she was slender in a languid, unmuscled kind of way. I thought again of Mr. Gichuki, so whip-thin that he had to cinch the black pants he always wore tightly to his waist. He had a body worn down to its tough essential cords. And he was black. Wendy had the whitest skin I have ever seen.

I agonized for days about inviting Wendy to my house. What would she say when Mr. Gichucki sat down to eat with us? My solution came to me like a gift from above. Or somewhere. I waited until my parents announced plans to go out for the evening, and then I invited Wendy. We lounged in my room listening to singles on the tiny (and tinny) record player, but I made sure to jump up at exactly six o'clock. My plan was to set the dinner table myself. When it was done, I called Wendy and we all sat down—my brother, sister, and the two of us. I soon heard the shh-shh-shh of Mr. Gichucki's slippers coming down the hall; he was bringing the dish of steaming Shepherd's pie. When he got to the dinner table, he placed it on the hot mat, and then looked around at the four of us, all ready with our napkins in our laps and our water glasses filled. Four places, four people. Even after all these years, I can still hear his soft exclamation—oh, oh, oh—as he looked for his own place at the dinner table. He waited a moment, and then made his soft, shuffling retreat back to the kitchen.

"Isn't Gichuki's?" my brother started to say before I kicked him under the table.

"He's got a plate in the kitchen, remember?" I stared at him.

My brother nodded uncertainly.

I ate miserably, wondering if it were true, or if Gichuki sat alone at the kitchen table, an empty plate in front of him. But Wendy was here, sitting beside me, her pale skin glowing in the lamp light. She nibbled a tiny portion of shepherd's pie, then asked for coffee. When I said we didn't have any, she jumped up.

"Come on," she said. "We'll walk to the cafe at Westland's."

I had meant to offer to wash the dishes, as an apology to Mr. Gichuki, but I quickly forgot my good intentions and followed Wendy out the door. Better for Mr. Gichuki to eat alone in the kitchen, I figured, than for me to sit friendless in the school cafeteria.

My excuse, as such, was that I was fourteen and came to the city of Nairobi straight from the farm in New Jersey, where I had lived for all my previous thirteen years. I was inhabiting that uneasy territory between childhood and maturity, and my new life in Kenya brought with it a whole crop of doubts and puzzles.

I remember that my room in our new house faced the back, toward the squatters' towering cornfield and our own scraggly plot. I shared the room with my five-year-old sister, who slept through everything. Even being robbed. I always shut the curtains tight after sundown. There were no streetlights in back, only the cornfield that harbored the mud house, filled with dark-skinned people I did not know. Strange insect sounds, the hoots of unfamiliar birds, and mysterious rustlings filled the darkness. And the thieves came out at night. They were Africans, I knew that, dark people whose skin would blend with the shadows.

One night, I closed the curtains as usual, but left the windows open; it was hot. I went to take my bath, leaving my sister curled up in bed. When I came back, something seemed strange. Suddenly, I realized the comforter wasn't on my bed anymore. It was dangling halfway out the window. And still moving. I yelped and leaped to grab it, but quick as thought it slipped out of my grasp and disappeared silently into the night. Terrified, I looked at my sister's bed. She was still sound asleep. I heard nothing, not even footsteps.

It wasn't the only time things disappeared in the night. My watch wasn't on my night stand one morning. Cans of food flew out the pantry windows. A sweater wafted off its peg. The thieves were experts at manipulating fishing lines and snags, reaching into the rich houses with skill and care, seeking the necessities they lacked. I only truly regretted one loss. That was a new mini-dress I was sewing. It was tent-style, gathered at the neck and falling as short as I dared to make it. I was proud of the fabric. It had a wavy op art check pattern. Really mod, I told Wendy. I worked on the dress all one Saturday, then went to eat supper and left the almost-finished dress hanging over the back of a chair. Too close to the window. When I came back, it was gone.

For a while, I looked for a Kenyan girl wearing what would have been the most mod dress in all of Nairobi. Every time I saw a flash of purple and pink, I stopped and stared. It was never mine. Kenyans didn't wear mini-skirts, so it must have been given to a child. Maybe she wore it to feed the goats or to gather firewood or to splash in the creek. I hope she liked it. I wish it had been a gift.

Wishes

Anne Whitlock

If wishes were Euros and I could untwine
in the afternoon with a glass of red wine,
order salade niçoise, le poisson du jour
from a beau garçon on the Côte d'Azur
away from Washington, safe from news,
four thousand miles from Boehner and Cruz,
where the president's mistress is no one's concern
with a French paperback or something by Verne
on a sandy beach in the land of romance
where they pamper their pets, I'd winter in France.

If wishes were Francs and I could devise
a timepiece that ran counter-clockwise,
I'd wake up again in that Swiss chalet
under feathers and down and start the new day
with butter and cream, strawberry jam
and climb down the Gornergrat mountain again
and autumn would follow just as before
in a country that shows no interest in war
where they bank on peace, invest in hope
and their only crime is guarding the Pope.

If wishes were Krone and pockets were deep,
I'd summer in Norway and go to sleep
in an old hotel where water pours
over the rocks of the Sognefjord,
where cows and sheep on the mountains roam
with GPS collars to guide them home,
where North Wind shields her babes in her wings,
caring for animals, people and things,
water is pure, you can breathe the air—
just for summer, I'd stay there.

If wishes were Dollars and peace was for sale,
I'd buy all the banks that are too big to fail,
spread out the wealth like icing on cake

and bring back our troops to celebrate.
I'd make politicians be gone or be nice
and give all the polar bears plenty of ice.
I'd sweep the drugs and guns off the street,
tax corporations, help women compete.
Then I'd light a torch at the harbor door
to welcome the sick, the hungry and poor.

Spring

Bella Hollingworth

Pear tree petals thick on the brick walk
Follow us in like obedient dogs
Scattered white on indoor rugs,
Begging to be acknowledged.
We scoop them up tenderly.
Put them outdoors for the night
Hoping they find a welcome elsewhere.

Two Eggs, an Orange, and Six Black Olives

Muriel Sandy

Izmir, Turkey, known in ancient times as Smyrna, had a campsite. Unfortunately, it appeared a bit rundown, so I suggested to Bob, my husband, that we look for a spot to free-camp.

We hadn't gone very far down the road when I noticed a small empty field on our left. "Let's have a look, shall we?" I said. He turned onto a side road, and then onto the field and parked under a large shade tree.

I climbed into the back and opened the sliding door of our VW campmobile to catch the breeze, rolled out the screened louvered windows for cross ventilation, pulled up the table, and got out my Corona portable typewriter. Bob settled in the front seat with his latest read. We had an hour before I would start dinner.

Perhaps it was the sound of the typewriter keys that attracted attention. In any case, I heard a slight movement outside the sliding door. I looked up. There stood a short, middle-aged lady in street dress with a bowl in her hand.

I smiled. "Good afternoon. Is it all right to stay here for the night?" I asked in English.

Bob stopped reading and watched.

The lady nodded and held out the bowl in my direction. Not wishing to frighten her by hopping out, I stayed in the camper, slid over on the bench, and extended my hands to accept her gift.

"Thank you very much," Bob said from the front seat. I thanked her as well.

She began to speak hesitantly. "I no speak good English. My son, he speak English very well. I send him to talk when he come home." She smiled and left.

In the bowl were two eggs, an orange, and six black olives. Bob tasted an olive. "Delicious, they're marinated just the way I like them."

Sometime later, while we were eating dinner, a young man in his thirties knocked on the sliding door. Bob opened it. "You must be the lady's son," Bob said.

"Yes, I am Hassan. My mother asked me to come and tell you, you may stay here overnight if you wish. You will be safe. My mother asked me to invite you to our home tomorrow evening. Will you come?"

Bob looked at me, and said, "We will be pleased to come, thank you. By the way, please thank your mother for the eggs, orange, and delicious black olives." He handed Hassan the bowl with our thank you note in the bottom.

"See you tomorrow about 8:00 o'clock," Hassan said. He headed back to his house.

"Well, *mon cher*, that was an unexpected surprise," I said. So instead of driving south the next morning, we drove into the city, where we immersed ourselves in Anatolian archaeology at the Izmir Museum. Later in the afternoon we returned to our private camping spot for dinner. A few minutes before eight we closed the windows, locked the doors, and strolled over to the house.

Hassan greeted us and directed us through a hallway into the living room. Three people, deep in conversation, were seated on overstuffed chairs. Hassan waited a moment, then introduced his father and explained that he did not speak English.

Bob and I took turns making a slight bow to each person in the room, and said, "Hello." We remembered not to shake hands, a custom not used in the Muslim world. Then we were introduced to their neighbors. Hassan told us they too did not speak English, but that they had come to meet someone from America. Then Mama joined us. She invited us to sit, extending her hand towards a Western-style sofa.

A black-and-white TV sat in the corner of the living room. Playing on a ten-inch screen was a 1930's Laurel and Hardy comedy in English with Turkish subtitles. Papa turned down the volume.

Hassan began by asking how long we had been in Turkey.

"About a month," Bob replied. We waited while the question and our answer were translated into Turkish.

"Have you been to Istanbul?" Hassan asked. "Did you like it?" They all smiled when they heard we thought Istanbul was a very exciting city, like no other capital we had ever seen.

The conversation continued. First Hassan's question to us in English, then his translation of his question into Turkish and our English response into Turkish. While we waited, it struck me that here was an example of how secretaries of state conduct foreign affairs. While Hassan applied his skills, Mama said something to him. He asked if we would care for a drink of water. We replied that that would be very nice.

Mama left the room and returned with a tray on which rested a water pitcher and two glasses. First, she offered Bob a glass. The other glass was offered to the gentleman neighbor. When Bob finished drinking, he sat holding the glass.

Mama looked at me.

I smiled.

She took Bob's glass, filled it and gave it to me.

Meanwhile, the gentleman guest finished his drink. Mama took his glass and filled it for his wife, and when she finished Mama used the glass for her husband, her son, and finally herself.

After an hour or so had passed, Bob whispered, "We should be thinking of leaving." I nodded in agreement.

Before saying goodnight to each one, I asked Hassan if I might use their toilet. He escorted me through the hall to the side door and pointed to the garden. There I found a wooden toilet shed just like those we had used numerous times in Europe. Inside was an immaculate white porcelain squat toilet plate. I turned around, faced the door, placed one shoe on each corrugated section, then lifted my long shirt, adjusted my clothes accordingly, and squatted to relieve myself. I was pleased to see a roll of toilet tissue hanging on the right-hand wall. Even though there was no running water to remove human waste, the hole in the ground was deep, so the shed smelled fresh from the cool evening air. Even if it had not been clean, I would have used it. Our own portable chemical toilet in the camper was not as good as the real thing.

I found my way back into the house and signaled to Bob that I was ready. We thanked Mama and Papa, their guests, and Hassan for a very pleasant evening, and again for their permission to free-camp. Hassan escorted us to the front door and directed his flashlight towards our camper.

Assured of our safety, we slept well, thanks to the completely unexpected kindness and gracious hospitality of strangers.

Face to Face

Nancy Sandweiss

I peer through a window at the dark young man on my porch.
Well-groomed, earnest, he starts his pitch. I cut him off:
Sorry, not today.

The encounter troubles me. Often I pause before a stranger
at the door, sometimes open it.
Why not today?

In the hallway I halt by a picture of my grandson Quinn;
his luminous eyes reflect traces of a Chinese grandmother;
latte skin reveals a grandfather's African roots.

Quinn is a new blossom on my Eastern European tree,
moves easily from room to room. His life's more spacious
than my own – he'll open doors for me.

Our First Valentine's Day

Yasue Aoki Kidd

It was Valentine's Day in 1974, the first one after our marriage. I was the only married lady working at the Chittenden County Superior Court in Burlington, Vermont; all the other women were either divorced or single without a boyfriend at the time. I was not expecting anything, so I was surprised to see a young black man show up with a large bouquet of gladiolus for me. There were so few black people in Burlington that I had not seen one yet. He was tall and good-looking, and I did not doubt that he was a delivery man from the flower shop. Naturally, the bouquet was from Bruce, and I was touched. All the staff, and the lawyers who happened to be in the office, cheered for me.

It was a nice surprise, but I was even more surprised when the young man said, "*Barentain omedetou. Bruce, Aishitemasu.*" He had said, "Happy Valentine's Day, (this is from) Bruce. I love you." I thought it was a nice touch to send a delivery man with a Japanese message. Bruce must have tipped him well for the extra service on this busy day.

When I got home, I found out what had happened. Bruce had gone to a florist to get a bouquet of flowers delivered to me, but was told they were so busy that it would not be possible. Too many men were eager to send flowers to their sweetie pies. Then Bruce looked round and found a man who was also in the same predicament.

"Hey, if you deliver the flowers to *my* wife, I will do the same for you," Bruce suggested.

The man thought it was a splendid idea, so they exchanged the addresses for delivering the flowers. The man, Sam, from South Africa, happened to be a graduate student at the University of Vermont, and his wife was from Russia. They thought it would be cute if each man would speak a short message to the unsuspecting wives, so Bruce memorized a message in Russian for Sam's wife, and Sam did the same in Japanese for me.

I was delighted to hear the story behind the delivery of the flowers, but I was a little embarrassed that I had automatically thought Sam was a delivery man from the flower shop. I wondered what Sam's wife had thought of Bruce.

Meanwhile, when Bruce went to Sam's apartment and knocked on the door, out came an Oriental-looking lady who was Sam's wife, which was a surprise. But he delivered the flowers and the Russian message to her. She was as equally delighted as I was when she received the flowers and the message in Russian.

Every time I see gladiolus, the memory of that first Valentine's Day comes back. It was long ago, but the memory remains fresh. It still makes me feel happy all over again. These days, since our house is surrounded by beautiful flowers of many kinds, grown mainly by Bruce, he gets me a box of chocolates and cuts flowers from the yard to make a big bundle of whatever is flowering on February 14th.

"Bruce, do you remember the first Valentine's Day? You delivered the flowers to the Russian wife, and her husband came to the court for me?"

"Of course, I remember! I can still say the message in Russian. *Sprivieton ot Sama*."

"What does it mean?"

"It means 'Love from Sam.'"

Then I asked Bruce the question I had been wondering about all these years, but never asked: why he chose gladiolus on that day? Were roses all sold out when he got there?

"That was because it was the biggest and the most beautiful…and the *cheapest*." He smiled and we both laughed. It was our most memorable Valentine's Day.

Myriad Faces of Change

Ida Jean Smith

It's Sunday morning. A warm spring day ushers in a gentle breeze that caresses the beautiful lavender blossoms on the jacaranda trees that neatly line the sidewalks on both sides of the long, narrow streets. As I drive down the quiet lane, I smile to see a little squirrel quickly run across the road in front of me and scamper up one of the nearby trees.

It's 1963. My husband, Gary, and I have just moved to this neighborhood in Los Angeles, California with our three children, Janet, Vickie, and Gary. We're having fun sightseeing and exploring the area. Although there isn't that much to see, it's new to us. How nice to look at the pretty storybook houses with their wooden shutters and colorful flower beds sprinkled across plush green lawns.

Turning the corner to reach my house, I notice a small church across the way. Service is just letting out. People are coming out of the building, and some are standing outside, visiting with each other. I cannot help but notice that all of the parishioners are Caucasian. I look closely at the marquee. It says: Park Windsor Baptist Church. My heart skips a beat. We're also Baptist. This would be a nice church for us to attend…right down the street from where we now live. We wouldn't have to travel far across town to attend our old church. This would save us time, gas, and energy. Also, we could squeeze in a few extra winks on a Sunday morning. That should sound good to Gary.

I can hardly wait to tell my husband about my gem of a discovery. Less travel time and the idea of a church being in the neighborhood within walking distance is very appealing to us both. We decide to make a visit to Park Windsor Baptist church.

The next Sunday, as Park Windsor's church bells are tolling in the neighborhood, Gary and I take our three children and join the throng of morning worshippers making their way into the sanctuary. We are barely seated when a Caucasian lady with salt and pepper hair and wearing glasses sits down beside me. She smiles broadly and introduces herself.

"I'm Olga Brighton. I live right across the street from the church."

Olga appears to be in her early forties. She extends her hand to me. I shake her hand and say, "I'm Ida Jean Smith, and this is my husband, Gary, and our children, Janet, Vickie, and Gary."

She smiles at the children and reaches across me to shake hands with Gary. Just then the call to worship is heard and everyone gets quiet. Service has begun.

After church, Olga invites us to step across the street and see the flower garden in her back yard. "I love tulips. I grow different varieties and colors. You'll see."

She has a storybook house with grey trim and white shutters. A white picket fence with an archway leads into a front yard dotted with white tulips.

"How lovely!" I exclaim.

She takes us around to the back. We see a field of tulips of every hue, size, and shape. It's breathtaking. After picking a bouquet for me to take home, Olga invites us to come inside for some lemonade.

"Thank you so much," I say, "but we really have to be going now. Hope to see you next week. Thanks again for the beautiful bouquet."

With that, we make our exit. On the way home, Gary asks, "Well, what do you think?"

"I think she's just curious about us," I reply. "She says she was born and raised in that house. Her husband is out of town, and that's why we didn't get to meet him."

Gary looks at me and smiles. "She seemed to take a liking to you, babe."

"She's nice," I reply, returning his smile.

"Why does that lady have so many flowers?" asks Little Gary.

"Yes. she's got too many," Vickie chimes in.

"Where did she get all of them from?" Janet, our oldest child, wants to know.

We both laugh. "You kids stop asking so many questions. Just enjoy the beauty of it."

As time goes by, Olga and I become better acquainted. Olga is full of questions about me, my family, my job, how we arrived at coming to this part of town and to this church.

I discover that she is the church secretary and has been a member of Park Windsor all her life. She is an excellent cookie baker and gives our children a little bag of her homemade cookies every Sunday.

I miss my old neighborhood…colored people all around me except for old man Edwards, an elderly white gentleman who lived alone in his house there on the corner. I miss the warm, friendly greetings, the hand waves and smiles as one passes by, the spontaneous chit-chat as you go in and out of your house, the over the back yard fence conversations with neighbors.

But our children are getting bigger. We've outgrown our small two-bedroom house. We had to make a change…a change that is bittersweet. After looking at several houses, we decide on a spacious four-bedroom house in an all-white neighborhood. Our presence there is met with a conglomeration of attitudes and exhibitions. Fear and apprehension immediately grip the neighborhood. Giggles and outbursts of nervous laughter shatter the atmosphere like a display of firecrackers on the Fourth of July. Others play the Peek-a-Boo game from behind closed curtains in their homes. Whenever we come out on our front porch, we hear doors slamming shut. Stubborn anger runs amuck. Our white neighbors gaze at us like we're wild animals escaped from the zoo. We are met with attitudes that run the gamut of negativity, resentment, and hatred. Everything except a burning cross has challenged us.

Before long, FOR SALE signs start popping up in yards all over the community. We watch as white flight takes off with jet liner speed. Some houses are abandoned before actually being sold. As soon as the whites move out, Negroes move in, invading the neighborhood like an army. Gary and I are not dismayed by any of the behaviours demonstrated by our white neighbors. We hold our heads high and tend to our own business, that being to make a home for our family, to teach our children by example to be good, upright citizens, and to honor and have faith in God.

To help support our goals and desires, in 1964 Gary and I join Park Windsor Baptist church. Attending Park Windsor is a totally new experience for us. Service is short and to the point. Afterwards, a coffee and donut social is held in the dining hall. However, social intercourse between white and colored worshippers is guarded and minimal. Some whites keep their distance. Others do not speak at all, completely ignoring us. Many avoid any eye contact with us. A few boldly glare at us, not blinking an eye. Some give us restrained smiles. We receive fingertip and lukewarm handshakes. A few give pure, warm, heartfelt greetings that strike a golden chord of harmonious melodies, comforting the very depths of our souls. I am both amused and puzzled by the responses our presence provokes.

If looks could kill, I think to myself. *But how can they sit here in church so pious and at the same time…oh, well…* I shrug it off with a soft chuckle to myself.

After we join Park Windsor Church, we witness an influx of Negroes looking for a church close to their new residences. Many join the church, but this action proves disturbing to many white parishioners. Nevertheless, the coloreds keep coming. More and more join every Sunday.

One Saturday afternoon our doorbell rings. It is John Springer, our white pastor. Throughout the process of colored migration to the community and Park Windsor Church, Pastor Springer's demeanor has mirrored deep sincerity, while extending hospitality towards everybody.

We invite Pastor Springer to come in. After exchanging pleasantries, Pastor Springer speaks very candidly, coming right to the point. "I want to personally welcome you to our fellowship. God respects all persons and so do I. There are those here who feel the same as I do, however few in number. As you know, I've been canvassing this community, reaching out to people, especially newcomers, and inviting them to our Sunday services. My activities are meeting with resistance from the vast majority of members. In fact, they invited me to a private meeting over at one member's house. To my surprise, most of the church members were there. Right away, they started expressing their fears and concerns."

Gary and I look at each other. Then Gary asks, "What are they afraid of? What are their concerns? Look, we're not trying to make friends with the whites or get in their circle. We go there because the church is close to our house…it's convenient. We have our own families, our own set of friends. The whites don't need to worry about us."

Pastor Springer looks down, then replies, "Yeah, I know, but they're in the majority, and they've asked me to resign, which I will do, but I want you both to know from me why I will not be at the church anymore."

A wave of emotions rushes through our bodies: anger, impatience, disgust, sympathy, compassion.

Pastor Springer goes on speaking, "I'm ashamed to say this, but a few do not want their children in Sunday school class sitting beside the little colored children. They say their children are scared to be around them."

Gary and I sit staring at the Pastor in stony silence, trying to process all the things we have just heard.

The Pastor stands up to leave. "The whole thing in a nutshell is this... our white members are afraid that the colored members will soon outnumber them and will rule over them." He shakes his head. "I'm sorry."

Gary and I stand and reach out to shake hands with our pastor.

I ask him, "Will there be segregation in heaven?"

He looks at us, smiles, and walks out the door. We never see Pastor Springer again.

After he leaves, I say to my husband, "Gary, we can't let their prejudice and ill will create a stony path for us and our children to tread. This is just another mountain for us to climb. We can reach the top. We've done it before."

Gary agrees and takes me in his arms, cradling me. We both feel a sense of safety and security as we stand in our living room locked in a warm embrace. Unbeknownst to us, our comfortable blanket of confidence is soon to be ripped to shreds by attack dogs let loose by their owners.

After Pastor Springer resigns, the white members begin to hold clandestine meetings behind closed doors at the church. The rooms where these meetings are held are pregnant with malicious ideas that are utilized to establish a covenant... a covenant designed to allay fears of a Negro "takeover" of the curch.

One Sunday morning the church clerk reads the covenant to the congregation:

"Park Windsor Baptist Church members have voted to deed the church and all its properties to the Los Angeles Baptist City Mission Society." The reasoning behind the covenant is obvious: to circumvent the probability of the coloreds gaining control of the church. Negro members glance at each other with puzzled, yet knowing looks, as shock waves of disbelief permeate the atmosphere. The announcement thrusts a dagger into the hopes of members who want the church to remain an independent entity. Nonetheless, to the colored parishioners news is like water rolling off a duck's back. We just faithfully continue attending the church and Sunday school at Park Windsor. The white parishioners, however, vacate the church almost overnight. Only two or three whites remain. By this time the congregation is all Negro, including our first Negro pastor.

To my surprise one of the white parishioners deserting camp is Olga. One Sunday morning we come to church and we see a For Sale sign in her yard. The house is empty. All of the tulips in her front yard have been dug up. Olga never mentioned one word to me about moving. I was shocked. All the cookies, all the flowers, all the smiles, all the pleasant chit-chat was simply a masquerade. She didn't even care enough to say good-bye to me. There was no exchange of phone numbers, addresses, nothing. I couldn't believe it. I was momentarily hurt, but then reality kicked in, subduing my hurt feelings. I really feel sorry for Olga, as I harbor no hard feelings towards her.

Mrs. Lee is one of the whites who remained at the church. I asked her about Olga.

"Oh, yes, the Brightons had a new house built out near Torrance, and they moved out last week. Olga dug up all her tulips and the bulbs, even those in the back yard. She took everything with her."

She did indeed, I thought to myself.

I see Olga one last time at a general meeting of the Women's Missionary Society which meets once a year at a hotel in downtown Los Angeles. I am so happy to see Olga that I rush over to greet her and maybe give her a handshake, a hug perhaps. She looks me straight in the face, then turns her head without speaking. I could have kicked myself.

I tell Gary about it when I get home. He says, "Don't worry about it, baby. That's not the first time that's happened to you, and it sure won't be the last."

"You're right, honey. I wish you weren't right, but that's the way it is."

It's New Year's Eve, December 31, 1967. I'm standing at my kitchen sink, washing some of my best china plates that I'm going to be using tonight for our New Year's Eve party. The kids are over at their grandparents for the night. We're having some friends from church over after "Watch Meeting"…

watching the old year go out, watching the new year come in. Gunshots at midnight, car horns blowing, music, dancing, laughter, lots of good food and drink, everyone wishing everyone else a Happy New Year. What a beautiful season, full of enchantment and wonder.

I'm humming softly along with the radio, when I look out the kitchen window and see smoke. Lots of it! I then hear sirens that sound close to the house. I run outside to see what's going on. Gary is working in the front yard. We grab hands and hurriedly walk down the street, joining others doing the same. We come upon a scene of fire trucks, smoke, and firemen putting out a fire. And the fire is at Park Windsor Church! Everyone stands around, gawking at the devastation. Gary and I turn to each other. We both speak at the same time.

"Who did this?"

"Why?"

When the last fireman has left, we stand there in total disbelief and shock. The sanctuary is demolished. The trustee room and other areas damaged. I look at the water damaged piano and organ…all the mud on what used to be floors…the pews, furniture…everything gutted, water-soaked…

I begin to cry. Gary puts his arm around me.

"It's too much, Gary. Whoever did this…why? Why?"

"Now, now, baby. It's going to be all right. It's going to be all right. Don't you worry. Let's go home now."

That night there was no watch meeting at the church, no New Year's Eve party at our house.

My husband, Gary, and several other men of the church organize a watch force for Park Windsor, taking turns guarding the church day and night until it is rebuilt. To this day authorities have never determined the cause of the fire. The Los Angeles Baptist City Mission Society renovated the church and, on April 28, 1969, they transferred the corporation grant deed back to Park Windsor Church. What a day for celebration!

Gary and I have been married for sixty-three years. We are still living in the same house. Our children are grown and have moved out on their own. And now, fifty years later, Gary and I are still worshipping at the "small church across the way"…Park Windsor Baptist Church.

Gone Too Soon

Leona A. Jones

Oh, Martin, how I miss you!
Listening to your eloquent speeches
I weep... still.

Your passionate words,
Your pleas for non-violent action
Touched the hearts of thousands
Who had yearned for equality
Through decades of despair.

Oh, you weren't perfect—
Nobody is.
(Many believe Jesus was,
But, of course, He didn't have
The FBI bugging his telephone.)

You were the leader we needed, Martin
But you left too soon.
Just as Lincoln did.

Yes, the laws were passed, but oh, the aftermath...
Still tension between the north and the south,
Ongoing discrimination and hatred
Everywhere.

Perhaps if you'd lived
Progress would have come sooner,
Maybe you'd have groomed
A new, wonderful leader
To take your place.

But, Martin, I hope you know
Things really *are* better now...
Society is learning to look past skin color
To the content of character
And liking what they find.

We haven't yet learned
That peace is better than war
But you could only do so much
In the time you had.

Oh, Martin, I miss you so.

First Runner-up: Best Non-fiction Contest

Mississippi Memoirs

Irene Thomas

The movie "Showboat" had just appeared on the scene in the '30s, and I remembered the times I had spent trying to understand, as Paul Robeson did in the movie, just what that Ol' Man River was about. He sang, "It don' say nuthin' but must know somethin'…" Yes, I agreed.

My first acquaintance with the river happened when my Aunt Annie took me for a picnic lunch on the excursion boat, *Admiral.*

That day, being a Holiday, we were met at the pier by a band playing patriotic songs. There was an air of festival, and laughter and talk flowed easily as friends met who hadn't been able to see each other very often. Even the bright sunshine made the day something spectacular. This would be a visit with some of the wealthier people of St. Louis.

Unfortunately, my wardrobe wasn't acceptable; at this time (I was about ten) I was making my own dresses. I paid fifteen cents for a manicure job, fifteen for a hairset with "gooey" and, having previously bought a pattern, I found that fifteen cents would buy a remnant of material. I had paid a whole quarter for my white tennies, but they were unacceptable also. I had to first be taken to a dressmaker to have some dresses made and new shoes purchased. I happened to be in my tomboy stage, so all this finery was just so much overkill. My aunt and her friends were dressed in their finest—the ladies wore hats and some carried parasols. All were so correctly garbed, but I just felt stifled in my fancy clothing.

Young boys were hired by the boat owners to help the passengers, and many fancy boxes of gourmet food were brought to our table, along with ice to keep food from spoiling. Our green painted wooden table even had a white tablecloth, and silverware like I had never seen in my or a neighbor's home. Apparently, lack of money was something that hadn't touched these people. I had never seen such rich food and passed most of it up for a sandwich at noon. The sounds of gaiety continued, aided by the music of Eddy Duchin and his Band.

I guess my aunt felt safe in allowing me to roam the boat; where else could I run to, and probably some one would see me if I fell overboard. I was thrilled to have the freedom of the whole boat, and after inspecting everything I could walk to, I especially liked the ramp that connected the two floors. I had never seen anything like that before. But now I was beginning to feel blisters forming due to the newness of my fancy pointed-toe leather shoes, so I took the shoes and placed them in one of my aunt's cartons. It felt so good to let my sock-covered feet feel the freedom of the air.

Most of my time was spent at the side of the boat, watching the water wheels as they paddled through the water, up and around and up and around. I watched the water change colors as it rose, circled, and fell. I wondered at what was underneath all that greenish water, couldn't see anything...but the paddle wheels kept going and going.

I ignored the dancing in the afternoon, walked around some more and visited the powerful wheels often to gaze down into the dark waters. The rumbling sound of the wheels contrasted with the joyous sounds of the picnickers and dancers. It was a very good life for those aboard.

A few weeks later, I was to learn that all was not so happy on the muddy Mississippi. My father and I took a long walk down Angelica Street to the northern part of the St. Louis riverfront. It looked so different and sounded so different, or I should say it lacked the sound of music and laughter. The end of the street must have been a port at one time, for it was all red-bricked, and I could see where the water had cleaned it as it rolled by.

To a small girl the place had some fantastic features. I could see many doll houses, hundreds actually, all made of cardboard. They were four, five, six feet high, each one made according to the skill of the builder. One was quite fancy with hinged doors and windows, all of cardboard. Most homes were decorated with some form of remembrance of the owner's past homeland. All races melded together. If I'd been older, I'd have thought of them as remnants of humanity.

I ran over and started to look in a window, when my father pulled me back. "You can't look in there, there are people living there!"

Living! That was just cardboard! Yes, it was, and it was also the time known as the Great Depression. I could see small groups of people standing and discussing something that made them look very sad. A few cigarettes were handed around and put a brief appreciative smile on some faces.

In the distance I could hear the agonized cry of what had to be a sick baby. Then, suddenly, silence…followed by the piercing scream of a woman. Two ladies ran from their cardboard homes and rushed to embrace the mother and still child.

My father just shook his head, and we walked on.

Just then an old rickedy delivery truck came rattling down the street and did a U-turn. The driver leaned on the horn, and then both men got out and opened the two rear doors. People emerged from everywhere and lined up to receive the food that was being given out.

It was with shock that I saw my father get into the line. He motioned for me to remain just where I was. I could see he kept his eyes on me, but he stayed in line until he was able to accept the loaf of bread and piece of summer sausage from the truck. Then I saw the reason for his actions—a very old crippled lady was trying to make her way up the road to get to the truck, and without help she would never make it. I was embarrassed, though, when she accepted the food and tried to kiss my father's hands. I guess he was also, for I saw him reach into his pocket and pull out and give her the only money he had, fifteen cents he'd earned the day before shoveling a ton of coal into a neighbor's basement.

Soon everything had quieted down, and we walked closer to the gently lapping water's edge. Again I peered into the dark waters, but saw nothing unusual. As we drew nearer to a side of the street, we heard music. Two guitar players and what I think was a musical-saw player were singing accompaniment to the sad thrumming of the music: "Ah gets weary and sick o' tryin', Ah'm tired o' livin' and feared o' dyin', but ol' man river…" Suddenly, the sound was picked up and many people were singing and humming along. As they ate what was probably their only meal of the day, they knew a brief moment of happiness, stolen from hours of despair.

"…He jes keeps rollin', he keeps on rollin' along."

Big Daddy Plays and is Swept into the Night

Fred Bridges

Leaves of maples, elms, hickory, and other hardwoods now colored the foothills. Nature had painted a backdrop for the annual centipede two-step conclaves. The gathering brought thousands of dancing feet from every decaying log and other pieces of wood. It turned the dell into a mecca for centipede shoe salesmen and purveyors of fancy attire. The attire created prisms of color that matched nature's fall panorama.

A bandstand arose at the end of the meadow, and notes of jazz, bebop, and country western set the many feet into a frenzy. The stage was covered by a netting made of dragonfly wings. These filtered a soft blue light onto the stage.

On the sax was Big Daddy Doodle Bug; the bass, Joe Centipede; the trumpet, Hot Lips Catfish; and the drums, Sweeter Brown. Vocals were handled by the three Lady Bug Sisters.

Sweet notes soon filled the air. Glittering centipede feet began to swing and sway. These bedecked feet created a rhythm never before heard. Up in heaven The Duke, Count, Harry, and Glenn looked down and smiled.

Humans in nearby hamlets shook in fear. These feet were now generating a cloud of dust long remembered from the dust bowl years. Tidy housewives cowered in their homes. Too many boogying feet terrified the plain. Was there a hero who would save the day?

Fortunately, a convention of Hoover vacuum salesmen and Orca men were also in town. The two groups met and formed a plan. The airborne Orca men would attack from above while the Hoover men moved in from below.

D-Day was here and the masked adventurers moved in with great stealth. The dancing feet, now tranquilized, were swept into the night. The sweet tune, "When the Bugs go Marching In," was heard from the Hoover horns.

The Perfect Pitch

Helen Muriel Ganopole

My one admission to upward mobility was my enduring wish to own a baby grand piano. I wanted a smooth, ebony beauty with a tone and touch that suited my penchant for Debussy and Ravel and would sound crisp and clean when I switched to Chopin. Oh, how I wanted it!

Other pianos had filled whatever musical space I owned: all uprights, all adequate, one even a studio Steinway that had a sweet and lovely tone. Yet the domineering image of a baby grand lived within my mind and persisted.

When I suddenly inherited $5,000 from a generous relative, I banked it quickly and began to ponder possibilities. The pros and cons for investing in a baby grand took on major proportions as I began to consider the many ways $5,000 could go. Space was a problem. Finding the right piano at all for that price was a problem. Spending it all on myself was a problem. However, encouragement came from many sources, and the tide turned into a burst of optimism.

If ever I were to have that baby grand, this was the time. I yearned for it, frankly needed it, and so began my search, but always with a dialogue raging within. I visited our town's prime piano dealer, walking the aisles, stroking the surfaces of pianos, and playing chords and scales. The instruments were so beautiful and so expensive, far more than I could pay. Even second-hand, they were a reach. Touches and sounds were so varied; how could I decide anyway? Where was *the* piano that would make me feel like a great impresario, a gifted performer, a concert wannabe and, more realistically, a happy dreamer of a pianist, hidden away in her own little living room?

One salesman was sympathetic and especially helpful. He seemed aware of my inner dialogue. I sensed he knew exactly how I felt, and he lingered with me as I strolled the store. I returned home that day, and early in the evening my phone rang. It was the salesman!

He had a personal baby grand for sale, unused now and a sad memory of an unfortunate marriage, for she had arranged a new life with an even better piano. The orphan was a Yamaha, and I went to visit it and play it. From the moment I heard that exquisite sound responding to my particular gentle touch, it was mine, for $5,000. I had a skilled piano tuner come and look at it, and he proclaimed it a real bargain with exceptional touch and tone.

I bought that piano and, indeed, the hours of pleasure spent playing enriched my life. As years passed, that piano became part of me, and I relied on it in bad times. I had a duet partner and a violinist friend to play with, and family and even neighbors enjoyed my playing.

As years passed, my chosen life changes made it impossible to move the piano with me. My eldest son now has it in his family room back east, and grandchildren have taken lessons on it. Other accomplished musicians in the family have played it. Each time it is tuned, it is proclaimed a "fine piano." I play it when I visit, run my fingers over the beautiful surface, and never regret one moment of my decision to buy it. I found my perfect piano!

At the age

Una Nichols Hynum

when something breaks we don't fix it
at the age where every part of the body
has a different wake up call
at the age where we walk carefully, like a child
pushing a needle through her sampler, straight up,
straight down, embroidering the old virtues
Patience, Prudence, Hope, Faith,
the names of great aunts
at the age where medicine bottles accumulate
on the shelf, blood pressure gauge resides
beside the salt and pepper
at the age of remembering rain, wild,
wild roses twined along a split rail fence
a creek that speaks as it runs its hands over the rocks
camping under stars the night Sputnik went over
and we didn't know we were witnessing history
at the age where, in spite of all the harm
we've done, we can still laugh, holding our hands
out the window up to our elbows for the weather report.

Teddy Bear Picnic
a nursery song

Bobbie Jean Bishop

Laced in the shadows of middle-age I picture
    the charmed porch of childhood, screened to
keep out mosquitoes big as thumbs. My hair
    adrift in a sea of heat, I clip clop over tiles like
a pony in my mother's shoes, phonograph needle
    riding high on grooves of a lightly warped record.
"If you go down in the woods today, you'd better
    not go alone"—song spilling into my heart as I
skip toward where danger lies, "the never there was"
    realm of untamed bears. Little fazed by sounds
from my mother's vacuum, I clap and prance like
    Pan's child, unleashed into the wild. Bathed by
mists of memory, my aging self sways to refrains on
    a radio, tries a little twirl—hair loose and streaked
with white, eyelids drawn like blinds half-closed.

A Beary, Scary Mountain Visit

Helen Jones-Shepherd

The smell of coffee in that clean mountain air wafted through the campground one July morning at Twin Lakes in the Sierra Nevadas. We sat outside our motor home early that summer morning to sip freshly brewed coffee and discuss our plans for the day. Allen, my husband, began gathering our fishing gear together for the short trek to the rental boats and our quest to catch those large Rainbow or German brown trout, which he affectionately called "brownies," that were found swimming around in the lake located nearby.

The temperature was in the 50's and the sun was beginning to shine as we shoved off from the dock. My excitement mounted as the little boat with the outboard motor hummed along, taking us farther out onto the beautiful lake situated some 7000 feet high in the Sierras. Catching fish was a new adventure for me. Less than a year ago my husband, who had been enjoying this sport since he was a child, had taught me the basics of fishing. We fastened our lures, cast our lines out and began trolling, moving steadily and slowly through the water, anticipating a strike or a gentle tug alerting us to a fish nibbling on our lures.

We both savored the serenity and peacefulness as we looked about at the tall slim pines lining the shoreline. Suddenly, I felt a tug on my line and screamed, "I've got one! I've got one!" overwhelmed by the prospect of catching my first fish in this exquisite mountain lake.

"Careful," Allen cautioned. "You must set the hook or you'll lose him."

The trout thrashed about, spewing water everywhere at the end of my line. I was convinced he was hooked and quickly controlled my enthusiasm. I ever so slowly started to reel him in when the line went slack.

"Oh, no," I cried out. "I've lost him. I guess I didn't set the hook right."

"That's the sport of fishing," Allen stated, trying to console me.

After attaching the lure and casting again, I settled down in earnest and focused on improving my skill at manipulating the line successfully. We continued trolling for at least an hour, our only accompaniment the steady hum of the motor, when Allen caught a beautiful Rainbow, perfect for dinner. Shortly after that, I caught my first "brownie" and proudly announced, "Now we're all set for an excellent fish dinner."

Happy and content with our catch so far, but wanting more to put in the freezer, we trolled farther out toward the depths of the lake, marveling at the lush greenery of the trees and the intense blue of the lake water. A lovely cool breeze came up, which felt invigorating as we trolled through the liquid blue. But a few minutes later the sky darkened, threatening a summer thundershower. It was warm, however, so we were not concerned about a light shower and stayed out there, concentrating on catching those tasty fish.

Quite abruptly, the sky grew blacker, and thunder and lightning shattered the stillness. The crackling of the lightning bolts startled us, and we noted other boats leaving the area, heading for cover. Still not in a rush to leave, because we really love to fish, we stayed on the lake, but soon huge droplets began to pummel us. We watched in awe this magnificent celebration of nature, until a lighting bolt cracked and struck a tree on shore not 100 yards from us. The tree immediately burst into flames.

"Wow, that was close," Allen, exclaimed. "We had better head in."

A wee bit shaken at the proximity of this horrendous event, I readily agreed as I watched flames leaping about the tree that was struck.

Allen tried to start the motor, but it wouldn't turn over right away. As the minutes ticked by and the motor didn't seem to want to start, the rain increased in its intensity. By now we were drenched. We exchanged fearful glances, a silent prayer in our hearts, and the motor started up. By now the sky was ablaze with lightning, and thunder roared. Allen revved the motor, and we rapidly skimmed across the water, noticing that we were the only ones still on the lake. Lightning struck again, seemingly closer than before, and thunder raged with ear-splitting ferocity.

Fortunately, we reached the dock safely. As we climbed out of the boat, soaked through, the rental operator shouted with exasperation, "Didn't you hear my bullhorn telling everyone to come in? Being out on the lake in a summer thunderstorm is not the place to be—it's just too dangerous!" Thoroughly scolded and shaken, we ran dripping and cold to the campground for shelter, clutching our beloved fish.

Cleaning our catch was not my job, so I went about squeezing lemons, preparing to wrap the trout in foil with butter, pepper, fresh juice, and dill. I couldn't wait to devour those freshly caught fish. The near miss and danger was all worth it, as we sat on dry land, enjoying our delicious repast.

After dinner but before dark, we saw other campers scurrying about the campground and wondered what was going on. We saw a dark figure running through the campsite with many excited people and flashing cameras in hot pursuit. Apparently, a black bear, enticed by the smell of fish being cooked, had entered the camp to investigate and perhaps pick up a free meal. More and more men, women, and children joined the chase until the bear became so bewildered he shinnied up a tall pine and sat there, looking down at the humans below. His broad, upturned nose sniffed the air as food smells floated skyward to his safe haven above. He held fast to his tree and after awhile looked rather forlorn. The onlookers far below disbanded and eventually retired for the night. Our beautiful bear wasn't about to come down and stayed tree-bound until all was "quiet on the western front."

Early next morning at about 6:00 A.M. we looked skyward and, sure enough, our hairy visitor had left. However, later that afternoon, when Allen came around the side of the motor home, there stood another black bear between him and the way out, with a tree blocking his retreat in back. The huge bear stood upright, eyes darting to and fro, searching for a way out. Allen froze, not moving a muscle. I was looking out the window of the motor home and, shocked at what I saw, I said through the screened window, "You better get out of his way."

Since Allen was not threatening him, the bear hesitated, his massive body swayed a little, and then he backed up slowly and went on to the next campsite. We both watched as he rummaged through a cold fire pit, obviously foraging for food. The giant bruin dug and grasped what looked like a steak bone, then quickly rolled over on his back and gnawed away contentedly on his find.

Allen, breathing a little easier now, moved slowly to the safety of the motor home and watched this behavior with me. Our morning visitor appeared comfortable in this environment, invaded by us humans who did not discourage him from finding and enjoying food. He acted very unconcerned about the close proximity of people. To our relief this full-grown bear, after finishing his snack, ambled away, his nose in the air, sniffing for more delectable treats.

All campers are warned *not* to leave food or containers with food or leftovers outside at night, for nature's residents are late-night marauders and will help themselves to anything they find, and who is to stop them, or who wants to?

After witnessing nature and its glorious fanfare from the heavens above, plus a few of nature's creatures confronting, exploring, and foraging for food, we were grateful that no injury had occurred to anyone.

We then sat down, poured ourselves a cup of coffee, and reflected on the many gifts that nature provides us, especially in the mountainous regions of our beautiful state of California.

Woman in the Moon

Claudia Poquoc

Southern California – the most man-altered landscape
in the Northern Hemisphere – so much disappearing:
animal habitats, fresh water streams, native languages.

Two years after the forest fire, charred pine and
oak still struggle, half black – half green like scarred
and wounded women saddened by losses of youth,
unfulfilled lives, freedom to be alone at night.

Up the road small-faced flowers skirt a deer's jawbone
where waves of tall grass hide older scars. I cross the land's
invisible border to the lake's edge, inhale the twilight
before peering into quiet waters, offer up my feelings
of loss to a new phase of the moon.

The Deer

Lois J. Godel

At 2:00 A.M. my dog barks to go out.
Half asleep, I stumble downstairs, snap his leash on
and open the door to dark rustlings, swooshes and thuds.
My dog strains towards the sounds. I hold him back.
Shadows move across the moonlit grass: a convocation
of deer, arriving for a nocturnal feast. I call to them:
Bambies! Go eat someone else's bushes!
And then I see her, near the edge of our yard, lying on her side,
big as a pony, stretched out almost like my dog does, and deer don't.
Unsure of what is dream, and what is real, I close the door.

At first morning light, the deer is gone from the remembered spot.
Then there she is. Ten feet away, towards the woods
half sitting up; more like a giant dog than a doe.
My heart rushes to her. She must need water, but I am afraid to approach,
afraid of Lyme disease, afraid of her fear, of the hoof on her unbroken leg.
I am no vet, no animal technician. I call the county humane society.
They don't deal with deer. They connect me to
the sheriff's office. They will come and handle it.

An officer arrives. He rings my doorbell.
I come out and lead him to the deer.
He says it is too bad the deer isn't closer to the right-of-way.
The county won't take a dead deer from someone's yard.
That makes no sense, I say.
You should go inside, he says.
I wait for minutes. Finally, the shot rings out.
I go outside. The officer and the deer have vanished.
And then I see her.

Gun drawn, he had slowly approached the crippled animal,
who thrashed and hurled herself fifty feet
into the right-of-way. Convenient
for the county, an exemplary public
servant, he then shot her.
The deer came into my yard,
seeking refuge in the middle of the night.

Big Fluffy

Eleanor Whitney Nelson

"I can't imagine—not in my worst nightmare!" Who hasn't said these words?

On what started out as an ordinary Tuesday morning five years ago, I faced a nightmare that would rank high on anyone's list. On that day, my husband, Frank, and I were having morning coffee in the kitchen of our semi-rural ranch home in the Desert Southwest. It was about seven-thirty, and Frank, dressed in western boots and jeans, had just returned from feeding our horses. Still in my robe and slippers, I was enjoying a rare morning of loafing and reading the newspaper before digging into the day's activities. Pattie, our cat, lay purring on my lap.

Our two dogs were outside, barking in their acre-and-a-half fenced-in yard. Familiar with their woofs and growls, I knew their talk was about something of interest in the four-legged animal world—perhaps a passing coyote or bobcat. It was not a stranger-danger person alert. Whatever they were barking at was more interesting than the breakfast I had dished out and was waiting to serve them.

On most mornings Amber, our Golden Retriever, would greet us with one of her small fluffy toys stuffed in her mouth. She'd prance around the house until I called the dogs into the laundry room for breakfast. Slim, a large white and tan pointer-lab-retriever mix, would ignore his collection of toys until after breakfast. At fifteen, his hearing was mostly a thing of the past. He would lie on his mat until he sniffed food and saw me mouth the words "dog food." Once his bowl was licked clean, he would trot into the living room, select a stuffed animal and pounce on it, toss it in the air and chase it back and forth across the room until he was out of breath.

That morning, when the dogs finally came mulling and flouncing into the kitchen after their outside bark fest, I noticed that Slim had his favorite toy, Big Fluffy, with him. A crudely formed fleece bear, it was the size of a flattened football. Understood to be Slim's possession, Amber never played with it, but that morning the two of them were pushing and shoving, bumping shoulders, propelling Big Fluffy along between them. As the surging canine mass moved closer, passing inches from my bare legs, I noticed that Big Fluffy had sprouted a tiny black and white striped head and a rim of black fur below the mound of white fleece. More importantly, Big Fluffy was independently mobile.

"Skunk!" I yelled.

Headed straight in Frank's direction, the skunk was snapping at the dogs, trying to ward them off as they sought to tear through the thick fur on its neck. Frank lunged for the dogs, pulling them away; he kicked at the animal, which now focused on him. I leaped up, sending Pattie flying, and ran to get a broom.

A distinct, unpleasant aroma accompanied the intruder. Oh, God, please don't let it spray, I thought. But my second thought abruptly crowded out the first: I hope it's not rabid.

When I got back to the kitchen with the broom, the skunk had latched onto one of Slim's hind legs. A look of confusion crossed the old dog's face as he unsuccessfully tried to shake free of the creature. I jabbed at the skunk's head with the stiff bristles. I pushed and pried, but it hung on. Finally, I whacked it on the snout with the head of the broom. I felt the skunk loosen its grip and shoveled it away from Slim.

While Frank held the dogs' collars, the skunk scuttled across the floor. Steering it with my broom, I reached for the outside security screen door, flung it open and prodded the skunk, trying to force it outside. It snarled and charged me. I parried the crazed animal with my broom, forced the bristles under it and launched it out the door. Grasping the knob, I slammed the door shut. The skunk flung itself against the heavy metal mesh, its long claws scratching at the holes. The dogs wrenched free from Frank and rushed in for the attack. Crashing into the screen, they knocked the skunk to the ground.

For a moment it lay dazed, then slowly it dragged itself to its feet and hobbled away, hugging the wall of our semi-attached guesthouse. When it came to the front door, it rose up, clawing at the wood. Finding nothing of interest, it continued to the end of the covered porch and disappeared around the corner of the building.

"We don't know if it's rabid," I shouted. "Get a weapon. We've got to kill it."

Frank was already sprinting toward the hall closet.

Free to run, the dogs took off for the dog door in the laundry room. I raced after them, following a trail of skunk scent through the house into my office, which was next to the laundry room. Here the odor was strongest. Across a breezeway, which links the main house with the guest house, I saw the skunk forcing its way back toward me through the wire fence surrounding the dog yard and breezeway. I couldn't believe the football-sized creature was squeezing through the two-by-three-inch mesh. Looking like an engorged tick with its tiny head and huge body, the skunk was like a zombie trying to get back inside the house. Both dogs lunged at its face as it thrashed its way through the distorted hole in the fence.

I pulled Amber off and dragged her into the house, but before I could close the laundry room door, she struggled free and flew back outside into the fray. All the while I was yelling at the dogs to "leave it." Suddenly, Slim broke away and calmly walked off. Had years of training finally penetrated his aging ears? As I jerked Amber loose, the skunk slid through the wire and staggered toward the dog door. It must have smelled the dogs' food inside.

Just then, Frank appeared with a *nulla-nulla*, a heavy club carved by Australian Aborigines out of dense hardwood. He whacked the skunk behind the head, over and over, until the animal lay still. We double-bagged it in heavy plastic garbage sacks and hung it in a tree, where nosy animals could not bother it.

While we were lucky that the skunk never released a major blast of scent, there were traces of unpleasant odor throughout the house and breezeway. More worrisome was the fact that spots of saliva covered the floor throughout the kitchen and hallways, the laundry room, and my office. The dogs' faces, necks, and chests were soaking wet with saliva, but we found no bite marks anywhere on them.

We put in a call to the Animal Care Center, and an animal control officer was there within the hour. She jotted down our story and checked the dogs' licenses. From the information we gave her, she believed the skunk was rabid. Healthy skunks are nocturnal and are rarely seen during the day. Because there was no local lab, the skunk had to be sent to another town and wouldn't be transported until the next day. If the test came back positive, she said we would be notified immediately.

As the officer left, she jokingly said, "The skunk *is* dead, isn't it?" We laughingly replied we were certain it was, and besides, it would surely suffocate inside the sealed plastic bags. She told us later that, when she unwrapped the bags at the Animal Care Center, the skunk pushed out on its own power, quite alive. She said her scream brought all the other officers running. They promptly dispatched the animal and cut off its head for examination.

While our encounter with the skunk is, undoubtedly, the most dramatic part of the story, what happened afterwards is the real nightmare.

Since the dogs, cat, and horses were vaccinated, we judged them to be safe from the rabies virus. Neither Frank nor I had been bitten, but both of us had small scratches on our hands from working around the ranch and dry-weather cracks around our fingernails. With broken skin in contact with smears of saliva, we worried that we might be infected.

All the next day, Wednesday, we hovered around the phone, but heard nothing. On Thursday morning Frank called the Animal Care Center. They still had no word. We asked what we should do if results came back positive. They told us to call the County Health Department and gave us the number of the chief medical officer. She would be able to tell us everything we needed to know, as her department would be handling any treatment should we need it.

I called and found I had been given the wrong extension. After being shuffled from one number to another—at least four—I finally got somebody (whom I will call Rafael) who seemed to know what he was talking about. He said County Health did not give the shots. We should contact our primary physician if it became necessary.

About that time someone from Animal Control called to say the skunk was, indeed, rabid and to call Rafael at County Health. We phoned back and once again he said to call our primary care physician. He also said an officer would be out to the house with paperwork for placing the dogs in home quarantine.

As instructed, we called our primary care doctor. She said she didn't have vaccine and to call County Health. We called back and after being transferred several times were told to go to the emergency room. We drove to the ER at a local hospital and explained what we wanted. They looked at us as though we had lost our minds and said to call County Health. We said we had and they shrugged—not their business, they didn't carry the vaccine.

By then we were beginning to feel twinges of desperation. If we were to get treatment for rabies, we knew we needed to start before too much time passed. Two days had already gone by.

On Friday morning Frank called a nurse he had known for years at one of the local clinics. A specialist in overseas travel, she was adept at procuring vaccines of all types.

Yes, she said she could do it. We breathed a collective sigh of relief. She told us we had seven days from exposure—at the very most ten—to start treatment, so we should be all right. A short while later she called back and said we should go to County Health.

"We did!" we screamed.

She said not to worry—she'd get right on it. It took all day, but she finally found a laboratory in another state that would sell the vaccine. She also obtained authorization from the Health Department to administer it. The problem, we discovered, was that there was a worldwide shortage of rabies vaccine. Only three labs made it, but one had gone out of business, and another had shut down to upgrade its facilities. The third lab was in China and had questionable quality control. Consequently, no one used it. Luckily for us, one of the first two labs had a small stockpile. After much arm twisting, they agreed to dole out a few vials.

We were told the vaccine would arrive by Fed Ex on Monday, and we could come to the clinic to get our first shots. That would be seven days. On Monday we discovered that only a partial order of vaccine had been sent, but there was enough for us to get started.

Two different types of shots are needed. The first is rabies immunoglobulin. This gives you immediate immunity for up to three months. The second is a series of five rabies inoculations, which provides long-term immunity. Should one be exposed again in the future, two booster shots are needed.

We received forty percent of the recommended dosage of immunoglobulin and the first long term rabies shot that Monday—the seventh day. Three days later we got the rest of the immunoglobulin and the second rabies shot. We had just snuck in under the deadline. From then on vaccinations were given at intervals of seven, fourteen, and twenty-eight days. The immunoglobulin was injected in our backsides, which brought tears to my eyes, while the others were given in our arms. No longer is it necessary to endure the excruciating series of shots in the stomach, which was standard procedure for many years.

As with most vaccinations, people are affected in different ways. Both Frank and I had immediate reactions—we felt as though we were on an alcoholic binge. Worse than that, we felt stupid. We couldn't get our thoughts together. The effect grew stronger after each subsequent shot, and after each dose the symptoms took longer to wear off. For a month I was only semi-functional, but I'll take that over the alternative.

We soon learned that there had been a major outbreak of rabies in the skunk population in our area. Every time we mentioned our encounter to friends, we heard horror stories about skunks. None could match our ordeal. News broadcasts and newspaper articles spouted statistics about rabies, but after a few weeks the scare was forgotten and other subjects claimed the headlines. The dogs breezed through home quarantine. After forty-five days they showed no symptoms and were released by the veterinarian. Pattie and the horses were healthy, as well.

I wish I could say the nightmare ended there, but one morning recently, our new dog, Digger, who has distinctive barks for javelinas, coyotes, rattlesnakes, skunks, and unfamiliar people, sounded a warning that a skunk was trying to enter the yard at exactly the same spot where the first one had. What do they say about lightning never striking twice in the same place?

Animal Control came promptly and trapped the animal. After establishing that no one had had more than visual contact with it, they said, "You know, it's not normal for a skunk to be out in the daytime." I assured them we knew. Off they went.

We expected to hear some news in the next few days, but no one from their office called. Although curious, we decided that, since we had had no physical contact, they felt no need to notify us with the results of their tests. Now that we were immunized and knew what procedures to follow, worry about infection had been pushed to the back of our minds, and we had ceased to be proactive.

Three months later we received a phone call. A rather tentative voice on the other end of the line said, "Um…we're just trying to, ah, clean up some paperwork. Has anyone from this office called to uh…let you know the skunk was rabid?"

"No," I replied.

There was a long pause. "No one there had any contact with it?"

"No."

"Um…would you like me to put you in contact with the Health Department?"

"It's a little late for that," I said.

A rather sheepish voice said yes. I told him we were familiar with rabies and understood the situation. The relief in the caller's voice was palpable when he rang off.

The dog door has been replaced, but skunks remain a natural part of our environment, and I do, on occasion, hold my breath at night when I catch a whiff of one passing by our bedroom window. As the foul odor fades away, I breathe a sigh of relief. Another potential nightmare has drifted into the night.

WHITE SANDS, N.M. 1953

Betty Birkemark

Dunes that stretched beyond the eye
Interlocking sand and sky.
There was no shade for crawling things,
Or shadow of a swift bird's wings.
A Space Age Testing Ground, back then.
It's *history,* now…the *moon* saw men.

Powwow

Florence Korzin

The Indians hosted a powwow celebration
by the shores of Lake Casitas' rounded rim.
Represented there are many nations
Choctaw, Chippawa, Shawnee, Hopi, Algonquin.

In triangles festal fires burnt bright,
beaded macrame dream catchers hung there.
Bones of animal skeletons lay in sight
of far-flung fawns and foxes' vacant stare.

Pounding drums and chants enlivened our hearts,
two-step feathered dancers hop to the beat
adorned in shrunken skins and turquoise art.
Smoky air scented with musky mesquite.

Pensive wise men converse with fledglings of earth
on peace, power, knowledge, and wisdom's dearth.

Breakfast in Bed

Kathleen O'Brien

By "bed" I mean the living room sofa
since the offer of teen-age grandson's room
with pungent sweatsock-smell, I've declined.

I feel the heft of a plush blanket
carefully placed over me.
Toaster oven beeps on this early morning Saturday;
refrigerator door opens, closes.
Awake now, I play at sleeping; lie still.
TV tray appears near my head.
Half-open eyes squint at plate with one piece of dry toast,
golden as the marshmallows roasted last summer,
tall glass of milk in Sam Adams pilsner glass – and pretzels.
Something is tucked at my side, a small orange balloon.
Figure dressed in size eight Spiderman pajamas,
clears his throat, patiently awaits my reaction.

He tells me he woke at 6:13 before the alarm buzzed.
I picture the Yoda clock in his sunshine yellow room,
color perfectly matched to his personality.
Red Beanie Baby teddy bear, laid at my feet,
is mine to use, he says, but not to take home.

What can one say in Love's very presence?
Hugs and praise seem small recompense.

Next morning: L'Eggo waffle with raspberry jam,
chocolate sauce, maple syrup, and a mountain
of whipped cream.

December Brunch

Jean Brier Lusk

Mrs. Sorg and her mother, dressed in spotless aprons, served a bountiful brunch in their lovely North Shore home. We were four couples, each of us a student at Northwestern University. We had been invited to Jimmy Sorg's home for brunch the morning after an SAE fraternity dance held at an exclusive Chicago club.

The morning event climaxed a wonderful weekend. The boys wore tuxedos to the dance, gave their dates gardenia or orchid corsages. The boys borrowed their parents' cars, and we wheeled off, carefree and excited. We danced to Glenn Miller's band, laughed and twirled to "Moonlight Serenade."

At 2 a.m., the boys returned us to our sorority houses and, after a short night's rest, they picked us up again to attend the brunch.

Our hostesses, Jim's mother and grandma, were of Swedish descent and cooks par excellence. The food was delicious. The ladies served us, but left us to our idle chatter while they remained in the kitchen. Halfway through the brunch, Mrs. Sorg and her mother came into the dining room. They looked pale and distraught and made attempts to break into our laughter and chatter. At last, Mrs. Sorg blurted out, "Pearl Harbor has been bombed, and we are at war."

I felt encased in ice. My mind repeated, *It's a mistake. That is my home. Daddy worked at Pearl Harbor all of his engineering career, and he knows how safe it is. He always told us how protected Oahu was because of this Naval Base.* Suddenly, I heard myself voicing these thoughts to my friends. Our hostesses shook their heads and sent us back to school, the remaining food uneaten.

The car radio kept repeating the same words: "Pearl Harbor has been bombed."

"No," I said to my date, "there is some mistake."

He shook his head and dropped me off at the sorority house.

As I walked in, the girls were gathered in one room. I could hear them talking, and the radio was on. When I entered the room, they fell silent and turned the radio down. Someone gently said, "It is true."

I ran to my room as the terrifying thoughts rushed over me. My family—were they dead? The radio said they were bombing near my home. What should I do? I was tortured with these thoughts for ten long days. The boys on campus were enlisting and leaving school, all headed for my beloved homeland. What would happen to them?

Ten days later, the telegram came for me. Our housemother intercepted it and joyfully brought me the news that my parents, brother, and sister were alive and well. The relief was great, and I cried. I still do when I think of those fearful ten days.

During those days, my life changed forever. I was offered and accepted a part-time job to cover my room and board expenses, and I settled into my studies. Later, my highly improved grade point average reflected these efforts. I was never a carefree girl again and was determined to become a responsible young woman, prepared for whatever life might bring.

The Strongest Man

C.A. (Chuck) Peters

Beset by embarrassment and humiliation, the young Marine was endeavoring to disappear in the noisy, crowded squad bay. He could not. All hands in that barracks had read the bulletin board and knew where he was going. Even if they had failed to peruse it, he was attired in the "go to meeting" dress uniform of a new "butter bar." The butter bar pejorative reflected their boot-officer status as advertised by the gold bar—a symbol of rank worn on their shoulder straps and collars. His classmates were dressed for training in green utilities and the Corps' signature gung ho caps. There were five dozen so-designated young men in the barracks that dark day in 1956, but the cherry officer was all alone.

As is customary in the military, when an individual is in deep do-do, all others avoid him lest they become collateral damage or "catch" whatever trouble he has contracted. No one made eye contact, smiled, or spoke to the infected man. Had the situation been reversed and some other poor SOB been in his situation, he would have behaved in exactly the same manner. He was, indeed, all alone.

The anxiety-ridden lieutenant had been ordered to plead his case before a panel of highly decorated combat veteran colonels. A humble plebe venturing up Mount Olympus in ancient Greece could have been no less intimidated. He was so nervous, he feared he would "pump his bilges." His grievous sin was that he could not read a map. If they found him guilty, he would be summarily discharged from his beloved Marines and the Corps' Basic Officer School at Quantico. The irrevocable decision would be in the hands of the gods he was shortly to appear before.

Decades on, in retrospect, he concluded his unfortunate deficiency was a congenital weakness. He recalled many occasions sitting in the back seat of the family car while his mother endeavored, unsuccessfully, to read a road map and direct his father, who was driving. His kid brother had confessed that he, too, had nearly walked the plank at Quantico for the same deficiency. Their failure gave validity to the military maxim, "The most dangerous thing in the military is a second lieutenant with a map."

That day, out of the busy, noisy crowd, another lieutenant approached him. He hardly knew the man's name. Butter-bars were much too busy to socialize outside of their assigned squads. When he got close, the newcomer dropped his big arm on the shoulder of the dressed-up Marine. This was the late fifties, when men rarely did the physical touch thing, and even more rarely in the macho testosterone-driven Corps. This was "Tim." He was known as the "strongest man in the company." He had won a lot of money arm wrestling other Marines, providing convincing evidence that he had truly earned that title. On that dark day, he was strong enough to risk the military taboo of approaching a comrade in trouble.

He inquired, "Do you know how many of these assholes would secretly like to be in your place? They really want out."

Nearly in tears, the distraught butter-bar plaintively responded, "But I want to stay in. I want to be a Marine lieutenant. I've always wanted to be a Marine."

This was a slight exaggeration; perhaps not quite "always." Certainly since he was a nine-year-old kid, a Junior Marine, growing up on the home front during World War II. He and his playmates had used white chalk to create a stripe down the outer seam of their blue jeans in the belief that real Marines always wore one on their uniform trousers. So attired, they had wiped out hundreds of Japs and Nazis with the rat-tat-tat of wooden submachine guns. One of his earliest memories was of an impromptu parade he and his playmates had staged the September day in 1939 when the Germans invaded Poland. They had no idea where Poland was or why that country had been invaded, but they paraded chanting, "We are the Yankees, we fight for our bread" in their high, squeaky preschool voices.

His benefactor looked deep into the troubled lieutenant's damp eyes and, after a prolonged pause, pronounced with great intensity, "Then that is how it will be." He then gave the lieutenant's arm a squeeze sufficiently hard to make him wince.

On cue the shrill whistle of a recorded boatswain's pipe was heard over the public address system, quickly followed by an authoritative voice announcing, "Now hear this! Now hear this! Marines scheduled to go to mainside lay up to the battalion office at once. Transportation is standing by."

He knew that meant him. He received another squeeze on his bicep and heard a half-whispered, "Walk tall, Marine. Semper Fi." It was time for him to trek up Mount Olympus.

The thirty-minute ride was a blur followed by a sergeant-orderly ushering him into the impressive temple, where the gods sat waiting. Behind them, the American flag and the scarlet colors of the Corps seemed to blaze. On the bulkhead hung portrait photos of the President of the United States, the Secretary of Defense, and the Commandant of the Corps. All were equal in size. He suspected that, if regulations had not forbid it, the commandant's would have been larger then the other two.

He knew the drill. He came to attention and reported, "As ordered..."

Someone ordered, "Sit!"

The adjudicators were arrayed behind a long table with a hard, straight-backed chair about six or seven feet in front of them. He sat at attention. The half dozen gods all had name cards facing him. He recognized some of the names from books and after-action reports he had read of the Korean and Pacific Wars. These were career offices; some were "mustangs" who had been promoted up through the enlisted ranks for exceptional service. All had "Seen the Elephant" (been in combat). Reading the fruit salad on their chests, he noticed all had purple hearts for wounds received in action. He was in awe.

Then the chairman barked, "What is your story, Lieutenant?" But before he could respond the colonel added, "Why should your commission not be revoked?"

There is a ritual in the Corps when a Marine has fouled up and is asked such a question. There is a set response. He gave it: "No excuse sir!"

Another colonel said, not unkindly, "We know there is no excuse. So what is your explanation? Why should you not walk the plank?"

And he told his story. He told how, as a kid, he read books about the Corps under the blankets at night by flashlight, of the chalked stripes on trousers, of the toy submachine guns, of Marine veterans of both World Wars and Korea he had known and idealized, and his desire to be an infantry Marine. He was striving to keep his voice steady and maintain eye contact with his interrogators, but was not sure he was succeeding.

When he paused for breath, another colonel asked, "Who is this army paratroop-colonel who has written to us? He says if we dump you, he will get you commissioned in the army and send you to jump school. He thinks highly of you. Much more highly than your platoon leader or company commander or your record suggests he should."

"A friend of the family, SIR! I worked for his company on vacations and some summers. I was his foreman, SIR! He tried to get me to go army, but I was committed to the Corps, SIR! He jumped with the 82nd Airborne on D-Day, SIR!"

So it went for thirty minutes or so, until finally the chairman announced, "You are dismissed, lieutenant. Your company commander will advise you of our decision later today."

He jumped to his feet, came to rigid attention, did a smart about-face and marched from the temple and away from the gods who held his fate in their hands.

It proved to be as Tim had predicted. Perhaps it was the paratrooper's letter that tipped the scales. The Corps hates to give anything to the army—even a fouled up second lieutenant. Had it not been as predicted, this painful sea story would never have been written.

After he was placed on probation, the lieutenant who-could-not-read-a-map was grateful and bought his oracle several drinks in symbolic payment for the unexpected gesture of camaraderie. After they graduated, Tim went to the east coast and his friend to California, where he quickly forgot the hefty arm on his shoulder from the strongest man in the company.

Fifty years later, when the class reunion was being organized, someone called Tim to determine if he was going to attend. His wife reported that he had Parkinson's and was far too weak to muster. When the once-young lieutenant, now an old man, read Tim's name and explanation for his failing to attend, this story came rushing back like a painful, long repressed and forgotten dream. One that had to be memorialized.

And so it has been.

Wielding your machete

Diana Griggs

you slice through roots
that entangle ankles,
sweat drips from your
sun bleached hair
as Xlasma trees are felled
with a single swipe.
Ear buds pipe reggae tunes
Instagram and surf reports
regularly checked.
Man child, college student,
surfer, partygoer,
hoping to save the world,
now in need of extra cash.
Yet I'm watching a boy,
face painted with finger paints,
stalking tigers
deep in this boundless jungle.

Two Gems Came Out of the Hills
[ask author for accompanying photo]
Fred Bridges

The 1st Marine Division had landed on the North end of the island of Okinawa. Resistance had been light, and we encamped near a town called Nego. Okinawa was different from other islands in the Pacific in that it had evergreens on its north end and the nights were cool. Rice paddies and sugar cane fields were abundant. Our valley stretched from a tranquil bay and ended at a scenic waterfall.

Our engineer company busied itself building roads and radar stations. One morning we were gathered around the mess tent enjoying ebony coffee when our attention was diverted by two small girls, who came out of the trees. Dressed in homespun cloth, they had bowl haircuts and smiled with tiny white teeth. The men soon supplied them with goodies, and the cooks found mess gear for them. They seemed to be ill at ease with our utensils.

They soon left, clutching goodies, and disappeared into the hills. The next morning they appeared with their father, who bowed and smiled through yellowed teeth. His clothing appeared to be of homespun cloth, and he also wore low-cut rubber shoes. He was so thin that the bones of his rib cage protruded. Of course, he too was fed and enjoyed a Lucky Strike. We also noticed that he had large ulcers on his legs. We called this jungle rot, which was caused by tiny cuts received from coral.

Our corpsmen looked at the sores, made a salve from Barbasol Shaving Creme and Penicillin, and then placed a clean compress over them. The man and the two gems disappeared into the trees. Several days later, they appeared for breakfast and his sores were healing. They disappeared again, and we too moved south to the deadly battle along the Naha Shuri line.

I hope these two gems remember us for our kindness and not for men who came to conquer their land.

Mark's Chair

William Killian

It must have been Mark running to the bus—
I wondered if the driver would wait for him,
but I was distracted by the folded chair
lying in the median stones
at the stoplight where he hustled all day.
"Mark's chair" was printed on the back.

I stared at Mark's chair,
forgot about the bus
and waited for the left-turn signal.
There'll be a thousand cars
passing that chair before Mark returns,
and no one will bother it.

I've seen him there before—
newspaper corners sticking out around his sign:
"Homeless Vet trying to make a buck" —
Mark sells a lot of news,
waves to every car, four lanes deep.
He's proud of his uniform—an orange safety vest,
long-sleeve shirt in the Tucson summer,
jeans and cowboy boots.
His smile reveals four slanted teeth
and hair falling over his face
as he limps up and down his narrow path.

If he gets to talkin'
or you give him a buck,
I've seen him make cars wait two lights.
Horns don't bother him,
he just waves, smiles, says *Have a good day*,
lifts his sign up real high
with his middle finger on the word 'Vet'—
everybody laughs, honks and speeds off.

We all know he earned this chair.
It probably started off in a church potluck hall,
made its way through rummage sales,
ended up in the garbage,
then Mark branded it for himself.

When he looks at you from the corner,
you know he has hundreds of stories to tell,
but he's got work to do,
papers to sell
before he gets back to camp,
probably in the *Rillito Wash.*

I glance over at the Bus Stop—
no Mark to be found.
I'm sure that driver knows Mark real well.

Welsh Cakes

Diana Griggs

Mother hates to cook, yet on summer Sundays
she makes welsh cakes on the griddle.

From my seat at the scrubbed wooden table
I watch her hands sift flour through her fingers.

I add sugar and raisins as our weekly ritual fills
the kitchen with dreams of lengthening days.

Wasps buzz through an open window, the ones
who didn't stop to sip from a water-filled jam jar

resting on the outside ledge. Already it fills
with drowning bodies. On days I am alone

I insert a stick into the struggling mass
collect those able to climb aboard,

lay them in the daisies and delphiniums
where their wing shadows hum in the dust.

My Dad's Sad Story about the War

Ruth Moon Kempher

I was nine-going-on-ten—in fact it was almost my birthday—so that what happened here came between Christmas and my best birthday yet. I was scrawny, bespectacled, a loner, good mostly at reading and catching cold. It was already well established that I was good at imagining things. And nightmares. Still, in my wildest imaginings, never could I have dreamed up what really happened.

First had been the unexpected phone call from my father. After weeks and weeks of uncertainty, trying to figure where he was on war maps, carefully inked oceans in the newspaper, the call came. The *Thomas Jefferson* was in Norfolk! Could we come?

My mother, frantic, ran through the neighborhood, trading sugar stamps for gas coupons—then a wild drive south in Nanny Tower's Buick, sliding out from Trenton, skidding on icy streets, pushing ever farther south 'til the sleet turned into rain, dark night, and the ferry boat into deep blackness, all lights muffled for the war.

I had kept waking and sleeping through all that incredible ride, so when we finally did meet up with my father at the ferry, everything he said, or we said, whatever we did had the hasty jumbled qualities of a dream. But who could have dreamt that Daddy would take us to a YMCA? That was supposed to be only for men. And there was my mother, fair-skinned, dark-eyed, clearly the most beautiful, most feminine woman in the world. I was nothing to speak of—with my gold-rimmed glasses and the skinny braids—but still. Clearly a girl. Yet there we went, all three, to the darkened Y.

As we shoved through the revolving doors I could feel smells coming out of the old walls to greet us, old bathroom smells and onion and cabbage, lye soap and disinfectant all mixed up with the heat smell of steam heat. It was a quivering, live smell that came at you all at once. And there were bodies everywhere. Because of the room shortage, the lobby was strewn with sleeping men—young sailors and older Chiefs, aged civilians, all with stubbly, tired faces, sleeping in the lobby chairs.

"There's a bad housing shortage," Daddy whispered, picking up our keys at the front desk. "We're lucky to have a place."

"Don't tell me," my mother murmured, echoing the phrase we'd heard all down the road as we looked for gas, or places to eat. "'There's a War on.' Oh Lord, I know."

I was fascinated by the sleeping men sprawled every which way in the lobby chairs, curled up or stretched out, rasping, snoring.

"Dolly!" Mommy pulled me closer to her side. "Don't gawk, for Heaven's sake!"

But there was so much to see. Up five flights, by our door just down from the elevator, someone was sleeping on an old couch pushed up against the hall wall. A faded quilt completely covered whoever it was, rising and falling regularly with the breaths of his sleep.

"We have a suite," my father said, pushing me ahead of them into the rooms. "Time for you to get some real sleep, Punkin." His smile was tired, but his eyes shone. "I bet you've never been up roaming around this late before. At least, I hope not."

I didn't want to sleep. There was too much to see. I would have been happy just sitting and staring at my father, tall and lean in his crumpled khakis, clearly the most handsome man in the whole wide war. But as soon as my head touched the cool, clean pillow, I slept. When I woke, it was dark yet. The elevator, somewhere near, whooshed up and down in the walls. There were feet sounds, and broken laughter, trucks honking at each other down on the street. I slid out of the strange bed, and went to tap on their door. "I woke up," I sniffled. "I'm all hot. I guess I caught a cold."

My mother, in her lovely blue woolly gown, chuckled sleepily and went to pluck a thermometer out of her small suitcase. "Welcome home, Daddy," she reported soon. "Her temperature is a hundred and three."

It was strange, being sick in a YMCA. The doctor who arrived later in the morning was a frail, elderly man, storklike, who pulled at his stringy grey beard and said things like "Ummmm," and "Ahhhhh," and "My, my," and finally, "Mastoiditis, as I live and breathe."

Daddy had to be away on the *Jefferson* through the days, of course, so Mommy spent most of her time going up and down on the elevator, fetching orange juice and tomato soup from the cafeteria for me, doling out a variety of pills. I kept thinking I'd be better any minute, but there was a complication when I turned out to be allergic to some of the new sulfa drugs, so I turned more bedridden and miserable than before.

My father sat on the edge of my bed one night and said, "You know, Punkin, I think you planned things this way. Do you know that I'm the only officer on the ship besides Captain Wall who gets to come home every night? That's because of your emergency."

I was hot and itchy, but I wanted more than anything to keep Daddy talking, so he wouldn't go away. "Is Captain Wall nice?"

"He's okay. He has a beard. Very British navy."

"Like Doctor Ritchie's?"

"Oh no. Not old and grey. Very sharp and black, like shoe-polish."

"Is the *Thomas Jefferson* nice?"

"Oh yes. If you ever get your temperature down, I'll take you and your Mommy over, and you can see my cabin, and my office—"

"I'll get well right away!" I was ready to leap out of my blankets then and there. "Doctor Ritchie says I'm gaining every day. Amazing re-cup-er-a-tive powers, he says, now I'm not on those dumb old sul-fa-nil-a-mides. Tell me a story about the *Thomas Jefferson* and the war."

"It might be a sad story," he said, with a small suggestion of a smile.

"I don't care. Just so it's about the *Thomas Jefferson* and the war, it can be sadder than sad. I'm feeling sad, anyway." I nestled back in the pillows. "Just don't put anything in it about sulfa-nil-a-mides." I was scratching my stomach under the blankets as I said that, but I remembered my manners. "Please."

"Punkin, you can talk about sulfa drugs and it won't make you itch."

"Not me. All I have to do is think of them."

"Sit still," he ordered. "This is going to be very sad." His face was sad, except for his eyes. "It was Christmas Eve," he began. "And the *Thomas Jefferson* was somewhere in the middle of the North Atlantic."

"This Christmas Eve? This Christmas Eve that just was?"

"Yep. That's right."

"I didn't like this Christmas. It was awful. You weren't at home."

"Are you telling this story, or am I?"

"You are. I'm sorry."

"All right. It was Christmas Eve and it was storming. The waves were rolling higher than anybody'd ever seen them before. It was a terrible storm, but besides that everybody was very sad. The sailors were all thinking of their mothers, and the officers were all thinking about their wives…but mostly everyone was sick. Seasick."

"Not you," I interrupted, certain of that.

"I'm telling this story, so I don't count."

"All right. But I know you were never seasick."

"Umm. Well. The waves were like mountains of water crashing over the decks, and the poor old *T. J.* was going up and down, up and down. It was cold, too. When the watch came in from the bridge, he swore he had icicles on his nose."

I giggled at that.

Daddy frowned. "It wasn't very funny. It was very sad. Down in the galley, the cooks were all cursing. That was bad of them, of course. But they'd had to put padlocks on the oven doors to keep the turkeys from flying out, and the salt and pepper shakers kept falling into the potatoes they were trying to mash." He shook his head. "The messboys were all huddled in one corner, being seasick, and the cooks kept yelling at them to keep from being too seasick themselves. There was one cook, I heard him myself, he kept saying, 'They ain't nobody gonna eat this feast no ways, no how.'"

I was delighted.

"Even Captain Wall was sick."

I cheered.

"But it was Christmas Eve," Daddy went on. "And that's a special time, even when you're in the middle of a terrible North Atlantic storm; even when you've been hoping, with a little luck, you might be home. But, you know, a funny thing happened. Everybody came to chow."

"Everybody?"

"Everybody except the people on watch, and they all ate later. Even the sickest person on board came to chow. And that sick, sick person was a man named Ensign Green."

"Green!"

"That's right. He was a passenger. That is, he wasn't part of our regular crew. We'd picked him up in Scotland, and he was on his way back to the States. He'd flown over, so he'd never been on a ship before in his life. Oh, he was very, very sick. Everybody called him Green Green."

"Green Green!"

"Yes. Well. Because the messboys were all too sick to serve, and the storm was making it too hard to eat off a plate anyway with the ship lunging and plunging the way she was, we were all eating off trays, the way the sailors do."

He paused, dramatically, so I could think for a minute how that had been. Then he went on. "Green Green came down a little late, staggering, because, you know, he'd been sick. By the time he came in, everybody else had been served. He was very pale, and his hands were shaking, but he went rolling over to the serving table and picked up a tray. Captain Wall said to me, 'Chappie,' he said…"

To my delight, my father used a pompous voice for Captain Wall, and stroked a precisely-pointed pretend beard. "'Chappie,' he said, 'I admire that man's spirit. His *esprit de corps*.'" Daddy took a deep breath and went on. "The steward must have admired Green Green's spirit, too, because he took his tray and piled it high with double helpings of everything."

"Everything?"

"Everything. Double turkey. Double dressing. Double peas. And a triple heap of mashed potatoes with a quadruple flood of gravy!" He stopped. "You know what happened?"

"No!"

"Green Green took his tray in both hands, very cautiously, and started back for his table. He was right in the middle of the wardroom when the old *T. J.* hit a tremendous wave, and dipped, and pitched, and flew down the side of a swell harder and deeper than she'd pitched all day. Poor Green Green. Next thing he knew, he was sitting smack dab down on the deck."

I clapped.

"Everybody went 'Ahhhhh,' and Green Green just sat there a minute, stunned. Right beside all his food. Double turkey. Double dressing…"

"Double peas! And triple mashed potatoes!"

"I thought, myself, it was the triple mashed potatoes that did it. That, and the quadruple gravy. Because the ship lunged again, and Green Green slid into the potatoes and gravy, all the peas and stuffing, too, and before anybody could even try to help him up, he went sliding down, down, down the whole length of the wardroom floor. Crash! He slid into the bulkhead. He tried to brace himself, but the *T. J.* dipped again, and whoosh, he went sliding back, back to the other side of the wardroom, and he banged into that bulkhead, too! He'd almost get up, and the ship would dip or lurch again, and off he'd go again, only faster and faster, faster every time because the peas and gravy and all in his path kept greasing his way, slicker and slicker every time!"

I grinned. "Poor Green Green."

"Poor Green Green. Lieutenant Cumberland said, 'Green Green, you damn fool, you're supposed to eat the turkey, not wear it,' and everybody began to laugh."

"Poor, poor Green Green."

"Yes, indeed. But after that, it was a very wonderful thing. Nobody was sick anymore. The cooks and messboys had all come running out of the galley to see Green Green sliding back and forth on his slide, and they forgot all about being sick. The people up on watch all heard about it, and when they came down, they all ate tremendous dinners, because they had been laughing and feeling so good."

"Everybody was happy?"

"Happy as they could be."

"Good old Green Green." I skrunched down in the blankets. "He was a hero. But you said you were going to tell me a sad story."

My father stood up and stretched uncomfortably. "Well, it was sad. In a way."

"I guess you wouldn't tell me anything really bad sad."

He looked down, somewhat surprised. "No. I wouldn't. You're growing up kind of fast, aren't you?"

"Not fast enough." I sighed. That was an old complaint with me. But I remember thinking then that I did seem to have learned something, almost accidentally, that night. In a crazy, shapeless, immature way, I'd found something important. I just wasn't quite sure what it was.

Years later, in another life, I tried to write Daddy's story as best I could. By then, he was in his nineties, living next door. Very hesitantly, I gave him a first draft to read.

He was rather disgusted with me. "It wasn't Norfolk. It was Newport News."

News to me. I was a kid in love with names. Kiptopeke Beach. Rehoboth. I'd have sworn it was Norfolk. God knows, I don't know for sure. I argued a little. It didn't seem possible I'd been wrong about where I was for all those years, but I didn't argue much. I was still too pleased to have him home.

Little Star's Midnight Journey

Aleane Fitz-Carter

It's a warm summer night. A gentle breeze flows through the air and white fluffy clouds play peek-a-boo with a big full moon. The sky is sprinkled with stars. Every night they come decked out in their fanciest and shiniest star suits. Making a grand entry, they parade around the heavens, putting on a spectacular performance for the earthlings below. They call out to one another and vie for the first place of importance.

"I'm the most important star," says First Star, "because I'm the first one people see every night. They've even honored me with a poem…Star light, star bright, first star I see tonight…"

"Oh, that's nothing," says Twinkle. "I'm so important that they've composed a song about me…Twinkle, twinkle little star…How I wonder what you are…Up above the world so high…Like a diamond in the sky…They think I'm a diamond."

Dusty comes out with a big bag of star dust slung over one of her points. She starts throwing it up in the air and watches as the dust floats down, settling in lover's eyes. "See, I'm the one who puts stars in the earthlings' eyes. If it wasn't for me, there'd be no love. Keeps me busy manufacturing the stuff that makes the world go round. The world needs love. That's why I'm the most important one around here."

"That's all very well and good, but there are more serious matters in life to attend to. I'm the most important star because I've been given an important mission to carry out. I've been designated to guide people to safety and keep them from hurt, harm, and danger. I give off a bright steadfast light. All they have to do is follow me. In the far distant future I shall lead African slaves to their freedom up North. I am destined to do great things. I'm North Star."

"Oh, North Star, people can't go around being serious all the time," says Shooting Star. "All work and no play makes Jack a dull boy. People need a little fun and entertainment. That's why I'm the most important star here because I give the people what they want – a good show. I dazzle the earthlings with my fancy moves and lightning speed. First, I'm over here; then, I'm over there."

"Yes, but when you reach the earth, your light fizzles out! It's all over," says Wishing Star. "But take me now. I forever give light and hope to the world. Dreamers look for me every night to wish upon. That just happens to make me the most important star in the galaxy."

"Well, I'm important too."

The stars all look around. It's Little Star. He's sitting in his orbit listening to the other stars bragging about how important they are.

"You?" they chorus. "You're not important! You don't do anything or go anywhere. You just stay in your little orbit night after night."

"Yes...no one looks for you like they do me," says Falling Star. "I get to travel down to the earth every night, and when people see me coming, they run to meet me. Everyone wants to catch a falling star. That just happens to make me the most important star in the universe."

"You stars have been doing a lot of talking and flapping your points. But all of you have to go to bed early. I'm the only one who gets to stay up late 'til it's the morning. I'm Morning Star. I'm the first one to greet people every day. Moon has gone to bed. Sun hasn't gotten up yet. I have the whole stage of heaven to myself. I draw the curtain on night, then I take my bow. Surely you must realize that makes me the most important star in the skies."

Little Star listens as each star boasts about how important he is. A tear drops from one of Little Star's points. He feels so insignificant and alone. Why can't he have people wishing on him or trying to catch him?

"Come on, you guys, let's play follow the leader," hollers Shooting Star, and with that he dashes across the heavens. The other stars follow, creating a shimmering, glimmering hail of light. The earthlings look up and cry, "Ooooooooh!" and "Aaaaaah!"

Little Star gets so excited that he jumps out of his orbit and scoots after the other stars. "May I play with you?"

"Go on back to your orbit. You cannot play with us!"

Little Star turns away. Tears roll down all his five points. How come he can't be like Shooter and explode across the heavens? Angrily, he digs one of his points into a drifting cloud, tearing off a piece of its fluff. As he watches the fluff float away, he thinks, *If only I could be like North Star and lead people to freedom and give them hope and joy.*

LITTLE STAR'S MIDNIGHT JOURNEY

One cold winter night Little Star is sitting in his orbit, watching the other stars dance about the heavens. Shooting Star is cutting up with his antics, Twinkle is winking and blinking at the earthlings. Dusty is throwing stardust in people's eyes, and Wishing Star is luring people to make a wish, when out of the midnight sky a voice booms out. It's like the sound of many rolling waters. Each star stops in its tracks. Their points perk up like antennae. It's the voice of the Ancient One. Each star stands at attention and waits for Ancient One to speak.

"Tonight is a special night, and I need a very special star to perform a magnificent and courageous task."

No doubt he's talking about me, thinks North Star. *Because I'm the only courageous one around here.*

I know he's got me in mind, thinks Shooting Star, *because not only am I courageous, I'm magnificent when I shoot.*

Falling Star thinks, *Courageous? That's me – who else? It takes a lot of courage to fall from heaven all the way down to earth without a parachute.*

While the stars are making mental assessments of their credentials and qualifications, Ancient One speaks. "Little Star, I choose you for this assignment."

The stars' points droop in shock and disbelief!

"Little Star? Did he say Little Star?" they all chime.

Little Star can't believe his ears. "Me? You choose me? Nobody ever chooses me for anything. I can't…I won't…I'm not…I don't…I haven't…"

"Little Star, your time has come. Prepare for a long journey tonight. A party of travelers will need you to provide starlight for them to find their way to a city far away. Sharpen your points and turn on your bright lights."

"Yes, Sir." Little Star takes three deep breaths. Each breath pumps light and energy into his points, making them grow bigger and bigger, brighter and brighter, longer and longer…so long that they reach the earth.

The other stars gasp in amazement. Is this Little Star? But now he is Big Star, *bigger than any star they've ever seen!* The stars all cheer and clap with their points.

Little Star blushes. Looking down he spots a group of travelers sitting on camels and dressed in fine robes. Each one is holding a package in his hand. They seem to be waiting for someone.

Little Star looks over at Ancient One. "Sir, could they be waiting for me?"

Ancient One nods his head and smiles. "Yes, Little Star. You may begin your journey now. Be brave and of good courage."

"Yes, Sir." Little Star slowly begins to move westward. The stars all watch as the travelers follow Little Star's long, bright, beautiful beams of light. Little Star carefully leads them over hills and mountains, moors and fountains, stopping by day to rest and continuing their journey by night. After a time and a season, Little Star comes to a halt. He spreads his shining points out over a little hut.

The travelers descend from their camels. They thank Little Star for a safe journey, then they go inside the little hut, carrying their packages.

Little Star smiles and breathes a sigh of relief. He is glad it is over.

Then a voice rings out of the midnight sky. "Little Star." It's the Ancient One.

Little Star stands at attention.

"Little Star, a job well done. Your feat tonight will go down in history. From this time forth you will no longer be called Little Star, but you shall be known as the Eastern Star."

Little Star is thrilled beyond measure. His points tremble with excitement. At last, he has accomplished something worthwhile in life, something for which he will always be remembered.

A Christmas Lesson

Bonnie Papenfuss

It was December of 1961, and my horse-loving little sister had just turned five. Since she was too small to ride our other horses, my mom and dad decided it was time to get her a pony of her own.

So three days before Christmas, an aging and docile Shetland pony named Butterball was covertly stashed in our barn. My older brother and I were tasked with keeping the secret by making sure our active and precocious sibling stayed away from the barn. It was a frigid December in Minnesota with two feet of snow on the ground, so we managed to keep our sister busy inside with games and coloring books. With rare camaraderie, we executed our assignment in a spirit of eager excitement and delightful deception.

Everyone except my father attended candlelight services that Christmas Eve. Instead, while we were singing carols, Dad was busy in the barn currying even the smallest dirt clumps from the thick winter coat of little Butterball and combing out the countless tangles from his long, multi-colored mane and tail.

After an overnight snowfall, Christmas morning dawned crisp, clear, and full of all the usual childhood delight. As the three of us children were gathered under the tinsel-draped tree opening the last of our presents, my father quietly snuck out of the house. A few minutes later, we heard a tap, tap, tap on the living room picture window. There was Dad, standing in the glittering, new-fallen snow holding the halter of a plump brown and white pony with a red bow around its neck. The expression of sheer glee on my sister's face brought me more pleasure than any gift under the tree, and I realized it really is better to give than to receive. Thinking about that morning so many years ago still warms my heart to this day.

Time Is...Slip/Sliding Away

John Barbee

Jacob Marley's ghost still walks among us. I know, because he spent an hour with me this Christmas Eve. I didn't see or hear him, but I felt his presence. I know he was there, and it changed me. This may sound strange, but I have proof!

Over a hundred and seventy years ago, Dickens told the story of Marley's ghost in his tale, "A Christmas Carol." Where the ghost has been all these years and how he got from England to Southern California, I do not know, but he was here. It happened as follows:

Each year I get older and slower. As a result, this year I didn't finish Christmas preparations until late Christmas Eve day. Because I had turned down the heater before leaving in the morning to do the last of my shopping, I came home to a cold and lonely house. After stamping the last envelope and wrapping the final present, I collapsed in my recliner with a cup of hot coffee. Arthritic old bones and the start of a headache drove me to take a Vicodin. Christmas has changed and I dislike change; it's just not like the good old days.

The silver clock on the desk showed 7:15, much too early for bed. Not wanting to read or listen to music, I turned my head and watched the condensation on the window, where the warm air was causing trickles of moisture to run down the glass. Time passed, and when I looked back at the clock, I received a shock. The clock was distorted and seemed to be melting. The pain pills had never done this before! I felt a tugging sensation, my vision clouded, and I seemed to float away. Then the haze cleared and I was watching a long ago Christmas.

My children were small and played around the tree. My wife in her new mandarin style housecoat sat holding a new puppy. Joy filled me until tears came to my eyes. The year was 1968, and there had never been a better Christmas—nor will there ever be again, for tragedy destroys innocence and tempers happiness. In two years my wife would be gone. Grief flooded in to dilute my joy, but it could not eradicate or spoil the wonder of that moment. The happiness of that day can never be taken from me; it will live in my heart forever.

Fog once again clouded my vision and, when it cleared, another Christmas was playing out before me. Recognition was slow to come; some people looked familiar, while others, mostly the young, did not. Then I saw my youngest daughter sitting in my favorite chair. Her hair was white and on her lap were two young children. I realized they must be her grandchildren. I was seeing Christmas yet to come.

A woman at the table reached out and pressed down on the back of a plastic moose, and it pooped out a brown jellybean. They all laughed. A grandson, now a man, told her how I had loved the moose and the gumdrop tree sitting nearby. They then took turns telling stories about me and the silly things we all had done at Christmas parties long ago—all of the wonderful celebrations we'd had, and the good family life we had lived. I wanted to stay watching, but the mist was returning.

Then, there I was back in my chair once again. My aches and pains were gone, and I was no longer sad, tired, or lonely. Instead I was filled with love and a sense of satisfaction. It had been a fine dream and seemed so real. Turning back to check the time, I was shocked...the clock had melted, oozing across the desk, half of it hanging over the edge. It still kept time, but it was now 8:15. So it hadn't been a dream, but what was the explanation? I had none. All I could think of was the ghost of Jacob Marley. I hate change, as do all old men, but change is inevitable, I told myself, so suck it up and learn to live with it.

Having learned my lesson, I advise you to do the same. Life moves on and cannot be stopped or even slowed, so we must learn to accept changes. Live life as best we can, for we are only here once, and a visit from old Marley to remind us of the joys of life is not recommended. If perchance you don't believe my story, stop by my place anytime and see my melted clock. It's still there, hanging off the side of the desk, and still keeping good time.

The Twelve Days of Christmas

Leona A. Jones

I'm just an old-fashioned girl, you know? I don't make a lot of money at the dime store, but I was able to move out of my parents' house this year. I just love having my own small place, and I have been decorating for an old-fashioned Christmas with a few things I could afford from the dime store. My boyfriend, Billy, has been pushing me to let him move in with me, but he needs to realize that I expect the traditional engagement ring and wedding before we live together. We had a big fight, and I told him I didn't want to see him anymore. He has a really good job working for his wealthy parents. But I don't want his money. I just want a man who loves and respects me. I got a telegram from Billy saying he was going to prove how much he really loved me between now and Christmas. He sent a copy of the words from "Twelve Days of Christmas." Next day I received a package marked "Handle with care. Live contents. Perishable." I thought, "He must have gotten me a kitten. How sweet!" When I opened the package a bird flew in my face, a partridge I suppose, since there was also a small potted pear tree in the box.

Next day when UPS rang my bell I began to get a sinking feeling. The package held a live dove with a turtle and a note, "Darlin', no one seems to know what a turtle dove is, so I'm sending one of each. I love you so much!" Next day, doorbell, UPS, I dragged my feet to retrieve today's package, which was postmarked, "Paris, France." Sure enough! Three hens and a note from my ardent suitor. "Honey, I flew to Paris to make sure these are really three French hens. Nothing but the real thing for you, my best girl!" Apparently, Billy hadn't noticed that one of the hens was a rooster. The hens began clucking, and the rooster crowing, and I was trying to remember the remaining gifts from the song. I referred to the copy he'd sent me. Oh yes, four calling birds. Sure enough, the four calling birds turned out to be peacocks. I guess they had been sleeping on the trip, but now they spread those beautiful tail feathers and started calling what sounded like, "Help!

Help!" My small house was filled with flying birds and bird droppings. For the first time in my life I used the word cacophony along with some four-letter words I rarely use. Oh well. The next day would be five golden rings. Now maybe I would get my diamond.

I greeted the fifth day with anticipation, but the rings turned out to be huge. The note explained, "I know you've been wanting a gym set. These are for the jungle gym." From there, things just got worse. In order to accommodate six geese and seven swimming swans he sent a huge above-ground pool and arranged to have it installed. It nearly filled up my whole back yard so that when the eight milking maids arrived there was hardly any outside room for them and their cows. And I still had more than forty people coming in the form of dancing ladies, leaping lords, piping pipers, and drumming drummers. I kept a few of each as they arrived and sent the rest to my parents and neighbors to add to their Christmas merriment. I guess Billy had forgotten how small my place is! He could have sent small things like a dozen red roses. (Someone told me red roses mean "I love you.") Or a nice box of Whitman's chocolates. Or while he was in Paris he could have bought a little bottle of Chanel #5. Things like that would fit nicely in my tiny house. Sometimes I think Billy just isn't very smart.

On December 26th I met Billy on the front steps. "Now may I move in?" he begged.

I surprised him. "Yes, you may. Here's a key. You have one month to get rid of all these creatures and clean up this mess. I'm moving in with my girlfriend. I'll be back in a month and we'll talk then."

I'm just an old-fashioned girl, you know?

Birthday

Helen Benson

I rose at dawn
To see the sunrise
So that the entire day
Would be my gift.
I walked to the gate
Where I could see the mountains
Dark against the silver summer sky.
All around me
The morning chatter of the birds
Harmonized with the whisper
Of the drying leaves
Rustled by the dust-scented breeze
That blew wisps of hair
Across my face.
As I watched,
The eastern sky turned brilliant gold
To usher in the master of the day,
Whose brightness first touched
The far hills, then the tree tops,
The barn roof and, finally, me.
The glory of the morning
Lasted all the day.
When the last color faded
From the purple evening sky
It left a star
For me to wish on.

BIRTH~DAY

Happy 16th · Good Luck · Happy Luck · Happy Luck · Good Luck · Happy

Dear Kenneth,

So you reached the first step of Maturity
The magic "sweet kissing" 16 year ❁ stage
With all its new mysterious opportunity
You will find at this magic age
Life holds a lot for youthful visions today
Compensation measured only by your own
          work or play
So give it all ~~in proper~~ you have in
          proper balance
The returns are always ~~measured~~
up to you not only to chance
Your ambitious Dad and True and
loving mother gave you a good start
a comfortable home, good teachings
to mention only in part

It's Thanksgiving: "Daddy's" Here!

Kenneth A. Yaros

The Thanksgiving feast has always been a proud tradition in our home, but one special holiday turned out to be unforgettable. Grandmother and "Daddy," as my mother's father relished being called, occasionally came to our house for Thanksgiving. Memories of Thanksgiving 1967 still bring laughter, and sometimes a tear to, this very day.

Usually, they would ride the express bus to Philadelphia, and then take the train to Reading, where we lived. Dad would pick them up at the station and bring them to the house for a few days. It was the only time of year they would make the trip. Time had, however, taken its toll. Daddy and Grandmother, now both walking with effort, could no longer make the trip via public transportation. My dad would need to drive to their home in Atlantic City, pick them up and bring them to our home, the trip taking the better part of a day. Our tired 1957 black Chrysler Saratoga grumbled as it climbed the final three blocks up the mountain carrying our two special guests. The sun was about to set. Our holiday could now begin!

That year they came to the house on a Tuesday. I took the train home from school on Wednesday, arriving just in time for lunch, which was already sitting on the kitchen table. When I came in, Daddy called, "Kenny, Kenny!" and both grandparents rushed over to give me a hug and kisses. After all, the oldest grandson coming home for a visit is something special!

Mom did her best to make sure Daddy and Grandmother had a gourmet lunch. On display I could see aged Limburger cheese, filling the kitchen with its unmistakable odor. Since this was definitely *not* to our taste, my brother and I decided to skip lunch altogether. However, Daddy and Grandmother knew this cheese was a delicacy and eagerly helped themselves to an ample portion, along with crackers, pickled onions, and thinly sliced hard boiled eggs.

Frankly, our family isn't known for its great cooking. Mom probably had few cooking skills because *her* mother was nearly clueless in the kitchen.

One evening, while I was still living at home, Mom baked four large meatballs as our entree. My brother and I tried to spear them with our forks, only to find them impenetrable.

"Oh oh!" I shouted, as our two meatballs shot off the table, fell to the floor, and rolled/bounced to end up in some dark corner under a cabinet! For a few seconds we sat motionless. My brother and I looked at each other, bursting into laughter. Poor Mom, embarrassed, ran out of the kitchen, sobbing. Dad did his best to look indignant.

"It's not so funny boys, no allowance next week!" Dad scolded.

Cooking mishaps ran through the generations. Dad told me that, when he got engaged, Grandmother and Daddy threw them a party that included a home-baked, multi-layered chocolate cake. Grandmother worked all day on the creation and hid it from view until the party was underway. After the official announcement, she went to fetch it off the back porch, where it had been cooling. Voila! She uncovered it with panache, placing it on the dining room table as the centerpiece.

Guests gathered around the drooping pastry. "What kind of cake is that?"

Grandmother sheepishly announced that she had baked a seven-layer cake but, "It sort of fell."

My other grandmother squinted at the pastry and stated, "I think it collapsed. It's only one and a half inches tall!"

Everyone laughed. Who could blame Mom for being a reticent chef?

But Dad was a competent cook. Even though he seldom spent time in front of the stove, today would be an exception. Cooking for Thanksgiving was Dad's contribution to the holiday. First of all, *he* had to select the turkey, but not just any turkey—it had to be a fresh tom turkey from a local turkey farm. He insisted on choosing it himself, bringing it home the night before. The bird was stored outside on our back porch until next morning, which was okay since it was always cold in Pennsylvania that time of the year.

"Kenny, hand me the box of salt from the top shelf," Dad called out. Soon he started koshering the enormous bird (an ancient tradition of covering fowl with a thick layer of kosher salt for a time, then rinsing thoroughly in cold water and patting dry before seasoning), making sure it was in the oven no later than 10 a.m. Afterwards, he would turn his attention to peeling and cooking the potatoes, making gravy and stuffing, steaming the string beans, slicing up the cranberry jelly, and finally whipping the heavy cream for the pumpkin pie.

From 10 a.m. on, the kitchen was out of bounds for everyone except Mom and Dad, but Mom was only there to help. We spent the day playing cards, listening to music, and talking to uncles and aunts, who would call long-distance to wish us a happy holiday. To be sure no one went hungry, Mom put out plenty of punch and soda, nuts, candies, cheese and crackers, dried fruit, and something new: mini-pretzels, which no one had ever seen before.

Thanksgiving turned out to be a beautiful day. The afternoon's yellow-orange winter sun reluctantly slid through the trees, casting dancing shadows through our oversized dining room window onto the mirrored wall.

After a stroll through our neighborhood, we were greeted by the unmistakable aroma of a well-cooked bird, further sharpening our appetites! The turkey would soon come out of the oven, and Dad would cover it with foil so it could "rest." From that moment on, the activity in the kitchen picked up in intensity. The sound of utensils clanging, dishes rattling, orders being shouted, and the electric beater whirling through pounds of potatoes could be heard through to the living room. We could only guess how the meal was progressing on the other side of the closed louvered doors that led into the dining room.

Just as the sun was beginning to set, Dad yelled out, "Okay, everyone, dinner is about to be served—please take your places in the dining room!"

As we all filed in, Daddy went to his armchair at the head of the table. He was walking with the help of a cane now, a little unsteady on his feet. Once six feet tall, by age eighty-seven he had shrunk to five feet seven, a shadow of the man he used to be. Moderately hunched over, face wizened, he appeared to be nicely tanned (from the salt air, we guessed). His snow-white hair surrounded his ears, a thin wisp neatly combed across the top of his head. His brown horn-rimmed glasses would slide halfway down his crooked nose when he smiled. The lenses were badly scratched, but they did not diminish his sparkling blue-gray eyes.

"Ugh," he moaned as he eased himself into his chair. To his left sat Grandmother, beaming at us all, dressed in her shapeless, matronly attire, but sporting a colorful apron. My brother and I found our chairs. Mom and Dad would sit at the opposite end of the table, nearest the kitchen.

The ritual began. One by one, Mom and Dad quickly brought in the heavy dishes from the kitchen. A huge plate of roast turkey was soon followed by a large bowl of steaming stuffing and two pitchers of gravy. Next came the vegetables and cranberry sauce. Once the dishes were placed on the table, two tall candles were lit. Boy, were we ready!

But before we began filling our plates, Dad lifted the turkey platter up over our heads and brought it over to Daddy, insisting that he take the first turkey leg. For a few seconds Daddy waved his hands, "No no," protesting this was too much. But Dad insisted, saying, "This year the honor of the first turkey leg goes to Daddy, and that's that!"

So, with shaking hands, Daddy reached for the enormous leg and placed it on his plate; it barely fit. Grandmother also protested, shaking her head no. "He couldn't possibly eat all of that, Everett," she said, laughing. "He wouldn't eat that much in a week!" But it was too late. Daddy wasn't about to refuse the honor.

Dad stood, actively passing the food dishes around; it seemed quite a while until he finally got to sit down. There was little talking for half an hour. Almost before we were through, Mom started to clear the table. When Dad said, "I'll help," she smiled and said, "Sit, you did enough already."

While she put away the leftovers and prepared coffee and dessert, Dad started to reminisce about the early days when they first were married. "I remember our first Thanksgiving, when we celebrated with a roasted capon and Lipton onion soup for gravy. We could barely cook on that ancient gas stove in our tiny kitchen." Yes, they had come a long way, now with two sons they were proud of and a prestigious home with a large modern kitchen.

The sun was now setting and Daddy would have a chance to reminisce, as well. He wondered how he fit in anymore. Life clearly was passing him by. He'd raise all sorts of questions like: "Why do families need two cars?" He had managed to go through life with none.

"Speaking of cars, Everett, I heard a new Chevrolet costs nearly $3,000! Can you imagine that? Who can afford a car anymore?" He went on to elaborate. "Gas at the Atlantic station is now thirty-two cents a gallon, over six dollars just to fill up!" he would exclaim. And he would continue, "What's so good about the Beatles and all that hair? Why do kids like Rock and Roll? You don't listen to that stuff do you, Kenny?"

I just looked down.

Daddy could not see any reason for a garbage disposal. "How long does it take to carry out the garbage, and who wants to clog their pipes with chopped-up food?" Same for the dishwasher. "I could wash all the dishes with one hand faster than the machine could do it." Of course, he would never want one of those newfangled 'radar' ranges sitting in *his* kitchen! "Two freezers in the house? Who could eat that much food?" Daddy would ask, shaking his head.

Although Daddy admitted life was simpler years ago, there were some things he appreciated. He liked getting his Social Security check. "Well, that money comes in very handy each month." He also thought that discovering the cure for polio was wonderful, and putting a man on the moon was amazing. "But what good is *that?*" he queried.

He and Grandmother enjoyed watching TV a couple of hours a day. A favorite program was "All My Children" at noon, after which they took a nap. Also important was the 11 o'clock news with Douglass Edwards, Edward R. Murrow, or everyone's favorite—Walter Cronkite. "And don't forget the Ed Sullivan show, and Uncle Miltie," Grandmother would chime in.

There were only three TV stations then. They actually used the radio more. Their large high-fidelity, beautifully veneered floor radio was the de facto focal point of the living room for nearly forty years. All day Grandmother tuned into the Philco, which delivered delightful symphonies, comedies like "Amos and Andy," mysteries, local news, and human interest stories.

"Let me have my radio anytime!" Grandmother said.

Daddy told us their all-time favorite TV experience was listening to and watching a famous orchestra and conductor. Yes, it was New Year's Eve when they tuned in to hear the following words: "Broadcasting directly from the Waldorf Astoria hotel in New York City, featuring Guy Lombardo and the Royal Canadians, we invite you to come celebrate the New Year with dancing and a champagne toast." How special they must have felt to be part of the celebration!

By Saturday morning, Daddy and Grandmother were ready to go home. Mom and Dad had packed at least ten pounds of turkey and fixings into meal-sized packages, which were wrapped in wax paper and secured with a rubber band. All was frozen for them courtesy of our second freezer in the cellar. The meals were placed into a picnic cooler, then set in the trunk next to their small suitcase for the long trip back to Atlantic City. Mom would go with them for company.

Bundled up with heavy jackets and scarves, they slowly made their way, step by precarious step, down two steep flights of moss-covered stairs to the sidewalk. They clung to my brother and me, as there was no handrail. Grandmother and Daddy had hugs and multiple kisses and smiles for us. I can still feel his stiff whiskers scratching my cheek, and remember the faint scent of toilet water on Grandmother's clothes. One final wave and they were on their way down the hill in the trusty Chrysler, the backs of their heads barely visible in the rear window.

That was the last time I ever saw Daddy; he passed away the following March. He was a lovely man in every sense. He lived through two gut-wrenching World Wars, and sobbed when he had to send his only son to fight in Korea. He barely survived a fifteen-year global depression, then witnessed the extravagant expenditures of space exploration. He saw horrible diseases cured, ran a business for his brother for nearly forty years, raised two fine kids, gave unselfishly to his community. And he never missed an opportunity to vote Democratic, because "They care about the little guy."

It is hard to believe he has been gone nearly forty-five years now. I still miss him today. I do. That special smile and loving advice freely given could never be replicated. I remember and safeguard a long handwritten letter he artistically designed to mark my sixteenth birthday. It contained poetry and wishes from both Grandmother and Daddy.

Over the years, he and I spent many hours discussing what I wanted to do when I grew up. I chose dentistry for my career; he urged me to become a journalist.

This is for you, Daddy!

Because I Am Human

Mark S. Fletcher

Because I am human, I have in me the ability to let *wrath* guide my path. Blinding rage, holding grudges, and seeking revenge for real or perceived wrongs can, and will, become fundamental character traits if allowed to flourish.

Because I am human, I have in me the ability to let *greed* flow freely through my heart and mind. The desire for more and more material things can become a master of my choices if I let it run unchecked.

Because I am human, I have in me the ability to let *laziness* consume me. Letting myself squander the hours of each day lounging about caters to only one person: me!

Because I am human, I have in me the ability to let *pride* define my interactions with others. A dangerous thing, this pride. It fills my ears with my own words so loudly that I cannot—or, more precisely, will not—hear the advice of others.

Because I am human, I have in me the ability to let *lust* fill my eye, seeking pleasure for myself and myself alone.

Because I am human, I have in me the ability to let *envy* turn my heart bitter from wanting the things and relationships that I see others enjoy.

Because I am human, I have in me the ability to let *gluttony* run rampant in my life. Not only through eating, but in excess consumption (hoarding/stockpiling) of many other things, like: toys, tools, shallow relationships, number of Facebook friends, or the size of my savings account.

The preceding seven items have all been focused on inward satisfaction and are selfish in their general nature. The following seven are more outwardly focused and, as such, are more servant-like than master.

Because I am human, I have in me the ability to let *contentment* dispel the need for gluttony. Being satisfied with my circumstances allows me the opportunity to enjoy my life rather than compete with others.

Because I am human, I have in me the ability to let *helpfulness* overcome envy. Spending time giving encouragement, praise, physical assistance, or financial support to someone else is a wonderful way of defeating that green-eyed monster, replacing it with a sense of satisfaction.

Because I am human, I have in me the ability to let *love* replace lust. While lust is focused on my desires, love is more concerned with the other person. While lust is selfish, love is generous. While lust is cruel and consuming, love is kind and nurturing.

Because I am human, I have in me the ability to let *humility* soften pride to the point where I am approachable and willing to listen and learn. The humble heart can give and accept love freely.

Because I am human, I have in me the ability to let *liveliness* cast laziness aside and allow the mental, physical, and spiritual parts of myself to be productive. That benefits both me and those I care for.

Because I am human, I have in me the ability to let *generosity* replace greed, so that the blessings I have received may be shared. My time, talent, and money then become the tools that bless others.

Because I am human, I have in me the ability to let *forgiveness* expel wrath from my heart. This opens the door to healing relationships, rather than burying them.

The Healing

Joanne Johnson

Soft ribbons of morning light danced through the bedroom shutters. After unpacking boxes and arranging furniture for hours, I slept heavily. It was the first night in my quaint, adobe house.

The impatient sun grew stronger, demanding my full attention. Defiantly, I reached for the covers and pulled them over my head. Soon, a pleasant but boring little dream danced across my mind, assuring me I was asleep until reality struck. It was Saturday!

I exited my warm cocoon and, in my usual morning shuffle, arrived at the Holy Grail, the coffeepot. My first cup was drunk while staring blankly at the kitchen sink through squinty eyes. Suddenly, the blooming succulents and aloe vera I had hung on each side the window over the sink framed the oddest picture. In the distance loomed the usual view of the snowcapped mountain, Ski Apache, in Ruidoso, New Mexico. But what I saw that morning was a little orange fluorescent flag jiggling in the air, crossing from one side of the window to the other. It had to be traveling on the dirt road next to my historic retreat. It was too early to ponder such strangeness, so I poured myself a second cup of coffee.

I began drifting back in time to when I had been living with a tall, handsome man who had a deep voice, dark hair and eyes, and an overabundance of charm. I had felt fortunate then to have him as a partner. Women took notice of him when he passed them. Lucky me! I was in love and in the midst of a satisfying career. Life was perfect!

Then little things started happening. I realized, when all the glitter and frills of our relationship began to fade, that I was left paying the bills and buying the groceries. How had I let that ever happen? I guess I'd been accustomed to doing that, and it just continued after he moved into my house. It took several months before I realized he should at least share the expenses. Naive, stupid, low self-esteem? Maybe I was guilty of all of those things. To make a long sad story short, our relationship progressed into my being the recipient of psychological and sometimes physical abuse. I was one of those people who thought it must be her fault.

One day, the funniest thing happened. I ran into one of his daughters, a young woman in her twenties. After some casual conversation, she looked at me and said, "I never liked the way Dad treated you." Then she told me something that devastated me. "Dad was jealous of you."

He left behind some clothes to dispose of and his cat to feed. Many months passed until one day I heard he had been married for a year. He had only been gone a little over a year. This was another blow. How can anyone be in and out of relationships that fast?

I took my wounds to New Mexico, the Land of Enchantment, a place I had visited once, and purchased a cozy adobe house in one of the villages. I planned to retreat to it whenever I could. At first, I wondered if I had done the right thing, but my instincts said yes. I needed to heal and felt this was the right place for me. Equally as important, I wanted to get to know "me."

Why would anyone be jealous of ME? Who was I, anyway? Maybe I was someone I would enjoy getting to know better.

On a crisp, sunny October day, I quickly dressed in anticipation of one of the biggest events my new village offered. This time of year, the Farmer's Market was open in the city park every Saturday morning. The aroma of Hatch peppers roasting had filled the air the past few days, and I was anxious to acquaint myself with the large variety of famous peppers.

Before setting out by foot for the park, I glanced in the mirror and assured myself the wide-brimmed straw hat would make me fit right in. Catching myself in old mistakes, I threw the hat on the couch. They would just have to take me the way I was!

I let the screen door slam loudly behind me—my announcement to the world that this scorned and abused woman was not over yet. I welcomed the unknown. I dared the adventure to begin! The fresh scent of desert sage and crisp morning air greeted me. I had dressed for the chilly morning, knowing that by noon it would be hot. With the Farmer's Market now in plain view, excitement mounted as I saw the vivid colors of organic produce in crates and baskets set up under the shade of tall oak trees.

Occasionally, a farmer would proudly hand me one of his vegetables for my closer inspection. His rough, weathered hand in contrast to the smooth skin of a juicy, red tomato or dark purple eggplant was beautiful. I saw an abundance of peaches and pecans from local orchards. From farmer to table was definitely a more gratifying experience. Baked breads and pies, pickles, and freshly made jams were also for sale, displayed mostly on old fading tablecloths. Wonderful smells, bright colors, and new faces were medicine to my soul. Baking and canning were common skills here, probably learned at a young age. I imagined the many years these wise, now grey-haired women had spent in their warm, cozy kitchens, nurturing family and friends.

Everyone seemed friendly, so I attempted small chitchat with passing strangers. I spotted a vendor with a nice variety of ground peppers neatly labeled in small bottles for seasoning. I fumbled along in my very bad Spanish. She politely removed the lid from a bottle and held it out for me to smell. I breathed in the wonderful fresh aroma of ground jalapeno pepper, and suddenly gasped for air. I started coughing uncontrollably. The coughs finally subsided to every four or five seconds. I whispered, "Thank you." She stood there grinning, and I moved on, making a mental note to stay clear of her next time. Okay, I'm the new kid on the block and now everyone knows it.

I took my treasures and headed towards my safe haven. The newness of my recent purchases still excited me as I swung open the slightly rusting, blue iron gate that opened to a narrow brick path leading to my porch. I was kicking up sand occasionally as I trudged through my front yard in sandals, when a searing pain shot into my left heel. Later, I learned this was a burr the locals called a "goat's head." There was much I needed to learn about this new terrain. My wound stained the Mexican tiles of my porch as I treated it. I decided to leave my bloodstain on the floor, like an animal marking its territory. I liked the thought of getting in touch with "my savage." I knew I would clean it up the next morning anyway.

Once inside, I let my fresh produce gently drop into the sink from my basket and paid homage to Ski Apache. It was then I heard a strange sound, alerting me to something or someone on my property. Through the living room window, I saw two large dark eyes staring at me through the giant Yucca leaves at the edge of the porch. My heart leaped. Quietly making my way to the front door so the creaking old floor wouldn't give my location away, I listened, hearing that same strange sound getting fainter. I quickly ran to the edge of the porch and saw an adult tricycle with a fluorescent orange flag jiggling from its pole up in the air. There, on its well padded seat, sat a rather plump person with two thick black braids. She wore a colorful print dress and a wide-brimmed hat with a feather proudly displayed on one side of it. With the surprising skill of a NASCAR driver, my uninvited visitor quickly rounded the cactus at the end of my driveway and disappeared.

In the evening, I liked to sit in the porch swing while people in their trucks returned home from work. They drove down the dirt road out front and always waved to me as they passed. The friendly little parade made me feel welcome. It was then, sitting there, that I noticed what appeared to be my first batch of mail on the porch step. I laughed out loud, realizing I had experienced my first encounter with the mailperson. I wondered if there was an old mailbox accidentally hidden by time beneath the sage or other unfamiliar things growing in my yard. It didn't take long to find it, covered by the huge leaves of the Yucca plant where she had stood. Perhaps this rustic, older home had remained empty for some time before I purchased it. I felt something wonderful happening. This was where I needed to be.

A crow with its eerie sounding cry flew over me. I had to duck. I knew that, with time, I would learn to love that sound. For the moment, however, my environment was looking more hostile. I retreated behind my safe walls and peered at the world through my screen door with new humility.

Later, I placed a basket on the porch step where I had found my mail and went back inside to bake my favorite chocolate chip cookies. Tomorrow, I would make an offering to my "curious mailperson." Maybe a conversation would follow. Perhaps I had found my first friend.

I fell asleep that night, satisfied with my first bittersweet day in an unfamiliar place, and knew that this magical land would heal me, making me whole again whenever I was ready. I decided to leave my old job and look for a new one here. Something told me I would learn about self-respect, find peace, and my scars from the past would fade in this place.

Healing takes time, and the initiation had begun.

Recent Past

Bella Hollingworth

I thought he was all sweetness and light until I saw him walking
Jerking the dog's collar forward, muttering impatiently,
Striding—who knows where, absorbed in his own thoughts.
He had me fooled with all his fawning attention, fine manners.

When next we met, his receding hairline seemed more obvious.
His smile false; shirtsleeves worn at the cuff.
An uneasiness about him I hadn't noticed.

We talked of small things around our coffee cups,
His fingers tapping the table, impatient.
I said "Adieu" then and shook his hand as if we'd just been introduced,
Though we'd bedded together the night before.

The taxi, humming at the curb, waited to take me away.
To a distant place, I thought, the destination yet to be decided.

In the taxi's rearview mirror I could see his slight figure standing,
Waving, growing smaller and smaller; as we turned a corner, gone.

Ronda, Spain

Dolores Greene Binder

I

In the square tight-leaved pepper trees
        Gave nothing but scent.
The sun made glazed steps of stones laid
        In some past meant
For bare feet, raw sandals, rough wheels.
        Here was a place lent
For this moment of heat and still.
        We, greedy, grasped
The instant, reached for further time—
        Our now or its past.
Unwilling, it relinquished one
        Relic. A church cast
Its Byzantine shadow, slashing
        What hard light held fast.

II

We slipped from there to winding silent streets
        Empty, laid bare
By hours baked white; unfleshed bones
        Striking light and air.
We walked upward thru their dense heat.
Water, falling from the apex of those aching streets,
        Brought no relief.

III

There was no way then to more than pass through
Touching a stone there,
A flower here,
The head of a child
Somehow escaped this place in endless sleep.
Five years have passed
And still your thrusts to violate walls of time and place
Are useless and you are limp with old desires.

Our touching left it untouched
And we forever
Were never there.

Second Runner-up: Best Poetry Contest

Basting Threads

Ruth Moon Kempher

On my dining room table, a pig-shaped vase
(supposedly Sancho Panza's) sprouts roses
from the cavity in its head—

while in the rented kitchen, a pork roast
thaws for tomorrow—a house unnaturally clean
seems embalmed—smells of furniture wax, tallow

but everything, unpacked in a frenzy, fits in
like bone around its marrow, puzzle jigs
for a game—all the years of waiting

looking at watches—I gave
kosher directions, I hope, and am already
in the phone book, initials for Information…

surely he'll have a dime for the slot
and the fleshy visitation—must remember
to pare the roast's rind, the gored bristle…

With all its lights lit, this house sits
like a beacon; the street sheens downhill
otherwise asphalt grey, suburban with trees—

of all the avenues of approach, surely I gave
the best turns off strange roads, but
I'm still amazed at the number that's mine.

I wait. Behind the screen, the pup, uneasy
wonders what is it we're waiting for—
The older dog is fairly sure.

Moving On

Helen Moriarty

"I'm sorry it's come to this, girls, but we are going to have to sell the house," Mother said. With those words, our childhood came to an end.

I was twelve; my sister, Fran, fourteen. We had lived our whole lives at 38 Marion Ave. We couldn't imagine existence anywhere else. Yet Mother was telling us the unthinkable was about to happen.

We were mercifully dismissed after the announcement. I think Mother was afraid she would start crying. She would do almost anything to avoid crying in front of others. All through my dad's illness and death, she had never once cried—at least, not that we knew about.

"She is a rock," Aunt Mary had said.

"She's holding up remarkably well," Aunt Dolly added.

Aunt Helen said, "That's it, Anna. Never let them see you cry."

Fran and I went directly to our bedroom and closed the door.

"How could she do this?" I wailed. "Where will we move to? When is this going to happen? Do you think we can talk her out of it?"

Fran was indignant. "She has no right to do this. We were born here and should be able to grow up here. Susan and Beth got to live in the same house until they got married, and so should we." Fran started to curl her hair around her index finger, and that meant she was agitated. I could tell she was developing a plan of action. "First, we need some answers," Fran said. "Things must be pretty bad if this is the only way out. Maybe we can talk to Uncle John. He might be able to help. Or Aunt Helen. You know how proud mother is. She would never ask for help herself."

"Well," I said, "I heard her talking on the phone about a second mortgage. I had no idea that was bad news. And the roofer called to say she better make a decision soon, before the roof starts leaking again."

"She must feel like things are falling apart around her, and the only thing she can do is get out," Fran said. "But maybe there's another way."

We headed downstairs to face mother with our questions. We found her in the kitchen preparing a roast for dinner. She was crying. Hard. Never having seen her cry before, we weren't sure what to do. But we wanted her to feel better.

"It's okay, Mother. It won't be so bad," Fran said.

That only seemed to make her cry harder. "You know, girls, that I've lived in this house my entire married life. It was your father's wedding gift to me. We came here right after our wedding trip to Quebec. I thought I would live the rest of my life here." She seemed to shiver a bit, and then snap out of her reverie. And with that, the tears stopped. "So, what are you girls up to?" Mother asked, as if we had just walked into the room.

"Well," ventured Fran, "we were wondering where we're going to live after the house sells. Will it be nearby? Will we go to the same school?"

"Oh, dear," Mother said. "I meant to explain all the details. I guess I forgot. We're going to live in an apartment over on Carpenter Avenue. They have some lovely places there. I'm sure we'll have no trouble making a nice little home."

Fran and I rolled our eyes at each other. We might live in that apartment on Carpenter Avenue, but it wasn't going to be home. The house on Marion Avenue was home.

In bed that night, I worked the news over in my mind. It was bad enough to have our father die, but at least the rest of our lives had been left intact so far: school and friends and where home was. Besides, no one lived in apartments, not in Mount Kisco. People lived in houses, big ones, with lots of bedrooms and sprawling lawns. Apartments were for young couples with no kids and old people or maiden aunts who lived alone. But we were a family, even if we didn't have a dad anymore; we belonged in a house, our house, and nowhere else.

For the next few days, Fran and I moped around. We sat on the brick walk leading up to the house, absentmindedly picking at the grass growing up between the cracks.

When we were young, Mother often set us to this chore. "Little jobs for little hands," she would say, as she showed us how to dig out the weeds by the roots so they wouldn't come back. Back then, Fran and I would talk—or not—depending on our mood that day. Our hands would get dusty and sticky and had to be wiped often on our shorts. We'd catch the clean smell of new-cut grass from the next yard, or we'd see a butterfly land nearby.

But today we sat there, sad and angry, pulling the tufts of grass and weeds like it was an honor to do it, thinking about the time when we wouldn't have a brick walk leading up to a lovely white house on one of the nicest streets in town.

On Saturday afternoon after lunch, Fran gave me the signal that meant "Meet me in the valley." The valley was at the far end of our back yard. There was a natural depression there, with a lilac bush on one side and baby's breath on the other. Old logs and some brush had been tossed there over the years, and it was a perfect place to hide. In the middle of summer, it was a cool, safe haven. It was a delight to whisper to Fran, "I'll be in the valley" and head out the back door. We'd bring a doll or a book and slide into the cool greenness, knowing we were alone and could stay there as long as we wanted.

"You know," Fran said, when we were settled into the valley, "I don't know what we'll do without this place to come to. Apartments don't come with a valley."

Sunday was a rainy day, which gave Fran and me another excuse to mope. We lay sprawled across the sofa in the playroom, reading the Sunday comics over and over. The playroom was our favorite indoor place. It had originally been an open porch, enclosed before I was born. Mother had a green thumb, and there were lots of plants out there. "If Anna can't make it grow, it's not alive," Aunt Helen would say.

The sofa had slipcovers for summer and winter. Now it was covered in a splashy floral print; in winter it would wear blue corduroy. I much preferred the winter cover. The weak winter sun would come slanting through the windows late in the afternoon. If you ran your finger gently over the soft fabric, you could watch the dust motes dance, then slow, then settle back down.

"We won't have a playroom in an apartment, either," Fran said. She was becoming a harbinger of doom. But she was right. "I don't know what Mother will do with all the plants. Maybe she'll parcel them out to her sisters; they're always begging for cuttings. Of course, any she gives to Aunt Helen will die. Mother said that if she has a green thumb, Aunt Helen has a black one."

"I don't care about the dumb plants," I answered. "But I heard mother talking to Mr. Monahan, that creepy realtor. She said she'd be glad to sell some of the furniture along with the house, since it wouldn't fit into the apartment anyway."

"I hope she doesn't sell the blue tables," Fran said.

I looked at her in shock. Mother wouldn't—couldn't—sell the blue end tables in the living room. They were two simple mahogany tables, the tops inlaid with blue mirrored glass. It was such a pleasure to dust them. You could look at yourself as you did it (always an added benefit) as the dust disappeared between the table and your reflection. The lamp on each table had a base with hand-painted roses. If you jiggled the table at all while you were dusting, the lamp would rock back and forth. Somehow, the pleasure of watching those roses sway obscured the thought that the lamp might come crashing down.

About a week later, Mother asked us to pack up the books in the front sunporch. We dragged some boxes up from the basement and were desultorily filling them when Mother came out to join us.

"You know, girls," she said, "I'm counting on you to be pretty grown-up about all of this. I expect no 'lost' phone messages and no trying to subvert potential buyers with stories of snakes in the basement." She turned and left the room.

We were both chagrined. I had meant to tell her that Mr. Monahan called. I had just forgotten. And Fran hadn't told that little girl a story about snakes in the basement to scare her—she had only been trying to entertain her while her parents inspected the house from top to bottom.

"Did you ever talk to Uncle John?" asked Fran.

"Yeah, but it didn't do any good. He said if Mother had decided to sell the house, he certainly wasn't going to stand in her way. He said he'd be glad to help in any way he could, but that she would have to raise the subject with him."

"Gee, do you think he's scared of her?" I asked.

"Oh, yeah. Remember how he tried to convince her not to plant the rosebush on the shady side of the house? She almost bit his head off. And this is a much bigger deal."

"How about Aunt Helen?" I asked.

"Not much better. She said she had a nice little nest egg saved up, which she would give Mother in an instant, if it would save the house. But Mother would never accept it. You know how proud she is."

By now, the For Sale sign was in the front yard. Everyone knew. The neighbors were very nice about it, but some of them were more interested in how much we were asking and who would be moving in. They were concerned only with the future, and we were already the past.

One night, when Mrs. Boylan had let me stay for dinner, the conversation turned to moving. "We're going to miss you girls, and your mother, too," said Mr. Boylan in his thick Irish brogue.

"Your mother has lived across the street since before we moved in," Mrs. Boylan said. "I remember how kind she was when we had the fire. I'll never forget that."

Maureen piped up. "I hope you sell to someone with kids. We'll never make up a baseball team with you and Fran gone."

The Goloogly didn't want to see us go, either. Mrs. Goloogly brought over a pineapple upside-down cake the day after the sign went up. "Mrs. Moriarty, we are so sorry to see you go. You have always been such nice neighbors. The children will certainly miss Fran and Helen."

Even the Stacys, the crusty old couple at the end of the street, stopped by to wish us well and inquire where we were moving to. "We'll miss seeing your girls at Halloween," Mr. Stacy said. "And I always meant to fix up two of our old bikes for them and never got around to it."

We were usually out of the house when Mr. Monahan was showing it. We had to keep our room neat and clean all the time, just in case he brought someone by. One evening Mr. Monahan called to say he'd be over in an hour, alone. Maybe it was good news, we thought. Maybe he's coming to tell Mother he couldn't find a buyer, after all. Maybe we'd get to stay. But instead Mr. Monahan arrived with the worst news. Those snotty McNeills—the ones with the little girl who tattled about that snake story—were going to buy the house and most of the furniture in it. And they wanted it right away.

Mother came up to our bedroom that night, although she had long since stopped tucking us in. She said, "Girls, I know this is hard for you. But the offer from the O'Neills is the answer to my prayers. We've got to take it."

We assumed that Mother would send us to Aunt Dolly's the day of the move. She always sent us to Aunt Dolly's when something bad happened, like when Dad died, or when she had her gallbladder out, and even when our dog came home from the vet after being spayed. Mother was fierce about protecting us from the harsh realities of life. But she surprised us this time.

"I'd like you to to stay and help me the day of the move. Uncle Peter and Uncle John are coming over, and then Dolly and Helen. But there are some things I'd like to rely on you for."

"Sure, Mother," we said in unison. What else could we say?

Moving day was chaotic. The phone never stopped ringing, the moving van went to the wrong address, and Mother was having trouble remembering which furniture was staying and which was going. But toward suppertime, the process came to a close. The moving van pulled away, followed by several cars filled with aunts and uncles. They said they'd meet us at the apartment.

Mother, Fran, and I were left to go through the house one last time. Mother sent Fran upstairs and me to the basement. She took the first floor.

I walked down the narrow basement stairs, not at all sure what I was looking for. The main area of the basement was empty. The huge coal furnace—the bane of Mother's existence these last few years—was cold and silent. The laundry area still held the washing machine and the big old metal washtub we were leaving behind. Someone had pulled the car out of the garage, so all that was left there were some old paint cans and a few dirty rags.

There was only one place left to check: the compartment. This little room in the basement had been my father's workroom. We were never allowed in there when we were little. But after Dad died, Mother sometimes sent one of us down there to fetch a wrench or a screwdriver. I never entered this room without being struck by its organization. Everything had its own exact spot, shadowed by white paint on the wall. It stood in stark contrast to the devil-may-care attitude in the rest of our house, where one was never too sure where the scissors were supposed to be.

The room held long-ago scents of stale cigarettes and pungent paint remover. And somewhere between the smells from the past and the painted shadows, I sensed a masculinity that was lacking in our lives now. From this room, people got things done. They didn't apply makeup and giggle and act silly. There was order and purpose and can-do-ness here. As I stood there for the last time, I tried to breathe some of that in and carry it away with me.

Cookie Machine with Dad

David P. Cresap

A bowl for the flour by the cup in the throng,
Now with sugar and butter don't mix them too long.
At last to the bowl add our bounteous chips,
This brings us the treasure to pass through our lips.

Drop 24 cookies on each buttered sheet
With timing important you must move your feet.
Hands moving so quickly the teaspoons are measured
In each little drop a morsel is treasured.

If no chip is there a reject is made
And cookie police must surely be paid.
Four pans you must rotate as the oven is timed,
By a sip of his coffee, this baking is primed.

The technique remembered and measured by heart.
The sequence is followed to the end from the start.
They're laid on the table, their hot bottoms up
To cool until ready, to dip in your cup.

A surprise once did happen when memory failed.
A batch to be doubled was memory veiled.
So, doubled again, oh the cookies we churned.
On every flat surface, lay treasure unburned.

Oh, what a sight to see cookies galore.
We ate and we ate, and in three days no more,
480 were made and I did eat my share,
But not 180 as claimed by mon pere. (maybe 100)

'Twas usually Sunday when timing was right,
A time honored treasure you worked with your might.
This time spent in joy. It never was sad.
Fond memories made, making cookies with Dad.

Yard Sale

Norma Glickman

A short paragraph in the Business Section
of the local paper: Three siblings,
whose parents recently died – holding a yard sale
before selling their childhood home.
I took a casual, mostly out of curiosity stroll
to check the items spread across the front lawn:
dining table and chairs, a couple of
well-used recliners, two trestle tables invitingly
covered with books I made a bee-line for
but was side-tracked by a Formica table, onto which
had been emptied the contents of a catch-all
kitchen drawer. Putting my hand on the tangled heap,
I sifted through the usual everyday items: vegetable
peeler, can opener, soup ladles, one large, one small,
a slotted serving spoon, a garlic press, a set of
various sized rubber spatulas – but suddenly,
unable to pick up one single item – I was fighting
to dislodge a large lump in my throat and to
dispel the vivid image – a swarm of vultures
circling – waiting to pounce
on the tangled remnants of my life.

That Sunday

Rosa Needleman

In the early morning dark
   a flight of narrow stairs
At the bottom, a landing where
   the Sunday New York Times lies
   waiting to be collected
At the top, the kitchen, spare,
   the usual equipment and a
   table and 4 chairs
Where no one is sitting.

When the Times does not appear this morning
   someone will walk to the corner market
   to buy it, looking past the sleeping windows of
   ice cream parlor and dry cleaners
   deaf to the silent street.

Standing in the square room
   at the top of the stairs
   pencil in hand
   poised for the crossword puzzle, he waits.
She cleans the breakfast mess away
   postponing conversation;
Quiet wraps around the long moments.

The front door remains closed still;
   no steps are heard
   in the stairwell.
The kitchen clock whispers softly.
Grey shadows slide into the corners.
Sunday fades into dusk.

Someone does not return.
The morning disappears into time.

Memories of My Father

Laverne Gephart

William Jackson Dodd, a Civil War veteran, was a single parent and raised six children. Sonora Smart Dodd was one of his daughters. The year 1910 made history when Father's Day was founded in Spokane, Washington. The ceremony took place in the YMCA. Mrs. Sonora Dodd believed that fathers should be honored with their own day, the same as mothers. By 1980, Father's Day had become a second Christmas for men.

When I was young, I do not remember my family celebrating Father's Day. I do remember that my father was blessed with a strong Irish tenor voice similar to the great Enrico Caruso. My father sang in all the minstrel shows performed in Mount Oliver.

At the time, Mount Oliver was a thriving place to have a business, with medical and dental offices. The Minstrel shows always contained one person playing the part of the Interlocutor as a white man, along with white men whose faces were blackened to represent the black men, who were portrayed as simple-minded. They sang songs like "Old Man River."

My dad was known for singing "Let Me Call You Sweetheart." I have bought music boxes and one doll that, when you turn the key located in her back, she plays the tune, "Let Me Call You Sweetheart."

My dad attended South Side High School, but he left at the age of fourteen to work in a printing shop located on the South Side. He became an apprentice and later in life belonged to the Printers Union. When he first started to work, he was very young to be working on the large, heavy Lithograph machines. While working on the Lithograph machine, he caught his index finger in the machine and a portion of his finger was cut off. In addition, he was lying in a tray inside the printing press. Losing part of his finger made him self-conscious.

I am waiting in the OASIS office one day, located in Macy's Department Store, when I am asked to deliver copies to the Day and Night Printing

Company. They need to be printed for a celebration OASIS is having in Macy's auditorium.

The Day and Night Printing Company is located downtown on First Avenue. I walk over to First Avenue, thinking about how amazing this is. I am walking in the same direction my dad walked many years ago, all the years he worked for Day and Night Printing. I am enjoying this walk and thinking about my dad.

This is the first time I have ever been in the building where he worked. I am afraid to ride the elevators in this old building. I imagine I am standing in the same elevator my dad used to ride in. He starting working here at age fourteen and stayed until he was seventy-five. His only retirement pension was Society Security.

The new owner of the Day and Night Printing Company, part of the original family, has moved all the old equipment to a storage room. The old equipment dated from 1904 to 1915. The machines in the display room are large and heavy printing machines, along with lithograph trays that used to be inserted in the machines.

When I told the owner that my father was one of his retired employees, he surprised me by telling me my dad was known as the best mixer of colors. They would send him out on special jobs to be a teacher in other printing shops. He showed me pictures of the original staff. My dad is in the group picture. He looked handsome then. I guessed his age at thirty-six.

These pictures bring back memories of when my dad would come home from work. I would fill a basin with soapy water so he could soak his hands while we listened to "Amos and Andy" on the radio. After one hour of soaking his hands would be clean of the ink except for under his fingernails. The nails would have to be soaked and scrubbed again and again.

The next day he would go back to work to set the small inkpads that would eventually be readable when the paper came out printed. The small leaded ink stamps are loaded with ink. He was not able to wear gloves because the type he would be using to set the letters was so small. This is why his hands were stained with ink, and why the ink was so hard to remove from under his fingernails.

I am tired after my day spent visiting the Day and Night Printing Company and reliving my dad's memory. At home, I pick up the evening newspaper and reality enters my mind as I start to read. Modern technology has made printing the news so much easier. While reading, I happen to see an ad for what every father will want for Father's Day:

FOUR BURNER RED GRILLS
(It Has To Be Red Since Your Father Is A Red Hot Dad)

ARTISAN 165 PIECE MECHANIC'S TOOL SET
(He Is Always Being Scolded He Never Does Anything Around The House)

I remember how, on Father's Day, my dad opened his package and did not smile. He asked for the store's gift receipt. All he wanted for Father's Day was a new pair of work pants to wear while operating the printing press.

    These memories will always remain in my heart. Times have changed. Now the newspapers are filled with advertisements to remind you of Father's Day. If your father is still living, tell him how much you love him.

Smoke Rings

Marilyn L. Kish Mason

The pungent odor of tobacco smoke
clung to our curtains, clothes, while a white
cloud encircled my father's head as he lit
another cigarette, often off the one before.
I emptied ashtrays full of malignant dust.

My farmer father wore bib overalls
with many pockets. One pocket stashed
a tobacco pouch, with drawstring and tab.
He filled his pouch from a Union Jack,
or a popular Prince Albert tobacco tin.

Another pocket contained papers for
rolling. Deftly balancing thin tissue paper
between his fingers, he shook tobacco
from his pouch along the paper, rolled it,
licked one side to seal it, then twisted the end.

He carried matches in a third pocket.
Removing a match from the box,
he scratched the head along the rough leg
of his overalls. When it flared, the acrid
smell of sulfur assaulted the senses.

Nocturnal phone calls began in my twenties.
A heart attack first, by then he had opted
for readymade unfiltered Phillip Morris.
More attacks followed—pneumonia, cancer,
emphysema—he smoked until the end.

My father was my hero, my loss profound.
Like diffusing smoke rings, he drifted away.

My Father Used To…

M. C. Little

My father used to take off his hat and throw it on the floor when he was angry; then he'd holler or talk loud and fast about the situation—sometimes curling up his mouth and dark eyebrows while doing so.

It was a good idea to watch his hand during conversations about business or about a touchy subject. Watch his right hand; if it came out of the pocket of his insulated vest and started circling the brim of his hat—he may be getting a little upset. Be careful what you say. If things went over the top and he got really mad, then off came the hat, and whack! Down to the floor his hat would go. Most often, this would be accompanied by a tirade of words, either in Italian or a combination of English and Italian. Sometimes his hands would gesture and fly around in the air to accompany and emphasize his heated words.

When the "storm" was over, he would clear his throat, look around, then bend over and pick his hat up from the floor. He would always brush it off with the back of his hand, adjust the rim and re-form the hat, and carefully park it back onto his head…then, a smile.

Arm in Arm

Claudia Poquoc

Soon after my father's heart surgery
he lost his sight. We walked arm in
arm along deserted roads beside the
Salton Sea where he and my mother
lived in a trailer. For the next ten years
I visited him there – danced with him
to karaoke – his feet needing no eyes
to glide seamlessly along the floor.

He'd step deeper into his darkness
as we walked, no longer able to use
his cache of power tools – resenting
the extra weight he put on my mother's
hands and eyes – that God had forsaken
him – the sound of the dove always
pulling him up into a lighter dark.

Taking him for his final boat ride,
we scattered most of his ashes over
Lake Erie where he once loved to fish.
I placed the rest of mine in a music
box that plays *Amazing Grace*
the song we sang to him as we unplugged
his breathing machine and after the line,
I was blind, but now I see.

You Don't Have To Look Too Far

Nancy J. Alauzen

Did you ever receive a piece of advice that shaped your entire attitude and overall outlook on life, even a half century later? I was lucky to receive one piece of advice over fifty years ago from my dad, and it has had a tremendous positive impact on my life. At an early age, he would tell me, "You don't have to look too far." I'm not sure how much I comprehended at the time, but he repeated this lesson often over the thirty-eight years I was lucky enough to call him Dad.

He taught all six of his children many valuable lessons, but this particular lesson has been a guiding principle for me. Looking back, I'm certain his words were given in response to my rare metabolic bone disease, called rickets. Some of the physical characteristics I exhibited were short stature, a waddling gait, and severely bowed legs. My legs were bowed enough to put a basketball between them.

Today, I proudly stand 57 inches tall and, after several corrective surgeries and two total knee replacements, my waddling gait is markedly diminished and the bowed legs are part of my past. His advice initially was given when we encountered relatives of relatives, acquaintances, and even perfect strangers with physical disabilities. I now know that this valuable advice was to give his young self-conscious daughter three life lessons wrapped up in one message: "You don't have to look too far."

Over the years, this lesson has taken on a greater meaning for me than dealing with a physical disability, and I have learned:

1) to be grateful for everything I have in life,
2) the obstacles I face are minor compared to the challenges of others,
3) to put everything in life in perspective.

Today, I don't look too far, and I know that being genuinely happy is a gift from my dad.

"Don't stop talking on my account"

Sabine Ramage

Sunday morning,
Hiking boots laced tightly,
Knapsack packed and ready to go.
She smiles, her favorite hike at Point Reyes is awaiting.
Bright blue sky, wispy white clouds, majestic towering oaks along the trail,
Through the mist along the cliffs
The foghorn is resonating,
The waves come crashing onto the deserted, rocky beach,
Tall lanky pink foxgloves are in bloom.
The cool briny air feels crisp, a
Steady breeze is blowing.
He has been tagging along the entire time.
She is glancing at him, hiking alongside her, as if they're best of friends.
A peaceful, tranquil silence floats through the air!
His lips are moving without pause.
Silently she wonders what he is gabbing about.
Reaching the steep and narrow gorge leading to the beach,
She turns around and smiles at him.
His dark eyes gaze at her, then follow her descent to the beach.
A picnic beside the waterfall,
Hungry gulls circling overhead,
Suddenly he is sitting beside her.
His lips are still moving.
She is handing him a note,
"My hearing aids are not turned on."
Staring at her in disbelief, his lips now no longer moving,
She is smiling at him and hands him a second note:
"Don't stop talking on my account!"
Then suddenly, and with a twinkle in his eye,
His nimble fingers are gesturing gracefully in the air,
"Can you hear me now?"

Signals

Marie Thérèse Gass

There's a bomb in the roses, Rya said quietly. For a moment there was silence, then: Sure there is, from Joseph.

They both stopped talking, moving, and listened. The steady mini-siren they had been tracking for seventeen minutes kept whining at the same high pitch as when they'd first heard it. Oddly, it seemed to emanate from a spot in midair right over the breakfast table.

Joseph slammed the drawer that held batteries and the charger. Nothing in here. Maybe it's in the wastebasket. Did you check there?

Twice, said Rya impatiently. She furrowed her brow and tightened her lips, then picked up the container again, holding it close to her ear, but there was no increase of the irritating wail. In placing the receptacle back against the wall, Rya's head momentarily dipped beneath the shelf.

Hey! she said. The sound is coming from *above* this level, not under it. All that checking the radio, the drawers, everything that's plugged in—for nothing!

Rya automatically put the items back as she thought about Em, who might not be able to hear this siren at all. For the last ten years of their fifty-plus-year friendship, Emma's hearing had been bumped up by innovative machines so she was even able to take phone calls, but now that was no longer effective. It's so frustrating, Emma's sister had said on the phone yesterday. I shout and repeat, and I still don't know if she heard me.

What would life be like when her own hearing deteriorated? Rya wondered. The very thought of it made her shudder, and she remembered the trains. As a child, Rya sometimes rode the train with her grandmother from Kendal to Regina, from the farm to their outing in the big city where they had lunch at a counter and bought each other Christmas gifts at the Five and Dime. Rya would ask Grandma to: Stand right here—and don't peek! Then Rya would buy a china cup and saucer, get the clerk to wrap it in tissue, and proudly carry her bag out of the store. Grandma's teacup collection, from the English roses to the Japanese dragon, Rya now enjoyed in her own home.

But Rya could never replay that memory without including the overwhelmingly frightening sound they had to bear every trip: that of another train passing on the very next track. Grandma would wrap her arms around Rya, who closed her white-gloved hands over her ears and even squinted her eyes shut, but the deafening noise never went away until the train was gone.

Then one day a white-haired lady sitting across from them had shown Rya a small white plastic box with a black button. It's my hearing aid, she'd said. I can turn the sound off when I don't like it. And she did. Rya was astonished.

You don't hear *anything*? she checked, lest she had misunderstood.

The woman shook her head. Not a single thing, she said, and Rya believed her. How wonderful was that—to be able to choose the sounds you wanted to listen to!

Rya wished this incessant siren would turn itself off.

Since Rya had passed the stage of magical thinking where she'd live forever with all her senses and faculties intact, various bodily deficiencies had occurred, the most disturbing being hints of a possible decline in her hearing. It seemed ridiculous that such an insidious inference would have arisen from a little sound like "tic." It was Marc who'd convinced her to get a checkup. He always gave the car a careful once-over when he changed the oil and topped the fluids.

Could you please check the blinker system? Rya had asked with Old World politesse.

What's the problem—the lights are out? That's easy to fix, he had said.

No, Rya had said. There's no sound. I see the lights flashing, but there's no tictictic like there used to be. I keep wondering if the lights really are flashing or if the whole thing's giving out.

A half hour later, as he printed out her statement, Marc had told her that the blinkers were fine.

What about the sound? said Rya. I mean, I don't care if the sound is gone, but does it affect anything else?

Marc had looked seriously at her for a moment, then: Sometimes, as time goes on (Rya was glad he hadn't said "as you get older"), certain sounds aren't audible anymore. Maybe that's the problem.

Rya held her tongue. Marc was wrong, that's all there was to it. It was ridiculous to think that she was losing her hearing at her age. There was no other sign of hearing loss in her life. Likely the blinkers sounded intermittently, and they had just happened to be working while Marc was there.

Yet all the way home, Rya had found herself examining her life for other things she might not have heard. If I were to lose a sense, she thought, I would hopetoGod it wouldn't be my sight. All the paintings and sculpture she had thought about doing, but had never gotten to, would be lost. And hadn't Ola told her that Earth was the creativity place? Everybody wants to come to Earth, she'd said. Rya had smiled to think of how ordinary this talk of other lives was now and how strange it would have seemed to her even a couple of years ago. Earth is a plum, Ola had said. You can be best nurtured by creativity here—more so than if you spent your life in any other place.

If that's true, Rya told herself, I'd better get organized, spend more of my time in the arts, make the most of my chances. Her face softened, reliving the feeling that playing with oils always brought—like being cradled in a warm and fuzzy nest. How every brushstroke, even when thought out carefully, relaxed her brow and made her want to just be there, basking in the wonderfulness of the creative process.

What if she *were* losing her hearing? How would that change her life? Rya signaled for a turn with the tic-less blinkers. She'd have to be careful. Very, very careful. She'd only be safe driving in the very low ranges of hearing loss. Like what? a part of her mind asked. I dunno. How much is safe? What kind of sound would I absolutely have to hear for that? A child crying by the road? Horns tooting? She could still hear all those things. But wasn't that when accidents occurred—when one thought things were safe, so didn't take extra precautions?

Thank God it's not my eyes, she thought again, so loudly that she almost heard the words. Maybe she did hear them, but then, she was going deaf, so how could she tell? Rya laughed aloud.

Have to get new phones, she told herself as she parked at the Respite Care facility to pick up Joseph. Remind me to shop for phones tomorrow, she said to Joseph as she buckled him in. Okay, he said, though she knew very well that her own saying this aloud was likely the only reminder she would get. Rya sighed as she got into the driver's side.

What's wrong with the phones? asked Joseph, once they were on the highway.

I think they're dying, said Rya. I'm always having to say to people, Could you please speak up—I can't hear you. They're from the other house, after all. A chill came over her then. Was that me? How long have I been saying that/believing I can hear fine/it's just a coincidence/a new phone will take care of that?

Do you know how old those phones are? Rya asked Joseph as they crossed the river.

He stared down into the water. Fishing for steelhead, he said decisively. Lots of boats. All over the place.

Did you hear what I asked you? Rya repeated the question.

Joseph said merely, No.

Well, that was a worthwhile conversation, thought Rya to herself. Like most of them. I wonder if I'm going deaf because of the extreme stress of taking care of a brain-injured partner for nearly twenty years.

Lately, Joseph had been speaking more softly—when he wasn't yelling. Speak up, Rya had told him several times. A lot of times, now that she thought of it. Was that also my fault? she asked herself. Am I really going deaf? A tear stumbled down her cheek. That was the moment she made the decision to get her hearing tested.

And now there was this low-grade siren. If she were going deaf, who knew how loud it really was? Amazing that she heard it at all. Rya looked at each item on the shelf and around the table. She'd already checked the air cleaner and cleaned the filters. The carbon dioxide detector had the correct light on. So where was that sound coming from, and why?

Her eyes lit on the only photograph in front of her, taken before she was a year old, little Rya sitting on her grandfather's lap, back on his farm in Canada. A black and white photo in a striated grey/white frame. Grandpa's hair pure white. Rya had been a mother before she learned that his natural hair color was red. Red? she'd screeched. Red! Rya loved her grandfather but had always had an aversion to red hair. No one else in our family has red hair, Rya said to her mother. None of my siblings, none of our children. How come I'm this old before I know that Grandpa had red hair?

Rya's mother shrugged. I guess it never came up, she said. His hair turned white when he was forty, and you were born after that.

Why do you keep his picture here by the breakfast table, Ola had asked once. Well, said Rya, remember when I asked that psychic to find out why my father didn't see me for the first two weeks of my life? Turned out he was greatly disappointed that I wasn't a boy. Was going to call me Ryan. My grandparents were there for the conversation and Grandpa said, I told your father it was ridiculous, just because you weren't a boy. I've always loved you. You were the apple of my eye! And I seem to remember him saying that phrase while he was still alive. People did love me, but I especially felt that with Grandpa—I have so many photos of him holding me and smiling. So I keep this one here to remind me that I am indeed loved.

Ola had hugged her then. In case there's any doubt, she whispered.

Rya stared at the photograph, then said to Joseph, Maybe Grandpa's trying to tell me something. A siren—do you think it's a warning? What could it be for? In her mind, she flipped through lists of disasters: stroke, heart attack, sudden death, etc. Too many things that would cancel her plans. She took a deep breath and for the gazillionth time resolved to work in more exercise. To stop eating ice cream. To get more sleep. To remember to meditate. Rya looked at the photograph again. Grandpa's eyes looked back at her. What are you warning me about, she asked him wordlessly. To live a better life? To be more careful of each precious minute? To anticipate trouble and head it off at the pass? To tell me a friend has died? Help me understand.

The siren wailed all morning. Rya worked upstairs in the office where she could hear none of it. When Joseph came in from the garage, she called to him.

Is the siren still on?

What siren? he asked.

Siren—you know, the one that's been going all morning?

A pause. Oh, yeah. Just a minute, let me listen.

After a bit, Rya called impatiently, Well? Is it still going?

Joseph looked up the stairwell. No, he said. No siren here.

A Dance with Your Dead Father

Seretta Martin

To relive the dance,
play his much-loved music—
perhaps the *Bonanza* theme,
his untapped dream of owning a Ponderosa.
Play *They Call the Wind Mariah*—
the song of a Gold Rush
prospector longing for a woman.

On your father's Hawaiian guitar,
strum a refrain from the Sons of the Pioneers
Cool Water – a mirage in the desert,
a man and his mule.

To dance with your dead father—
face him, stand on top of his feet, eye level
with that silver and turquoise belt buckle.
Balance and hold on tight. Dance
with the weight of a child, gliding
as one – warmth between you
bringing blood back into his heart.

Bonsai Lessons
(Excerpt from the unpublished manuscript, *Evelio's Garden: A Costa Rican Life*)

Sandra Shaw Homer

I didn't become a gardener until my parents moved into their Costa Rican vacation home next door. My father decided to import his bonsai. I thought this was ridiculous, given they would be here only three months at a time. It was a multi-Ministry nightmare getting the necessary import permits, but finally my parents arrived at the airport with seven denuded, soil-free, fumigated, stamped-by-the-U.S.-Department-of-Agriculture bonsai hungry for repotting.

Three years later, half of them were dead…and I was divorced and living with Roger.

Their gardener had watered them to death; so, before returning to the States, Dad brought his last sad *ficus benjamina* for me to tend while he was gone. It was a peace offering. During a long and ugly divorce, both my ex-husband and my father had behaved so badly that I stopped speaking to my father for a year. He had sided with my ex, refused to help me financially and told me to go back to the States and get a job. I was almost 50, and I was forced to ask myself why I had remained in a marriage with such an abuser for so many years. The revelation: I had been trained for it. That's when murder entered my heart—and I saw the moment as a spiritual crisis and sought help.

It took as much emotional exhaustion as courage to tell Dad why I had been so angry. But even though he didn't fully understand how I had felt abused, he apologized, and we both tried harder after that, although the tension was ever palpable.

One of the ways he made me feel bad when I was growing up was by calling me irresponsible. Hence, turning over his bonsai to me was a statement that—at least for the moment—I was trustworthy. Of course, I jumped at it, just like the hungry puppy I've always been.

Taking this for the gift that it was, I determined I wouldn't kill his bonsai—but I was in no way prepared for what it required. I found a slice of log leaning against the bodega. The wood had curved inward as it dried, making a long, rustic tray. I laid it over a couple of cinder blocks under the grapefruit tree and arranged the three *ficus* on top.

How to deal with the scratchy black stuff on the edges of the leaves? Fungus or insect? The books my father had left all dealt with North American pests, and the instructions on the pesticide label were for *hectares* of Costa Rican crops. On the phone Dad and I agreed to try leaf-pruning instead. For someone used to whacking back tropical vegetation with a machete, this was not my kind of pruning! I carried a small rattan stool out under the grapefruit tree and sat down with the Japanese pruning shears, and the first thing I discovered was that I had to learn to see each individual leaf. Each one had to be carefully snipped so as not to damage potential shoots developing underneath. The open-handled Japanese shears felt good, the metal warm, the shape perfect in the hand. It took about two hours. When I was finished, my eyes were sore and my back ached. Hard work, bonsai!

The next day a few more leaves had to go. And then suddenly I started to see the trees themselves: the structure of the branches, the stumps left behind from bad limb-pruning. I took the curved trimmers—another wonderful Japanese tool—and attacked the stumps. It was like performing surgery; I wanted the bark to heal cleanly.

As I worked, turning each tree, I began to see the parts: the crown, the front, the curves, the balance of branches, awkward limbs, twigs crossing at ugly angles. The trees were in terrible shape.

"How are the bonsai?" my father asked the next time he called.

"A little better, I think," not sure exactly what to report.

"Are you enjoying it?" he asked. I wasn't sure what to say to this either.

Each day there were fewer and fewer leaves to remove, and I began to notice some new shoots coming. It took an act of courage to pinch my first shoot. Dad had been so worried about the trees' survival, he hadn't wanted me to remove any shoots at all. But I was developing confidence. Before each pinch I had to think: if this shoot keeps growing in this direction and becomes a branch, it will cross that branch at a bad angle, or it will throw the tree off balance. Or, if I pinch here, it might force the tree (the living tree!) to push out growth in another direction. As I snipped and pinched and trimmed, each cut would weep a sticky, white bloody sap. I had read that this blood was necessary to protect the wound from the elements and to bring specialized cells to grow new bark over the injury.

Dylan Thomas's line, "The force that through the green fuse drives the flower," trailed through my head like a mantra.

Every day there were more shoots, some unfolding into bright, shiny leaves with other tiny shoots nudging their way behind them. Even on the sickest tree: first one shoot, then three, then nine. I started to look more closely at the bark and recognize the difference between skin living and dead, and I learned that, as long as there was a living green fuse inside the trunk, any part of the tree could flower again.

My father was really pleased, the next time we talked, that the worst tree was showing signs of recovery.

There were insects on the trees—spiders and a Daddy-Long-Legs. Something told me to leave them alone. This is part of Nature too, I thought. Trees in the wild are host to a million creatures, many of which help them. Perhaps the spiders would eat other insects that weren't good for the trees. One day I found a spider's nest, four leaves drawn together with silk into a cocoon to hide the eggs from the birds. Daily I watched this nest. Which of the spiders made it? Was one of them keeping her eye on it as I was? There was another creature—with an exquisite black and white carapace—that skittered sideways like a tiny crab. I found a gecko living under one of the pots. He sat perfectly still, eyeing me, as I sat perfectly still, eyeing him.

Then one day I noticed that the bark on the sickest tree looked bubbly. I ran to the books and identified scale. Each book had something different to suggest, and one was opposed to the use of chemicals at all. In a panic, I mixed up a solution of dishwashing soap and water and, after picking each individual insect off the bark with a pair of tweezers, I sprayed the trunk with the soap to kill any remaining eggs. I hated to report this disaster to my father, especially since it was obvious the scale had been there for a while and I just hadn't known enough to see it. Its color was so close to that of the bark and the 'bubbles' so tiny that my father would have had to use a magnifying glass to find them. I think this depressed him.

My enthusiasm and confidence dimmed as, day after day, I struggled to find and remove the scale, and I imagined a new note of disapproval in my father's voice as we talked about the problem.

One day the farrier came over to shoe my mare, tying her to the grapefruit tree, as usual. Suddenly I heard her shriek—horses spook so easily—

and I rushed outside to find all three bonsai upended on the ground and in instant need of repotting. Back to the books and all their intimidating information about root pruning and soil mixtures. All I had available was black earth rich with the minerals that have been pumping for millennia out of our nearby volcano.

My friend Francisco always quoted a Chinese proverb: "If a problem has a solution, there's no need worrying about it…and if it *doesn't* have a solution, there's no need worrying about it." I took several deep breaths and cleared part of Roger's long workbench to make room for the job. The roots were in bad shape: long taproots had thickened and curled around the insides of the pots, and the feeder roots were poorly developed. Cutting away the taproots would leave very little in the way of a root system at all, but it had to be done. With more patience than I've ever exercised in my life, I washed and pruned and combed out the roots before setting the trees back into their pots with our local dirt mixed with a little sand for drainage. I was keenly aware that what I was doing could kill the trees; they were just barely recovering from the stress of the scale, and now I was stressing them big time.

Finally, brushing the new soil around them and carefully adding water so as not to disturb the arrangements, I stepped back and looked at the new bonsai, beginning to feel a little pleased with myself.

The rains came. Driving, torrential tropical rains sweeping the length of Lake Arenal, gathering force that threatened to swamp the *ficus* out of their pots. I cleared a tiny area under the shed against the bodega wall. Roger was building cabinets, and the shed was littered with lumber, tools and sawdust, but it was my only choice. Every morning the leaves were covered with sawdust. Every morning I would spritz them clean. When the bad weather settles in around the lake, the sun disappears. The *ficus* got waterlogged. On rare sunny days I took them out into the yard to get a blast of light and warmth to dry them out. It was a holding action, a five-month siege, during the middle of which my parents came back.

Gratefully, I carried the bonsai over to their house and set them up on the verandah out of the weather. I tore all the sheets off the furniture, lighted the water heater and the stove, made fresh ice. When I brought them home from the airport, Dad was disconcerted to find the bonsai on his own verandah. "I thought you'd want them back," I said. He grunted. I figured he was tired from the trip and I went home.

The next day he drove over with the bonsai. "I don't really want them anymore," he said. I was crushed. All that work and panic and heartache to save his trees! "I'm glad you've gotten interested in them," he went on. "You keep them." Once again my anger at him threatened to swamp me, and I felt tears burning. Not a word of thanks! But I turned away to lift a pot out of the trunk of his car to carry it back to the rustic shelf still straddling the cinder blocks under the shed.

I lived with my anguish for a couple of days before I got up the nerve. "I've been thinking," I said finally, as I drove him into town for some errands, "that you didn't want the bonsai back because they don't look as good as they did before."

"That's partly it," he admitted. "When I first bought them they were so full and green. But it's also true that I've lost interest." I read that to mean that he was afraid he couldn't care for them anymore, but there was nothing I could say. He was seventy-eight years old with cataracts and a bad neck. And he would always lack the grace to express appreciation for what I had done. My reward was to be the trees themselves. For Christmas he gave me $50 to go to a nursery in San José and buy an addition to my 'collection.'

Now the labor was all mine and I could start to love the bonsai for themselves, and not because I was trying to please my difficult father. The shift was noticeable. No more panic. A lot more patience. More courage in my design decisions. I could let the trees bring me into their peace.

I started to see big trees differently: those bent by the trade winds, all their branches reaching in the same direction; those clinging precariously to eroded banks, half their roots exposed; those sporting dead branches, perching places for sharp-eyed hawks; those with lightning-scarred and twisted trunks; and those with bleached and rotted boles for the squirrels.

I hunted down a small nursery in the dust bowl of the lowlands, where the proprietor wandered among his few specimens barefoot. My total investment in four wretched little trees in nursery plastic was about $4.00. But I brought them home, root-pruned and repotted them with all the patience and love that a Zen monk would lavish on a 200-year-old pine. My collection was growing.

Sometime later I met a bonsai artist who told me that an important quality of a bonsai is its history: whether physically old or not, where it comes from, who gave it to you—the emotional content—has value for the

Japanese. He told me that Zen monks see a tree as a ladder between earth and heaven, by which man can ascend to God and God can descend to man. He also told me there are no female bonsai masters!

Six weeks before their scheduled departure for the States, my mother broke her hip. The four-hour ambulance ride over the mountains to San José was agonizingly painful, and when they got back Dad drove over to announce that they were giving up on Costa Rica; they needed to live in a place where good medical care was more accessible. The decision was understandable, if painful, especially since they had just been talking about making Costa Rica their permanent home. Mom loved it here.

It was impossible, then, for me to accept their leaving without feeling it as a rejection, too, of me. Just as it was impossible for my father even to try to make me feel otherwise.

Taking care of the bonsai has been good training. My eyes don't tire anymore. I can shift my focus from close in (the new shoots) to mid-range (the health of the leaves) to miniaturized long-distance (the overall shape). Back and forth. Seeing, understanding what the tree needs, discovering how it heals itself.

Taking care of my father's bonsai has deepened my understanding of another living thing. To say that it is a miracle—this life form with its green fuse and white blood, its unfurling leaves, its innate thrusting out from the center—has been said before. But the bigger miracle here is me: the observer, the tender, the servant of these trees, the new lover of growing things, the one who is also growing.

Honorable Mention

The Pruning

Lynda Riese

Pinch the bud like this,
my father tells me,
his calloused hand guiding mine
to the joining of leaf and stem.

I stiffen at his touch but obey
as I've learned to lie still
when he opens the door to my room.
I pluck the knobby growth

between two fingers:
Good, he says approving
and lets me prune
the next two rows myself.

I move with care
among his prize chrysanthemums,
their gaudy blossoms large
as my baby's sister's head.

They stand taller than I,
these favored children,
stalks straight as rulers,
my father training them

when they were small.
They bloom for him
like obedient daughters
tethered to silence.

Attic Room

Rita K. Ries

Upstairs in my grandmother's house,
two draped closets
separated the attic bedrooms
with windows at each end.
The west one with light wallpaper
always seemed bright and open.
The east one had blue wallpaper
appeared darker, cave-like,
gave me a hideaway.
I spent much time on a small chest
by the two dormer windows.
There I peered into the parkway's huge trees,
saw leaves shake with squirrel games.
In the evening the green leaves turned black,
a street light glowed on the corner
and I could hear the zoo animals howl
at their evening feeding time.
At night in my bed under the slanted wall,
light swept around the room
as cars passed on the street.
Old house noises stirred my young fears,
making sleep come slowly sometimes.
Once I plugged my ears to block noises
and young people running by sounded
like mice skittering atop my shelved books!
My cousin and I told scary stories,
giggled a lot, checked each other's anatomy.
My big sister would scare me, call me "crybaby."
My bedroom
        my sanctuary
                my prison.

Moving

Barbara Scheiber

"Eat your food in small bites," the nurse tells my 52-year-old son as he lies in a bed in the hospital's Intensive Care Unit. He's been here for four weeks with a breathing tube down his throat and a feeding tube in his stomach. Now, the breathing tube is out and the nurse is telling him how to swallow without choking.

The phone call telling us that Robert was in the hospital ICU came the same morning my husband and I were waiting for the moving men to bring our belongings to a new home. We'd both decided it was time to do something practical about our old age, and we'd bought a house in Gaithersburg, a block away from our daughter and her family. The decision brought our own problems with swallowing as we said good-by to our home of 46 years—sorting old pictures, letters, children's drawings, stories that had collected closet dust as we'd rushed on with our daily lives.

While the moving van pulled into our driveway that rainy April morning, our son was leaving his apartment in Rockville to catch a bus for work. The fog was heavy, and he failed to notice a car coming down the street. But he can remember what he did see—a spin of color, the reds and blacks of a gas station—as he flew through space. The medics who received the emergency call and sped with him to the hospital didn't know if he would survive.

We come to see him every day and do our best to calm him as he thrashes his cast-enclosed legs against the bed rails and tries to pull off immense mittens that prevent him from tearing apart the paraphernalia inserted all over his body. The doctors say the blood on his brain makes him irrational; he doesn't know where he is. Our granddaughter brings an iPod and plays his favorite songs, and we believe the music soothes him, carries him closer to home.

We ourselves hardly know where our own home is. On the leafy suburban street we've left behind, or an unfamiliar house filled with unopened boxes? In the hospital, where, for lunch and dinner, we eat peanut butter sandwiches made hurriedly in the morning? I try to stop the ache that comes with every breath, and ask myself: Had I imagined that in our ninth decade we would be granted some sort of immunity to anguish?

Robert is the youngest of our four children. When he was born the doctor told me he had an inoperable heart condition and might not live to adulthood. I cried to myself for a week before I had the courage to tell my husband, and then we both cried. In his first few years, our son was so slow to talk and walk, we took him to a psychologist at the National Institute for Health for tests, and found out that he had a genetic condition that causes physical disabilities and below normal intelligence.

By the time he was twelve, Robert had undergone major surgery—a miracle of modern medicine—that corrected his heart defect. By the time he was thirty he was doing things the professionals had said would never be possible—reading newspapers, taking the Metro, working as a clerk for the federal government, living in an apartment by himself. An agency that provides help to adults with developmental disabilities sent a counselor each day to be sure he took his medications and kept his place clean. On weekends, he rode the bus to see someone he'd met through family friends—a young woman who lived in a group home for people with disabilities—and they went to the movies, or the Silver Diner.

That is his old world, one he wishes could reappear like magic.

Six months after the accident, Robert starts to learn to walk again. From the ICU, Robert goes to a rehabilitation hospital. His brain heals and he no longer has to stay in a net-enclosed bed to prevent him from climbing out and breaking his legs again. He learns to get up safely, to stand and hold onto an aluminum walker, to slide into the front seat of a car. He moves to another place—an "assisted living facility," where I watch the physical therapist try to teach him to take steps without the walker. She ties a strap around his waist and holds on. He stumbles, lurches, unable to get balance. Each day, he asks, in different ways, often with anger—when will I live by myself again? When can I cook my own meals? When can I earn a paycheck? When can I go home?

I don't know the answers. We talk about how far he's come. We take him to picnics with old friends, and he grieves for the difference between them and him. I can't pretend we know the future; he catches any false note,

Pollyanna-talk. But I say this: We'll wake up each day and see what happens. We'll use our brains and our love. We'll help you find new ways to be what you want to be.

And we—my husband and I—will look for new ways, too: quick moments outside the world of pain, times to nurture our selves. We have been living further and further away from ordinary life, hardly able to talk with old friends, as if they were speaking a strange language. We need to learn to live in this house we've moved into.

In our front yard, the leaves of the weeping cherry tree are gold, the holly berries red. I suck the colors into my lungs, try to see what lies ahead, and remember the words of the nurse when she taught my son how to eat.

We'll take it in small bites.

Minotaur

Anita Curran Guenin

I see you across
the supermarket aisle,
closely inspecting peaches.
You look up, a second passes
before the truth of us
freezes your flirting where
it should have years ago.

Under deathly neon,
we roll our carts
in opposite directions,
pretend not to know
each other, our history
when we burned
summer to the ground.

Youth fragrance wafts,
straightens your back,
renews your game as
you breech a darkened aisle,
stalk a maiden
with milky midriff,
study her tattooed signals.

Open mouthed,
she looks mystified by towers
of cans and bottles, but
sweetly, you offer to reach
honey on the top shelf,
while I push my silent dinner
through the check out line.

Food for Thought

Buck Dopp

One day, after chewing the last bite of breakfast, I turned to my wife and said, "What's for lunch?" Thinking back to that moment, it was the first time I realized I might have a problem.

She frowned. "We just had breakfast. You can't possibly be hungry."

"I'm not hungry now. I'm planning my day."

"All you ever think about is food."

I took that as a compliment because she used to say that about sex.

The good news about retirement is that I can do whatever I want to do when I want to do it. The bad news about retirement is that I can do whatever I want to do when I want to do it. After sleeping ten hours a night, there are fourteen long hours to fill, so spending as much of that as possible eating is a good thing. God made snacks because he loves us and wants us to be happy.

Planning activities around mealtimes became an obsession. A primal survival instinct told me I could starve to death if I didn't schedule regular provisions for hourly nourishment. A big bowl of popcorn slathered with butter and a tall can of Foster's to wash it down is the perfect nightcap to a busy day. Actually, it's just as good if it isn't on a busy day. It's also good in the morning. Easy to make, too—just throw a bag in the micro and four minutes later you're done. The only problem is that those skimpy bags don't make enough popcorn for a man-sized appetite like mine. There's nothing worse than waking up in the middle of the night with hunger pangs disturbing one's sleep.

I solved the problem by switching to a pot on the stove with an inch of oil in the bottom and drowning the popcorn in it. Seeing white kernels lifting the lid four inches above the pot, and then watching the kernels exploding in all directions on the kitchen floor is a thing of beauty, and the smell of popcorn is to die for!

In the mornings I would forage in the kitchen for food while waiting for the wife to wake up and cook breakfast. A bowl of cereal would do in a pinch to stave off hunger, but if I could find a cinnamon roll, heat it up real good, then carve a chunk of butter to put on top and watch the yellow streams melt into every crevice, it was heaven on earth. That would tide me over until breakfast.

It's good to have a lot of chocolate around the house for random snacking. It gives one a quick energy boost and keeps the blood sugar at the proper levels. Besides that, it's organic. I didn't write the catch phrase, "Chocolate is the answer, who cares what the question is," but I could have. I feel the same way. Being the health-conscious guy that I am, I prefer dark chocolate because, as everyone knows, it has more antitoxins. That way I'm not only satisfying my cravings for chocolate, I'm cleansing my body of dangerous poisons.

I noticed that t-shirts and sweat pants—my daily garb—began to shrink. The wife must have been using too much hot water in her laundry. I knew I had to carefully confront her and correct this behavior without hurting the little dear's feelings.

I broached the subject gingerly one night after a New York strip steak dinner that included a stuffed baked potato and chef salad. She had just set a chocolate sundae in front of me. I had chosen to wait for dessert to bring up this sensitive issue. That way, if the conversation took a negative turn, it wouldn't spoil my dinner.

"Sweetie, I wanted to discuss the laundry with you."

"What about the laundry?"

I could see her tense up, so I started with a compliment to soften the mood. "You know, Celeste, I really appreciate the way you keep my sweatpants and tees so clean."

"Thanks."

"Uh huh. There is one thing—just a small thing—I think you're using a little too much hot water. I've noticed my clothes are shrinking. Would you mind terribly, snookums, washing my sweats in warm water?"

"Howard Grimes, I've always washed your t-shirts and jockey shorts in hot water, your sweat pants in warm water. Nothing has changed in our thirty years of marriage except *you*. Your clothes aren't getting smaller, you're getting bigger."

"Maybe just a little, but are you sure you haven't been doing anything different with the wash?"

"Absolutely positively, I'm sure."

"Then it must be the cheap clothing you're buying—made in China by children—stuff doesn't hold up in warm or hot water. That's the problem."

She shook her head. "You're clueless."

I ignored her name-calling. Instead, I thought about Chinese children. It reminded me of Momma. She always said people were starving in China, so I should eat all my food and clean my plate. Momma's words of wisdom were always a good guide to live by. So I finished that last mouthful of my chocolate sundae and licked the spoon.

About two weeks after that incident, I was watching a game show on my flat-screen TV while scarfing down some potato chips, when it occurred to me that the wife might be right about me overeating. The next thought I had made me mad. My compulsive eating was all her fault. She was using me, constantly forcing food down my throat to undermine my self-esteem. I was the victim here. It was high time I empowered myself to throw off the chains of her oppression and dominance. She had been using food all these years to control and manipulate me.

I had seen the light. "Celeste! We need to talk!"

She poked her head around the corner from the kitchen. "Can we talk after dinner? I've got some things on the stove."

"Sure. What are we having for dinner?"

"Prime rib."

"Perfect."

I decided to have that conversation at a later date. There's no rush. After all, I'm retired.

Gargle

Margaret Golden

Good Gravy
Almost Always
Requires Roasted
Gobs of Garlic and
Luscious Lentils for
Everyone's Enjoyment

(A quick Gargle will restore your social acceptability)

Onion Eggs

Phyllis J. Seltzer

"I always wished I hadn't known *that!*" my wistful childlike voice whispers to me even now, sixty odd years later…

We lived in a red brick six-story building in the Hillside Homes community of the Bronx, the tallest of all the buildings in the community. The apartment kitchen only had a table for two that somehow we four managed to eat at, a small clock on the wall above it with its dark cord running down the wall. The table sat across from the small stove, next to which was a little sink, and adjacent to that what we called a Frigidaire. As I remember, only grilled cheese sandwiches and very good soups were made in there.

You needed to walk through the living room to get to the bathroom and two bedrooms, one of which I shared with my brother, Steve, until I became a bride at eighteen. This was not unusual when living in a city apartment, which is where almost everyone I knew lived. I knew very few people who lived in a private home.

My mother sometimes cooked onion eggs in the tiny kitchen, so narrow she could touch both walls by extending her arms. She served the eggs with tomatoes and toast for breakfast. Memory has dimmed the sizzling sound and rich aroma of the caramelizing onions and eggs dancing in the frying pan. Today my memory is not a mouthwatering one; it is, instead, stomach churning, evoking the tense and often worried conditions under which my mother, brother Steve, and I lived, under the glare and temper of our very angry father.

Our apartment, #6D, was just one flight down from the rooftop, where I often fled pretending to be at the beach, lying on a towel with my eyes closed under the clotheslines. The hot summer sun's kiss embraced my skin while I breathed in the happy smell of suntan lotion, which carried me off to coconut palm tree tropical islands. The melting tar of the roof softened and oozed its strange breath beneath me. The clean, sweet smelling clothes hanging on the line above sent me an occasional breezy kiss as they swung back and forth, providing welcome relief from the nervous anxiety pervading the small apartment below. But then…back down the flight of grey concrete steps and into the small entry hall, the familiar dark pulsating nervous anxiety pressing against my chest with a thud.

The small space contained one brown and tan folding chair, a black telephone on a shelf, and, right behind the front door, a cardboard box, home to my brother Steve's beloved guinea pig, Tony. To Steve's absolute delight, Tony would run up and down his arm and in and out of his blue-and-white-striped pajama sleeve. I admit I did not share the same affection for Tony as Steve did.

According to my mom, the black phone on the shelf received dark scary calls from a stranger whispering unspeakable things. She ultimately referred to the obscene caller as "Dick." As for Tony, one day our friend Eddie Reynolds came calling, leaned over Tony's box, and exclaimed in a voice full of wonder, "Jeez, he's stiff!" Poor Tony was dead.

Our community radiated closeness and support from neighbors and extended family. Hillside was a haven with its playground and tunnels and courtyards full of friends. My mother had three sisters, all of whom also lived in Hillside. My Aunt Belle and Uncle Bernie with their daughters, Mimi and Judi, lived right across the street. Aunt Sylvia and Uncle Murray lived on the first floor of my building with their children, Frances and Hank. Four streets down the hill lived my Aunt Lena and Uncle Mike with their daughter, Sondra, and son, Freddie. Unlike my mother and Aunt Sylvia, who did not seem to love cooking particularly, Aunt Belle's sweet and sour meatballs are still a delicious reminder of her wonderful-smelling kitchen. I can still taste Aunt Lena's pineapple fritters and cheese blintzes.

Being surrounded by family was a blessing in every way for me. Aunt Sylvia was my saviour, oftentimes pulling me away from my apartment and the thick black leather strap with the painful metal buckle that my father used to discipline me. She would take me down to her apartment and feed me her cabbage soup. I adored her. The other dish she was "known for" was "psghetti with ketchup," as Hank called it. She lived to be one hundred and three and died in 2012. She was my confidante till the very end.

Looking back at life as a young girl growing up in apartment #6D, I have mixed emotions. There was the terror I felt, living under fear and humiliation when my father would at times come threateningly into the shelter of our playground and drag me by the arm away from other children as we played board games, because he said it was going to rain and I should have come home. On seeing his face full of angry rage, my ears pulsed with the sounds of lightning strikes and dark heavy cracks of thunder, afraid he would hit me in front of everyone.

At the same time, I loved and felt loved by my mother, whom I admired so much. She was a very beautiful woman, and I wanted someday to grow up to be like her. She finally divorced my father, but unfortunately not until I was eighteen. She was first in her family to ever get a divorce, and it was a hard thing for her to do, as it was considered quite shameful at that time.

My aunts and my mother had strange names for various members of our family. At the time it was accepted without question or discussion, as were most things. Some of our relatives were known as "the snake" or "the mad dogs" or "poor so and so." It was only as adults that my cousins and I discussed these things.

I remember the night before I was to be married. I was eighteen and a virgin. I really needed more information, and so I told this to my mother.

"Close the light and come into my bedroom," she said. "Lie down next to me. What do you want to know?" she asked.

I said, "What is okay to do and what is not okay? What should I know?"

She said, "Everything agreed upon between and husband and wife is okay. Turn on the light, now."

In retrospect, it was good advice. But short and "sweet?" Not so much.

Looking back at memories of our pets and our relationship to them after Tony's death, at least we still had our beloved blue parakeet, Skippy, who lived in our bedroom. Skippy would fly in and out of his open cage at will until he flew smack dab into the mirror over our dresser with a bang, falling dead and landing on the back of a marble horse that stood beneath the mirror.

Tony was buried in the building's incinerator, across from the elevator on our floor, with many tears from my little brother's big brown eyes. As for Skippy…well, I carried one of his tail feathers with me in my wallet for at least twenty years after his unintentional suicide. I guess in our apartment #6D, history did in fact repeat itself, because the very reason the apartment was available for us to lease was as a result of the previous tenant having *hung himself in the shower.*

Years have softened the stomach-churning sensations, but my childhood voice echoes softly as it travels down through the tunnel of time, whispering, "I always wished I hadn't known *that!*"

Modern Myth: Equality of the Sexes

Irene Thomas

They were both four.
Intervening fence
six feet tall.

Acquaintance
became animosity.
Who knows who started the war?

Missiles flew,
toy cars, doll dishes,
tufts of grass, bits of stone.

He was innovative.
She was fast,
soon her side was clean.

Her stance of satisfaction
became
a glance of apprehension.

Thrust through knothole
a tiny penis.
Flood of yellow urine!

Body tensed,
fists clenched,
uttered primordial scream!

"MOM-MA!"

Second Runner-up: Best Fiction Contest

High Noon in the Garden of Good and Evil

Judith O'Neill

The year Sueann turned four, 1942, she was shocked by the arrival of three new cousins. Until that time, Sueann had reigned as the only grandchild on both sides of her family, and then suddenly, everywhere she went there was a soft little bundle with a tiny face peering out and an aunt or uncle saying proudly, "Sueann, Sueann, come and see your new little cousin."

The most intrusive came first. A miniature, curly-haired girl they called Julie, with huge black eyes now resided with her mother at Sueann's Grandma's house—the house where Sueann stayed every day. There was no denying that Julie was a beautiful baby. Everyone said so, and even Sueann had to admit it. They looked nothing alike. Sueann had inherited the blue eyes and blond hair of their English, Irish, and Dutch ancestors, and the new baby, she was told, had inherited the French, Spanish, maybe some American Indian characteristics.

At first, Sueann was drawn in by the excitement of the new arrival and liked to hold the small, warm, good-smelling (because nothing in her Grandma's house was ever allowed to smell bad), pink-blanketed doll. She was allowed to brush the dark curls with the soft, soft pink brush that did nothing for her own straight bangs. But it soon became alarmingly clear that the baby was going to be there every day and even stayed the night. One morning, as Sueann was dropped off on her mother's way to work, she came in to find her grandmother cuddling the baby and singing songs to it, the very songs she sang to Sueann. She told her grandmother loudly, "You *think* you're that baby's Grandma, but you're not!" Her grandparents had thought it was hilarious, and they repeated it to everyone who dropped by that day. They tried to show Sueann how much the baby liked her and how important it was to be a nice and good older cousin. She was not convinced. She couldn't bear the idea that a grandma might be something to be shared.

Sueann knew there was a war on, everyone talked about it, her father had come home from the Army injured, her uncles were far away. She was set on the front steps to alert the family to the mailman's approach. Letters were snatched from her hands and read again and again. There were blackouts even in St. Joseph, Missouri when they had to turn off all the lights and sit in the dark until the terrible, shrieking whistle blew again. She saw the men in uniforms. But she had no idea what a war was.

Her days were full and fun and busy. Even the baby, as long as it was not in her grandmother's lap, was entertaining. Sueann was delivered to her grandparents early in the morning on her mother's way to the overall factory, or later in the morning by her father, who was Bell Captain at a hotel downtown. Her job, as she saw it, was to accompany her grandmother around the house in her daily duties, go on errands or visits with her, or play in the sunny back yard while Grandma washed clothes in the silver tub on the back porch. She followed her down the rows of clotheslines, handing up the clothespins. Sheets flapped in the constant wind and her grandma hung clothes from their shoulders, so the long underwear, dresses, blouses, nightgowns, and slips all danced wildly on the lines in the breezes blowing up from the Missouri River. Sueann ran between the lines of clothes, winding herself into the sheets, making up stories, creating good and bad characters, giving them feelings, actions, and names in a kingdom ruled by her.

When her teen-aged aunts were home (the oldest one the mother of the new baby), Sueann trailed them, got into their things, sat quietly while they played with her long hair, and danced on their beds to their records. Her grandfather was a bartender, so he was home most mornings. He sat at the kitchen table and read, or visited with friends who dropped in, or entertained Sueann. Sometimes he took her with him fishing, or just downtown for ice cream. The old house, the long back yard, the cobbled street that ran alongside the house were full of things to see and do.

And then, into the house across that cobbled street, moved a woman who was an old friend of her grandparents, and with her she brought a large green parrot she called "Petey." One day, as Sueann raced around and under the hanging sheets, her grandmother called her from the porch. But when she ran to her, her grandmother laughed and said, No, she hadn't called her and she pointed across the street. And then the parrot called her again, in her grandma's own voice! How could that be? Petey went into a torrent of "Sueann, Sueann, Sueann, Sueann," and Sueann and her grandmother stared across the street to where the parrot sat on the porch on its perch, its leg securely tethered. The parrot began to call "Grandma, Grandma," and Sueann's grandma dropped her broom. "Now *that* is just weird!" she said, gazing at Sueann. Petey had not used her grandma's voice to call out "Grandma, Grandma," but the way he said it sounded very familiar. He did it again, and then Sueann knew whose voice that was.

She had heard the parrot speak before. Sometimes in the evenings, when the lady who owned him tried to take him from his perch and put him into his cage, he would draw all the neighbors out with screams of "Oh, no, no! Help, help! Murder, murder!" And sometimes he would call across the street, "Hello, hello." But always sounding very much like a parrot.

Now he began to mimic her every day. Whenever she was outside shouting, the parrot would shout louder. Worse still, when he called to her in her grandmother's voice, she couldn't tell the difference. She couldn't tell the difference! This enraged her. It seemed to her somehow not right, unnatural, scary.

The neighbor came over one afternoon and said to Sueann's grandmother, "Edie, come for lunch tomorrow and let Sueann see Petey up close. She'll like that, won't she?" Her grandma agreed and so the next day, with her grandmother carrying Julie wrapped in a lacy pink blanket, they went. It was the first time Sueann had been close to the large, nervous bird. It was the biggest bird she had ever seen, with green silky feathers and bright yellow and red around its beady eyes. It regarded Sueann with one eye, then the other, twisting its head from side to side.

The owner had set up a little table and chair beside the parrot, and she brought out a plate of tiny sandwiches, crusts cut off, and strawberries. She set down a flowered glass of cold buttermilk and said hopefully, "Your grandma says you like buttermilk." Sueann was pleased to sit surrounded by pots of sweet smelling brilliant flowers. The parrot was quiet for once.

"Mind your manners," her grandmother said as the two women went inside through the screen door. She could hear her grandmother's voice as the ladies talked and laughed and fussed over the baby.

She nibbled her peanut butter-and-jelly sandwich and watched the parrot, who watched her. The parrot began to make little noises. Little eating noises. When Sueann drank her buttermilk, Petey made glug-glug-glugging noises. When she burped, Petey burped.

Then it said, "Mind your manners, mind your manners!"

Sueann looked at the screen door, but the women were laughing inside the house. The parrot mimicked her grandmother's laugh.

Sueann jumped up and grabbed the parrot around its neck with both hands. It scrabbled loudly, trying to hang onto its perch, and flapped its wings about. It couldn't stab at her with its hooked beak because she had it right up under its head, her thumbs pushing in on that hated throat. She felt under her tight little hands, surprisingly, a wild beating.

She knew what that was. She had heard it often against her ear when she was curled up on her grandma's lap, her head against her grandma's chest. She had seen it on the top of Julie's head, the part she wasn't to touch, and along the blue-veined sides of the pale little face. She could see it in a mirror sometimes in her own throat.

She let go and sat back down. The parrot gave a squawk and scuttled to the far end of its perch. It did its side-to-side inspection of her, ruffling its feathers, smoothing them down, stretching its neck up and down, up and down, gasping, "Help! Help! Murder! Murder!"

Sueann's grandmother and her friend carried the sleeping baby and their coffee and some cookies out, and they all sat on the porch among the flowers, visiting. When they were leaving, the lady said to the parrot, "Say good-by to Sueann, Petey," and Petey said "Good-by, Sueann," in the lady's voice.

How Many?

Jeffrey Widen

They soared. Oh, how they soared. In the sky above them clouds floated, pushed by howling breezes like giant ships in an ocean of blue. The eagles' white heads and tail feathers reflected the orange and red colors of the sunrise, and their brown feathers flickered as they moved in the shimmering sky.

Keen eyes peered downward as the raptors darted from one updraft to the next, scouring the fast moving earth and water below. This was the first morning they'd left their two eaglets alone in the aerie. The first time they were willing to trust the maturing young ones to hop around by themselves in the great nest. Soon the hunt for food would be complete, and they'd return to feed their insatiable youngsters.

High in the tree the fledglings—one a male, the other a female—stretched their powerful young wings. They were eleven weeks old, and if they flapped just right, they could rise two or three feet above their twig and grass bole.

The male was more aggressive this morning. At the apex of his lift he gave an extra flap of his wings and rose high enough to be caught in a crosswind. He was blown to the side and toppled twenty feet downward, away from the nest. In desperation he reached out with his talons and grasped a branch, righted himself and perched, bewildered and frightened.

Returning home with their prey, the Bald Eagles heard the panicked screeching of the eaglets and darted back to the nest, where they saw the young female standing on its rim calling down to her brother. The female spotted her son on the branch below and swooped down, landing beside him. The male flew to the nest, placed his catch to the side, and nestled next to the eaglet to calm her.

Mom's look at her son was clear and direct, the meaning inescapable: "*How many* times have I warned you not to fly yet?" It would take an hour to rescue him. She flapped her two graceful wings and rose to a branch above, beckoning her fledgling to do the same.

Terrified but trusting, he followed her guidance, rose to the limb and alit next to her. Another flap, another rise, another branch. Limb by limb, they moved up the tree toward the nest. Finally, they hopped into the aerie. The mini-flaps and leaps had taken the young bald eagle from a place of fear to one of safety, where he was nuzzled by his grateful parents and sibling. He'd also gotten through his fear and was charged with confidence. He had no way of knowing that in two more weeks he'd be soaring with his parents, learning the secrets of the hunt.

The male and female tore chunks of the fish they'd caught and fed it, beak to beak, to their starved young raptors. While devouring his morsel, the young male continued to glance at the nest's rim.

A good bump from the female's wing snapped him back to reality. Mom's look was stern, the message clear: "Don't even think about it!"

How Many

Ila Winslow

Freckles has a redhead
Pennies in a can
Marbles in a jar
Words make a conversation
Fingers used in spanking
Rings on toes
People in a police line-up
Tickets before a warrant is served
Dog licks mean happiness
Slobbers can you take
Slurps in a 16-oz container
Rings in a 100-year old tree
Colors of the rainbow
Raindrops make a puddle
Feet down a fire escape
Twirls before you fall over
Snakes in a pit
Truckers with dogs on board
Vehicle makes in this generation
Styles of each vehicle
Shoes with 6-inch heels
Poor overworked umbrellas
Splashes before the tub overflows
People still laugh

Swan

Sarah Traister Moskovitz

My mother would come to me all the way across town
on two busses and a streetcar from West Adams to City Terrace
carrying Ball jars covered with wax paper, held tight with metal rings or
   rubber bands
containing meat rolled up in cabbage, doused in tomatoey sweet and sour
   sauce
or chicken soup with small egg yolks and gizzards to strengthen me
to care for newborn baby Debby.

I was so exhausted and yet couldn't sleep, between my baby's needy cries
too wired and overwhelmed with her demands,
afraid my milk was not enough, afraid I didn't know enough
afraid I could not be enough.

My mother came in softly, soothing as a swan
who lands and spreads her wings near waiting chicks,
her presence speaking wordless worlds of comfort.

She goes off to the kitchen to heat food with quiet footsteps calming as a
   lullaby.
Soon she returns and says, "*Kum ess, mine kind; du darfst makhn a
   mahmeh.*"
"Come eat, my child; you need to make a mother."
I hand my baby to her, so grateful for her outstretched arms
and wonder how did she ever manage with no mother to help her when I
   was born.

A Special Place in Our Hearts

Ruth Featherstone

We were having a wonderful Sunday afternoon celebrating our daughter Diane's fourth birthday with her four cousins and sister but, even with the excitement and fun of all the games, presents, cake, and ice cream, there was something I could not get out of my mind.

During our church service that morning, a representative from the Children's Society asked for volunteers to be foster parents to a five-day-old baby girl. She was due to leave the hospital right away. "Please phone as soon as possible," she pleaded. I had never thought about being a foster parent, but this baby girl did not have a home! I could not erase that thought.

When my husband, Matt, and I were cleaning up after the party, I told him what was bothering me. Unbelievably, he told me that it had been bothering him too. He immediately called our daughters, six-year-old Cindy and Diane, to ask them what they thought about having a baby girl live with us for a little while. No question about what they thought. "Yes, yes!" "Oh boy!" "When?"

The next morning, I phoned the Children's Society, and within the hour a representative came to our home. She interviewed me, checked out our home and asked for permission to interview our neighbors, friends, minister, and Cindy's teacher. We were amazed how quickly all this was accomplished. By 4:30 that afternoon, the phone rang. We had been approved! The representative would be back at our home the next morning with a seven-day-old baby girl that would need our love.

What a busy evening! We were all so excited and worked diligently to find and clean all the baby paraphernalia we had stored in the basement. The girls even searched through their toys to see what they could give to our new addition. We explained that she was too little for toys, but they could each put a small, stuffed animal at the foot of the bassinet. Finally, everything was ready and waiting for her.

Cindy had to go to school the next morning, but Matt, Diane, and I kept looking out the window waiting for the car to turn the corner and come into our sight. At 10 o'clock sharp they arrived. From our lookout post at the door, we smiled when we saw a small bundle wrapped in pink coming toward us.

What a thrill! A beautiful baby girl was placed in my arms. This tiny face, scrunched up and getting ready to cry, immediately won our hearts. When Cindy came home she joined in our happiness. Our new baby came with a beautiful handmade layette of sweaters, booties, matching bonnets, and pastel sleepers, which I knew had been made with love. This baby had been loved, but for whatever reason needed a home. One thing she did not come with was a name. We all thought about it and agreed her name was now Karen. Oh, what joy our little Karen gave us. Matt and I both felt she could have been our own.

Her parents had visiting privileges, but never came to visit. In their hearts, they must have felt it was best. After about three months, we were told by the Children's Society that they were close to selecting adoptive parents. Matt and I earnestly talked with them about adopting our darling Karen. We were immediately reminded about the paper we signed that stated we would not be allowed to adopt any foster child in our care because the birth parents had visiting privileges and knew where their baby was living.

Three weeks later, Karen was taken from us to meet and join her new family at the Children's Society's office. We sent her off with so much love, but we were devastated. Matt could not go to work, I was sick for two days, and the girls could not understand why she couldn't stay with us.

Never again! Matt and I agreed it was too hard on all of us. We were too emotionally attached. It was like losing one of our own daughters.

I phoned the Children's Society to tell them how we felt and to make arrangements to donate our entire collection of baby furniture and clothes. We would not be using them again. Maybe other foster parents could use them for another baby.

Little did I know!

About two months later the Society representative phoned me around 10 o'clock one morning. She thanked us again for giving Karen such wonderful care, but she desperately needed help and that was why she decided to call us.

A six-day-old baby girl, named Lynn, had to leave the hospital that afternoon. The representative had no available approved home in which to place Lynn. She knew we had said "never again," but asked us please to reconsider. Since Matt wasn't at home to offer his opinion, I knew this decision would be mine and mine alone. What would he say? Once again, I'm hearing a little baby doesn't have a home. How could I say no? I told the representative she could place Lynn with us. Now, to top it all off, she would be here in three-and-a-half hours.

After ending our conversation, all I could think of was, "What have I done? We don't have any baby furniture or supplies. Where will she sleep?" Knowing time was short, my mind quickly shifted into action mode. I started phoning neighbors, and within 30 minutes I was carrying a lovely white bassinet across the back yard. One neighbor called out, "What are you doing, Ruth?" I shocked her with my answer: "I'm having a baby this afternoon." No time for details.

It wasn't easy, but I was ready when our little bundle of joy arrived. The girls were so excited. They couldn't wait to hold her. So many questions followed. "Can we keep her?" "Does Daddy know we have a new baby?" "No, but he will soon!"

Matt arrived home right on schedule. I was visibly nervous when I opened the door, took his hand and said, "Close your eyes. I have a big surprise for you." As I led him to the bedroom, I kept telling him to keep his eyes closed. When he was at the foot of the bassinet, I slowly told him, "Open your eyes."

He was shocked! He stared in awe at Lynn, and then at me and asked, "Where did she come from?" Before I could explain, as if on cue, Lynn's little face puckered up, and she started crying as if her tiny heart was broken.

Matt immediately reached down and picked her up, wrapped her blanket around her and cuddled her on his shoulder. She snuggled, stopped crying and, by the look on Matt's face, I knew this was only the first step of a bonding that would result in eventual heartbreak.

Lynn was not at all like our girls or Karen. She was a unique individual. One or both of her parents must have had a volatile personality. This little one could express herself loudly when unhappy, but was very slow to show contentment. We all had one goal. We wanted to get Lynn to smile and respond. This went on for weeks until one day Matt quietly called us in to join him with Lynn. We were all thrilled as we watched Matt talking to her while Lynn smiled, moving her little mouth and gurgling at him. You would have thought we all had just won the lottery.

Lynn progressed beautifully and was a joy, except when things were not going her way. She let us know in no uncertain terms when she wasn't happy. It is hard to believe, but this tiny, pink, eight-pound baby girl managed to get us on schedule very quickly.

If we put her in her crib right after dinner, even the neighbors could hear how unhappy she was. Matt decided to try holding her for a few minutes while he watched television to see if that would help. It worked! In fact, it worked so well it became a nightly ritual that she would sit for at least an hour in the corner of the couch, under Matt's arm, watching television with him. Then, after having her bottle, she would go to bed like a little angel. We soon knew better than to try to put her to bed without her time with Matt.

We were all heartbroken when Lynn was four and a half months old and the Children's Society representative came around nine o'clock one morning to take her to their office to meet her adoptive parents. It was especially devastating for Matt, as he always looked forward to the time he spent every evening with his "little buddy."

The representative said she would call us when Lynn was all settled, so we would know everything was all right with her. We waited nervously all day, but it wasn't until 10 o'clock that night that we received our call. The representative was still at the new parents' home, as Lynn had just settled down. She had been very unhappy all day and would not stop crying. They had tried everything, but had not known how to comfort her. The representative wanted the girls to know that the only thing that finally did comfort her was when they put the mobile toy that the girls had given her on her crib. Something familiar! We were very upset that Lynn had gone through so much that day, but knew in our hearts that she would train her new parents very quickly.

It has been over 55 years since we last held sweet, little Karen and feisty, lovable Lynn. We have often thought of them and wondered where they are, what they look like and, most of all, if they are well and happy. We loved Karen and Lynn dearly, and they both have always had a special place in our hearts. We were blessed to have had them, even for only a short time, in our lives.

Next

Keven Bellows

The future has arrived at my door, like an infant
dropped on the steps of a darkened church
a small surprise in a beat-up box.
I guess I thought my future
would look more like my past—
opening out, promising—
a home, even an apartment, lightfilled
windows all around, maybe a door to a patio,
a place for the big painting, Jim's mother's desk,
opera tickets, Ireland, saving the polar bears
more like the life I've lived for 77 years—
nearly smooth trajectory from judge's daughter
to long cherished wife, now widowed—
transplanted to a windy hill,
four close walls in my daughter's house,
like that baby wide-eyed in her basket,
needing to be rescued.

The Island of My Choice

Carole Kaliher

In 1999, my friend, Cindy asked me, "How would you like to take a trip to Ireland?"

"Where did you come up with that idea?"

"One of my clients, for whom I do psychic readings, is a travel agent, and she's organizing a tour in October. It would be a week in Southern Ireland. If we took another week after the tour and rented a car, we could see Belfast, Edinburgh, Stratford on Avon, Bath, and London."

"Can we get all that done in two weeks? Will it be a case of *if it's Tuesday, it must be Belgium*?"

"No, it won't be like that. It'll be filled with sights, sounds, and fun; it'll be the trip of a lifetime. You have three months to think about it before they need a deposit."

"It sounds wonderful, but I'm not sure how I'll pay for it."

I considered using a dividend check that would come to me before October, and then dismissed the idea. A bill came in the mail with my husband's name on it, and the sight of it caused me pain. Over and over, I was reminded of what my life was with him, and now without him. I called the credit union and asked to have his name removed from our second mortgage. During the conversation the agent in charge of my account, said, "Let me check if there's an insurance policy on this loan. I'll research it and get back to you."

A month later he discovered the insurance policy on Jim. The result: absolution from the balance of the $25,000 loan and a refund of $7,000 that I paid on the loan after Jim's death. That money would pay for my trip and provide a down payment on a newer used car.

I recalled the Christmas present I received from Jim: a music box containing an IOU, promising me the island of my choice. He was on oxygen at the time and waiting for a lung transplant, so I knew it was a wonderful idea, but most likely a fruitless gesture on his part. The money for my trip to

Ireland was provided from his insurance policy; it meant that he was giving me the island of my choice, after all.

I called Cindy and said, "Count me in for the trip. I've found the money to pay for it."

On our first day, the four of us, Cindy, Judy, Terrel and I, boarded Virgin Airlines and flew into Heathrow Airport in London. Deplaning and walking through customs, I had flashbacks of old black and white movies featuring Heathrow with people wearing trench coats and hats, looking furtive and mysterious. I thought, *Where's a trench coat when I need one?* From customs we walked the tarmac and boarded a smaller plane that landed in Dublin. We met our guide and proceeded to Cabra Castle Hotel in Kilkenny, which would be our home base for most of the week.

The Cabra Castle Hotel and grounds are spectacular. We were met by a complete set of armor in the foyer and antiques placed artistically in the sitting rooms. We were shown to our rooms, and then went down to dinner. The Irish cooking is not haute cuisine, but delicious in its simplicity. Our bus driver/guide gave us a schedule for the next day and advised us not to be late for our start time of 8:00 a.m. Everyone was on time! After about an hour, the driver pulled to the side of the road and announced, "You have time to get out and take pictures this fine morning."

The view was of rolling hills, sheep grazing, blue skies, and white frothy clouds. We sat on one of the many rock walls to savor the moment and the beauty of our surroundings. I felt compelled to say out loud, "I can't believe I'm in Ireland. I'm a world traveler now!"

We were on our way to Cork, Bantry, and the Cobh Heritage Museum. Cork was a typical Irish town, a combination of the old and the new. Bantry is a small village on the coastline. The shops are set up like row houses—they're attached. We were given a few hours in each place to explore before returning to our bus. We had a lovely lunch in a pub. A custom for the Irish is to use the pubs as a restaurant, when not eating at home. The menu always consists of a choice of soup or the one entrée of the day. What bothered me most was seeing so many smokers who *continued to smoke* while eating!

The Cobh Museum had maps behind the glass and manikins dressed as the emigrants that used this port to leave for America and their new lives. It was both inspiring and sad to think that so many Irish had to leave their country to keep from starving. I was feeling compassion for those souls, when I realized that, if my husband's ancestors hadn't left their country, his family wouldn't have migrated to Minnesota first, and then California. I wouldn't have met and married that wonderful man! Their journey was a fine thing for me and our sons.

We returned to the hotel by 5:00 p.m. in order to freshen up and appear for our 6:00 p.m. dinner. After dinner we took a cab into a nearby town and stopped into a well-known pub. The custom at that pub was a spontaneous music session. The musicians were from all over, and no one planned ahead who would come and join in. The bartender said, "Every night, it's a different group. They don't get paid except for tips; they love to share their music with us and each other. They'll be happy to know that you Yanks are enjoying their music." It was a wonderful evening.

The next day took us to Kilarney (a lovely town), Ring of Kerry (could have missed that), Blarney Castle, the woolen mills, and Waterford for the crystal factory.

I was asked, "Are you going to kiss the Blarney Stone?"

"Are you kidding? Look at the stairs that go on forever. Then you have to hang upside down and kiss a dirty rock? I don't think so! The idea doesn't appeal to me. While you do that, I'll walk around town and visit the woolen mills."

The ladies thought that kissing the Blarney Stone was overrated, but they consoled themselves with the thought of having bragging rights.

We went to a cave dwelling called Newgrange, a Megalithic Passage tomb. Its origin is estimated at 3200 BC. The cave is carved out of a dome-shaped mound with grass on top. It looked like it was built by druids or aliens. We had to turn sideways to enter the cave. If an ordinary person tried to enter straight on, their shoulders would scrape the rocks. Newgrange has natural light only once a year for about seventeen minutes at Winter Solstice. The rest of the time, artificial lighting is required. I felt like I was entombed myself. It's an eerie experience.

After dinner, we were treated to youngsters in costumes doing Step Dancing to Irish music. Another wonderful day and evening was had by all!

After our usual hearty breakfast at the castle, we left to tour Kilkenny castle, once the medieval capital of Ireland, the fabulous gardens, and lastly the artisan section outside of the castle. I chatted with a young man who created jewelry. He was so pleased to speak to a Yank. I purchased his sapphire ring, and I'm sure *that* pleased him more!

"If you have any problems with your jewelry, my name and number is on the business card. Even if it's only to chat, call me."

Irishmen, young or old, are very friendly. The young men enjoy talking to and listening to women, even if they are not women they want to "hit on." Their attitude is so different from American men, who make older women feel almost invisible.

That day, I went to every small church I could get to, enjoying the murals, statues, and stained glass. Cindy would tell me, "You have ten minutes in this church; get it over with." She was enamored with cemeteries. If I found a church with an old cemetery attached, we were in business. She walked around outside, and I walked around inside. I never did understand why she felt drawn to graveyards. She especially loved the headstones shaped like the old Celtic crosses.

After our day on the tour was finished, the bus driver announced congratulations to a couple on their fiftieth wedding anniversary. "There'll be a special dinner and cake for them tonight."

I was so depressed because I didn't get to enjoy a fiftieth with the love of *my* life. I knew I couldn't plaster a smile on my face to watch their joviality and felt certain I'd probably cry, throw up, or both. Choosing to skip dinner and stay in my room was my option.

The phone rang and it was Tom, our bus driver. "Wash your face and get ready. I'll be up there in fifteen minutes, and if you're not dressed, you'll be embarrassed. I'm taking you for an Irish cure of the blues, a pub crawl."

Tom found a lovely pub with music, step dancing, and good company. "I haven't lost a mate, but I lost me mum, so I know the pain of losing someone that you love."

Cindy smiled after we got back to the hotel and said, "Tom was irate when he didn't see you come down to dinner. 'Where's your lovely friend?' When I told him what you were feeling, he picked up the phone and called you. He knew just how to get you out of your blue funk, didn't he?"

"He was so sweet to me. He's another gentle Irishman, to be sure." The next day, I thanked Tom once more for the night out.

"It was my pleasure, Luv."

The first of the planned two days in Dublin, we went to Christ Church, a magnificent Anglican Cathedral that's over a thousand years old. Frescoes, stained glass, three small altar sections, and murals abound in the church. Even Cindy enjoyed touring that church and not a cemetery to be seen. However, there were headstones in the floor. We went to Dublin Castle, built in 1204, once a center for British rule and later turned over to the Irish Free State in 1922.

In the newer part of Dublin city, there's a wonderful area called St. Stephen's Green Shopping Center. Stores from all over the world are featured. It's a shopper's paradise with blocks and blocks of every product imaginable to be found there. We stopped in a tea shop for a quick bite. For lunch, we were always on our own, so we chose a taste of the Irish fare by having tea and cherry scones.

The tea was wonderful. I'm not a tea drinker, so I asked the waitress, "What kind of tea is this?"

"It's tea," she said in a bored manner.

I guess I was thought to be a stupid Yank asking that question. Oh, well!

We spent one more night in the Cabra Castle Hotel, and then moved to Dublin and checked into The Dubliner Hotel for our last two days of the week. We had a view of Christ Church out our hotel window. We walked on the Ha'Penny Bridge over the River Iffey and enjoyed the older parts of Dublin. The homes there are mostly row houses, and they take pride in painting their front doors bright and vivid colors of red, blue, green, purple, and yellow. Each door is brighter and more cheerful than the next. We stopped to talk to a policeman.

"What is your title? I know you're not called a bobby."

"I most certainly am *not* called a bobby. I'm called a Garda!"

"I'm sorry to insult you in that manner."

He chuckled and said, "Got you, didn't I, Madam?"

Chatting for a while, he asked us questions about where we were from, and then he took a picture with us. If I didn't miss my husband so much, I would have felt entirely at home in this wonderful country. The people are warm and friendly…even the police!

Walking down the street, we spied a shop with steps leading to a basement store. Cindy looked and then said, "Carole, it's an adult store, want to go in and see what they have?"

"Do you seriously think I want to visit a porn shop? I can just hear my kids asking what I saw in Dublin and me answering, 'Do you know they have porn shops there, just like the ones in the U.S.?'"

"You're no fun at all. Why are you blushing?"

We didn't go in.

The last day we stayed in Dublin was a Sunday. We had breakfast, saw to the task of mailing presents home, and planned the day. My companions—Cindy, Terrell, and Judy—wanted to go to a concert. I wanted to find a church and go to Mass. I didn't want to spend another day in a pub watching two of the ladies hoping to get picked up by some man. They never had any luck, even though they're attractive. I think the desperation was rolling off them like steam. I told the girls, "Go to your concert, and I'll meet you back here for dinner. I want to go to church."

I received directions from the concierge, a crudely drawn map on a napkin. I started the trek to find a church, took the bridge over the River Iffey and turned right, as instructed. The walk seemed to take forever with no sign of a church. I thought, *I must have taken a wrong turn. Maybe the church is down a side street. I think I'm lost.*

I asked directions from a little elderly lady. "I'm looking for a Catholic Church. Have I missed it, or do I walk some more?"

"Why, you're here, Missy; you're just a wee bit early."

Turning in the direction she indicated, I saw a glass front building that looked more like a storefront than a church until I saw the name, Blessed Sacrament Chapel. I walked into the most starkly modern chapel I've ever seen. Planning to light a candle and say some prayers before Mass, I looked to the back wall of the chapel. Standing in front of the candle stand, I must have looked as confused as I felt. *Where are the matches to light my candle?*

The same lady who led me to the church said, "Pardon me for interrupting you, but if you're looking for a way to light that candle with a match, you'll be here long after Mass. Push the tiny button here, and it lights. It's a newfangled electric candle."

I smiled, thanked her and sat, waiting for the Mass to begin. During the walk up the aisle to receive communion, I felt a hand on my arm. There stood an elderly woman, and she felt exactly like my deceased mother-in-law, Gavonna. The touch, the texture of her skin, soft and wrinkled, and the shape of her hand, including the flat fingernails, was Gavonna's. I knew she was there with me. After Mass I left the church, and outside, another very petite, elderly woman looked into my eyes and said, "God loves you, don't you know? He really does. God go with you." I was so moved I couldn't speak; I just nodded, and then managed a whispered, "Thank you."

The whole walk back to the hotel, I reflected on my experience at the Blessed Sacrament Chapel. The chapel may have been extremely modern, but it moved me emotionally more than the ancient churches I'd visited thus far. I felt I shared that chapel with a community of the many souls that had gone there before me.

Cindy walked into our hotel room and started grousing. "The concert was terrible. All I can say about the musicians is that they were loud. The grandstand was shaky and moved back and forth every time another person went to sit down. I was sure it would collapse, and we'd all be crushed to death. How was church?"

I related the whole experience. I included the explanation of the emotions I felt while inside and outside of that chapel, and what it had afforded me, or rewarded me with, as the case may have been. It was a satisfying and cathartic event for me.

"Oh, my God, I'm the psychic, I get a crummy concert, and you have a supernatural experience. That's so unfair!"

"You could have gone with me, but you don't like organized religion, as I recall you mentioning many times."

This was our last night in Dublin. The next day we would be boarding a train to Belfast. What adventure would we have there? Could it compare to my time in Southern Ireland, a week I would never forget?

I had survived my first vacation without my husband. I was a widow for just two years at this time, and I went from being fragile to feeling stronger. I remembered the many times during my husband's illness, when he said, "You are the strongest woman I know. You can do anything you set your mind to."

This trip wasn't just about a person taking in the sights of a foreign country. It was a baptism into my new life as an individual and no longer a part of a couple. As Cindy predicted, it was a once in a lifetime trip, and it was to the island of my choice. Thanks, Jim!

Golden Ties

Margaret S. McKerrow

Sunday morning; she takes her
by the hand, she is the mother now

smoothes the flyaway wisps of straggly
grey hair, straightens her dress

they sit together closely, quietly
side by side in the middle of the pew

the older woman, like a nervous child
turns to whisper in her daughter's ear

gets the reassurance she is needing.
I watch them as they leave, hand in hand

roles reversed, kindnesses repaid
she is the caregiver now.

Remembering Kitty

Anna Mae Loebig

The week following May 12, 1987, the day Mum died, my sister, Kitty, invited Tom and I to her home for dinner. She didn't have to coax me; I was more than willing to get away for a few hours after the busyness of being Mum's chief caregiver for many years, and then attending to the details of her burial. We did a lot ot talking and laughing, recalling Mum and Pop's friends, old neighbors, school friends, etc., and we casually mentioned about the four of us taking a trip to Ireland, as I now had freedom to go. Kitty casually handed me an envelope, which surprised me somewhat. I was more surprised with the contents. Inside was a lovely thank you note with sweet words of appreciation from my siblings: Kitty, Fran, Bob, and Tom. Also enclosed was a check from them to cover a round-trip flight to Ireland for Tom and me with specific instructions that the check was for that purpose only. Fighting back tears and embarrassed, but excited at this lovely gesture, I mumbled a few words of thanks and accepted the check.

The following September, Tom and I left for Ireland with Kitty and her husband, Chris, for two glorious weeks in the land of our parents' birth. We traveled the first week on a tour bus with a group of friendly people from the Buffalo, Toronto area, visiting castles, pubs, lakes, the blarney stone in Cork, and many other tourist attractions. The second week we visited with cousins in Dublin, Galway, and County Meath. Our visit was climaxed with an all-night party at our cousin Lil's home in Dublin. From 10:00 p.m. till 6:00 a.m. we sang and danced on a bare wood floor (the rug had been rolled up), accompanied by a piano and a bodhran drum. To us, it was such a tribute and honor to be guests at a party to top all parties. We had a marvelous time.

I'm sure this sentimental journey, a gift from my siblings, was instigated by my sister, Kitty. She and her husband, Chris, cared for Mum many, many times at their home for several days to give us a break. As a mother of seven children, she was well aware of the work entailed in caring for a loved one for years and years.

She was there when we needed her the most, and we love and thank her for it. Sadly, she passed away recently—Rest In Peace, Kitty.

The General

Betty Birkemark

Almost fifty years ago, Linda and I met the General in a dusty, dimly-lit department store basement in the heart of Madrid, Spain.

My friend, Linda, and I were halfway through our nine-week trip to Europe. Linda had already bought enough souvenirs and dolls for her collection to warrant buying another piece of luggage…so we went looking for one.

While Linda was pondering over whether or not to buy a very smart looking plaid suitcase, I was nosing around in a dark corner among a sea of luggage, and there it was: a round, brown leather bag about twenty inches high. It had a second zipper that extended the bag four more inches. Stuffed with paper to make it stand up, it looked rather elegant. But what really caught my attention was what made me pull it aside and shout, "Linda, you'll never believe this. Here's one with WHEELS!"

Linda, being an unusual individual herself, was always intrigued by unique things. My discovery made her drop the plaid bag to come see what I'd found. It would be to my advantage to have luggage with wheels, because Linda was handicapped, and I was the one who carried everything.

We called the sales clerk over to ask about the price. It was more expensive than the plaid bag, but he kept trying to show us other *cheaper* bags. Strangely, he acted like we shouldn't purchase it. His attitude alone made Linda certain that this was the one she was supposed to buy. Maybe the clerk thought it wasn't suitable for two American women to be seen on the street with it. We didn't know enough Spanish to find out why he thought it wasn't for us.

After leaving the store that afternoon and rolling the bag along the streets of Madrid, more shopping was done. Pulling out some of the paper the bag was stuffed with, we'd put in what we bought. People gave us a lot of strange looks as we guided it back to our hotel. I doubt you could even find a piece of luggage without wheels now, but it was a rare sight fifty years ago.

At first, the suitcase had no gender, but before we left Spain to continue our journey, it had gender...and a name. Our hotel was located on Avenida Generalissimo Franco, so after we knew how much junk the suitcase held, we named him Generalissimo El Junko.

We got more startled glances when we were heard *talking* to him. I was doing just that when I rolled the packed General to the elevator before going to the airport, and a hotel maid heard me say, "Now, behave yourself, General, and get in the elevator." With four wheels on his bottom, the General had a tendency to go in the wrong direction. The story of a crazy woman talking to a bag was no doubt passed on in the hotel.

Somewhere on our trip, we got on a bus with the General and placed him in a space behind the bus driver, while Linda and I sat down in the first seats back of the space. It was okay until the bus made a sharp right turn and the General started rolling out of his place, headed toward a man across the aisle. I was able to grab the handles just before he ran into the man, who looked pale and paralyzed when he saw a big, brown blob coming straight for him.

The General not only had a name and gender...he also had personality.

We were going through Customs at the New York airport, when the Officer asked us, "Got anything to declare, ladies?"

"Well, Sir Officer," Linda said, "some of our luggage is here, but Generalissimo isn't, and we put our purchased items in him for easier inspection."

We waited aside for quite a while, watching everyone else's luggage come up the ramp to the inspection station. Still no General El Junko. We feared he might have rolled onto the tarmac and be out on a runway somewhere!

Knowing his personality, we weren't far off with our worries. When the General was finally brought to us, we were told what had happened: a dutiful airport employee captured the *bag with wheels* after he saw it leap from the luggage rack and speed across the room, heading for the door.

Finally, we got our wayward bag home to California, with no more escape attempts.

Epilogue

During the next two decades, the General made more journeys rolling around the world with Linda and a friend she loaned him to. It was always understood that I would inherit him, and I did in 1987, when Linda passed away at the age of forty-four.

The General's time had come and gone. Eventually, used and bruised, he went to wornout luggage heaven at the local dump. He looked very sad, all slouched over when empty, but when fully packed, he still stood tall and proud...as any old, retired General should.

Synchronicity
for Carl Jung

David Ray

Mid-morning coffee
with wife and we chat
about how the branches,
heavy with raindrops,
sag over our sidewalk.

Idly I pick up a book
and my eye lights upon
Mayakovsky's line
*The rain sobbed
all over the sidewalks.*

Synchronicity has struck
once again, unavoidable,
unpretentious. Sometimes—
as after grief or love—
it strikes with greater force,
but often arrives as gently
as morning rain—
a reminder that mysteries
do not always declare
themselves with fire.

Winner: Best Fiction Contest

The Last Act

Andrew J. Hogan

"One year," Sarah Mannion said.

"One year?" Brady Mannion said, looking at the *Woolly Mammoth*, the student newspaper of Mastodon State University.

"One year from today you will have put in your twenty-five years at the university. You can retire with full benefits, and we can go back home to Thunder Bay," Sarah said.

"Thunder Bay?" Brady pointed to an announcement in the newspaper. "We're doing *An Enemy of the People* again. I was supposed to be in that play my junior year, before I went to Canada." He paused. "Huh, this will be my final production."

"We were happy in Thunder Bay," Sarah said.

"Yeah, I was doing something there, not just making a living. But what would I do in Thunder Bay now?"

"Relax. Be happy. With me. Our son and grandkids are nearby in Superior," Sarah said.

Brady gulped his coffee. "I have to get to going. The set needs a lot of work." He picked up the newspaper and left for the Theater Department.

"Chief, you called me?" Officer Rafaela Jimenez said, knocking on the door of University Police Chief Calvin Clymer.

"Come in, Jimenez. Sit down." She did what she was told. "I got a call from a reporter at the *Woolly Mammoth* a couple of minutes ago. That's why I called you in off patrol."

"Did I do something wrong? Will it be in the papers?"

"Well, yes and no. Someone from Students for Fair Trade recognized you as a police officer. Apparently, there's a photo at *Woolly Mammoth* of you in one of the SFFT demonstrations." Clymer frowned. "I thought I told you to keep a low profile."

"I did, Chief. But I had to go on the march. That's when a lot of the members who don't show up for meetings get together. I thought the fringe elements might stage the protest against Pommeraie. I had to be in the march to get a chance to talk with them."

"Whatever. Cat's out of the bag now. I want every scrap of paper—reports, notes, memos, anything—on your undercover mission."

"How soon?"

"Right now. And I mean everything. When you've brought everything to me, take the rest of the day off. Go home and don't answer the phone. Don't talk to anyone from the newspapers, not the *Woolly Mammoth*, not the *Piainfield Patriot*. And don't come to work tomorrow."

"Am I suspended? I just did what I was told."

"Don't get your panties in a bunch. You're not suspended. You're ill." Hope flashed in Clymer's eyes. "You wouldn't happen to be pregnant, would you?"

"I'm not even married."

"When has that ever stopped you…? All right, look, you're going to be sick for a couple of days. Come back next Monday. I'll make sure that your sick leave is restored after this blows over. All right?"

Rafaela nodded.

"Now, get me everything, and then get out of here—and talk to no one!"

Banished to smoker's purgatory on the loading dock, Brady finished the second of his daily quota of five cigarettes. Taking a long last drag to extract as much nicotine as possible, Brady looked down at the *Woolly Mammoth* headline: "University Police Infiltrate Student Group." On the bottom left corner of the front page was a picture of President Paul Merton, standing next to a seven-foot bronze statue of former President Hank Joplin, which was to be installed in the garden in front of the administration building across from the Theater Department.

Brady marveled at the irony. Joplin had been university president when he was a student. President Kennedy named Joplin to a national task force on racial discrimination in housing, but Joplin refused to comment on the obvious pattern of segregation in housing in his own back yard of greater Plainfield. Joplin had been willing to recruit black players for the college football team—Mastodon State went from doormat to champion of the Midwest conference in ten years—but the black players had their own dorm.

This hypocrisy made Plainfield, a state capital with a large university, the perfect place for a major civil rights demonstration. In 1965 the Reverend Dr. Martin Luther King chose Plainfield from among hundreds of speaking opportunities to turn the screws on a popular Republican governor and a prominent university president in hopes of making some progress on housing discrimination in the Midwest. And it worked. Dr. King's visit embarrassed Joplin, who reluctantly hosted a meeting of local leaders to address Plainfield's segregation problems. Unlike the governor, who rolled with the punches politics threw at him, Joplin had, over the course of his twenty-five-year tenure as President, become an autocrat who resented being pushed around and knew how to push back.

Brady rose to return to the set for the junior class production. He had been scheduled to play Hovstad his junior year 35 years ago. Brady had cut back on his class schedule for that one semester to help organize the campaign against housing segregation in Plainfield that culminated in Dr. King's visit to campus on April 12, 1965, with a march down Central Avenue from campus to the state capitol and, later, a tumultuous speech at Birchfield Auditorium.

Brady had waited until the final day to drop the intermediate economics course he couldn't manage along with his outside activities. He had arranged to attend summer school to make up the dropped course and enter his junior year with a full set of credits. Somehow, the draft board discovered he was taking only 9 credit hours during the spring semester, and they revoked his student deferment.

Brady left for Canada at the end of the semester and only returned in 1975, after interest in prosecuting draft evaders subsided. It was then too late to resume his studies. He had married Sarah while living in Thunder Bay, Ontario, and had a son to support. He worked handyman jobs at Mastodon State until the stage manager position opened at the Theater Department in 1980. His undergraduate advisor had become chair of the department and was sympathetic about his lost opportunity.

Woolly Mammoth reporter Steven Jefferson was working at his terminal when he got the sign from editor-in-chief Bob Wilkins to meet with him and Opinion Editor Marti Spears. Wilkins was his normal calm self in the sea of chaos that always erupted just before the deadline. Marti Spears looked angry.

"Steve, Marti and I are putting together an editorial on the SFFT infiltration. Marti wants to cut off Merton's balls and put them in a jar in front of the administration building." Marti twisted out a smile. "But I want to double-check our facts before we go overboard."

Marti interrupted. "The big issue is how much Merton has been lying about the infiltration. Do you think he ordered it to protect his friend, Michel Pommeraie, from criticism about the way his bank finances international development activities to favor multinationals? That constitutes suppression of political speech, which is constitutionally protected, and—"

"Whoa!" Wilkins said. "Steve's here to give us the facts as he knows them, not listen to a speech." He turned back to Steve. "Go ahead."

"Okay, so here's what we know so far. February of last year, Officer Rafaela Jimenez was assigned to infiltrate the Students for Fair Trade, posing as sophomore Carmela Simonetti because *someone* suspected the SFFT could become involved in violent protests during the spring commencement speech of Michel Pommeraie, President of the International Development Financing Corporation. Pommeraie was personally invited by his old friend, President Merton."

"Who's the *someone*?" blurted Marti.

"*Someone* is a good question. Merton says the idea was Chief Clymer's, who consulted with his boss, the Vice-President for Administration, who decided to run it by Merton after they'd made a decision to go ahead with the infiltration. Merton says Clymer sold him on the idea."

"But?" Marti said.

"But Merton isn't very reliable. Shortly after the infiltration was exposed, Merton met with SFFT representatives and blew off accusations that he was behind the infiltration because of his friendship with Pommeraie."

Now Wilkins interrupted. "But he didn't specifically deny that he had prior knowledge of the infiltration."

"No. He was very lawyerly in his responses, sufficiently obtuse and indirect to avoid an overt lie," Steve said. "His answer to the accusation that he lied to the SFFT is that they didn't ask him the right question. Merton claims he went along with the infiltration plan to balance freedom and order—SFFT has the right to protest the IDFC's policies, but not to break the law doing so."

"Was there any evidence that the SFFT was going to break the law?" Marti said.

"None. The national SFFT had been involved in the Seattle World Trade Organization protests that turned violent, but no one from the local chapter participated in the Seattle protest. The administration tried to link the SFFT to vandalism of the university animal labs by PETA activists a couple of years ago, but that seems to be a pretext. There's no overlap between Students for Fair Trade and People for the Ethical Treatment of Animals. The animal rights activist who was caught in the vandalism case wasn't even an MSU student—never had been."

Steve expected an interruption, but hearing none, continued. "The Greater Plainfield American Civil Liberties Union got almost nothing back from its freedom of information request about the infiltration. The administration's explanation is that the case was closed; since there had been no disruptive protests at Pommeraie's commencement speech, they got rid of the case files. But the animal labs vandalism case has been closed, the vandal convicted, and those case files still exist. Apparently, once the infiltration was exposed, someone went through and destroyed most of the documents in the files. Why would that be necessary if Chief Clymer had ordered the infiltration based on reasonable police information? The better guess is that Merton ordered the infiltration for 'political' reasons—an abuse of police power—and so the records had to be destroyed."

"But you have no proof?" asked Wilkins.

"No. The proof in all likelihood went into the shredder."

"And what do the esteemed leaders of our board of trustees have to say about all of this?" Marti said.

"Nothing," Steve said. "Both Davidson and Jacobs initially refused comment on the grounds that they didn't have enough information; they weren't consulted. Since the infiltration was an operational issue, not a matter of university policy, Merton wasn't required to consult with the board."

"It would be a matter of university policy if Merton was using the university police to suppress political dissent," Marti said.

"Sure, but the trustees seem to prefer not to know this; they appear relieved there isn't any evidence they have to act on publicly. The trustees are focused on developing a policy to avoid such controversies in the future," Steve said.

"Thanks, Steve. Marti and I will hammer out an editorial."

"Brady, nice to see you again. Have a seat. How about a latte, or do you still like old fashioned coffee?" Simon Hendricks said.

"Regular coffee's fine." Brady could see that Hendricks was trying too hard. Something was wrong. Brady hadn't spoken with his old political science professor except to exchange passing pleasantries for ten, maybe fifteen years. Their real discussions had taken place back in 1965, when Hendricks helped him decide to go to Canada rather than be drafted. When Brady returned in the late 1970s, he and Hendricks discussed his decision to leave, and Brady told Hendricks it was for the best. Hendricks wanted to hear he had given Brady good advice, but it wasn't a conclusion Brady was completely honest about. So they drifted apart, their earlier friendship degrading into mere acquaintanceship.

Hendricks came back with Brady's coffee. "Well, it is nice to see you again. We haven't really talked in years. How's Sarah?"

"She's fine. How about Vivian?"

"Not so good. It's her mind. Maybe Alzheimer's."

"Sorry to hear that," Brady said, before sipping his coffee. Hendricks still wasn't ready to take the lead in the conversation. "So I read in the Bulletin that you retired from MSU, but you're keeping busy with the ACLU. You've been involved in the SFFT infiltration case?"

"That's what I wanted to talk with you about. You probably read about it in the papers. We filed a freedom of information request and got next to nothing from the MSU administration. Then we sued."

"And you got nothing again, if I read correctly."

"Yes, on the SFFT case. But when we sued we thought we might need to establish a pattern of behavior by the university. So we asked for all records of university infiltration of student groups or spying on individual students."

Brady felt a chill.

"Your name came up," Hendricks said.

"How?"

"Joplin was spying on you because of the King visit, back in '65, before you left for Canada."

"What'd it say?"

"I brought copies with me. The judge has enjoined us from releasing any of these records because of the Buckley Act; it protects the privacy of student records. But since these documents are about you, I think you're entitled to see them."

Hendricks lifted a manila envelope out of his briefcase and extracted copies of two hand-written documents. He laid them on the table for Brady to read.

Uncle Hank,
The student you told me about, Mannion, who is causing trouble with the Negroes, just dropped my economics class. I think he might not have enough credits to keep his deferment.
Paul

INTEROFFICE MEMO
Date:3-15-65
To: Joyce
From: HJ
Ask the registrar to find out how many credit hours Brady Mannion is carrying.

"Who's Joyce?"

"Joyce Hildreth. Joplin's executive assistant," Hendricks replied.

"Uncle Hank?"

"That's what Paul Merton called Joplin, an old friend of the Merton family. It was Merton's uncle, Phinneas Merton, who nominated Joplin for the presidency of Mastodon State Agricultural College. Paul Merton's father was Phinneas' youngest brother."

"So Paul Merton was spying on me for his uncle, Hank Joplin?"

"Right, and not just on you. Merton wasn't the only student who was spying for Joplin. They spied on Cecil Jacobs for the same reason, because of his involvement in the King visit."

"So Merton ratted me out, and I got drafted."

"It looks like it. This is all we have pertaining to you. We only asked for documents related to infiltrations and spying. Communications with the draft board wouldn't be included."

"Could I sue? For damages?"

"Probably not. Your deferment was based on your maintaining full-time credits. It's not clear that the university did anything wrong updating the draft board on your change of status."

"It would probably cost more than it would be worth."

"The university has a lot of money to fight lawsuits. But I could help you write a request under the Privacy Act, if you want to."

"I'd better think about it."

"Okay. I thought you'd want to know."

Even though he had long suspected what he had just seen, Brady was still stunned. "Thanks for thinking of me. It's been a long time."

Hendricks returned the documents to the envelope. He patted Brady on the shoulder and said, "It's been a long time, but after all these years, it still stinks."

"Where have you been?" Sarah said.

"I stopped by the coffee house. Simon Hendricks wanted to talk with me about the old days," Brady said. "Did you see in the paper how the administration infiltrated the Students for Fair Trade? It's the same as when we were in school."

"When *you* were in school. I'm Canadian. We don't do that sort of thing."

"Well, they're doing it again here. I'm thinking about writing something for the newspaper."

"Haven't you learned anything about being an American?"

"What are you talking about?"

"I'm talking about the last time you stirred up trouble, you got more than you could handle. You're only a year away from retirement. You've got high blood pressure, bad lungs, and God knows what else is wrong with you. We need the health insurance when you retire. If you get yourself fired, we'll have to wait three years before you can get Medicare."

"So I should let them get away with this again?"

"That's right. Think about yourself and me this time. You've kept your head down for twenty-five years. You can do it for one more."

"These bastards ruined my life. I could have finished my bachelor's, maybe gone to grad school. Hell, I could have been teaching theater, not acting as a stage manager and flunky for somebody else's kids."

"Well, that's a compliment. Your life with me, your son, that's all a ruin? If you hadn't evaded the draft and met me in Canada, our whole marriage would never have happened."

"I didn't mean that. I just meant—"

"I know what you meant. You consider your life a failure. You didn't accomplish the big things you planned, and the little things like being a good husband and father don't really count."

"You'll never understand. You never tried to be anything better."

"If you don't keep your mouth shut, you sure as hell will make things worse for us."

Brady waved his hand in disgust and went into the guest bathroom. He knew Sarah would go to bed soon. One or another version of this argument had been replayed so many times there was no need to continue; they each knew their scripts by heart. He needed to think about what he could do to redeem, if only by a miniscule measure, the meaning of his life.

Brady told the faculty advisor for the upcoming junior class production he was taking his lunch break early, but that the set was almost ready. In spite of the blustery cold, Brady ate his lunch outside on the quadrangle. Clancy Construction Company workers were finishing the installation of the seven-foot bronze statue of President Joplin. According to the *Woolly Mammoth*, President Merton had personally financed the last ten thousand dollars for the installation of the statue.

Brady had been observing the installation on and off for the last two days. A large reinforced concrete pad served as a base for the statue's pedestal. Steel rods were anchored into the base, and holes had been drilled into the bottom of the pedestal so it could be lowered onto the steel rods. The same had been done to connect the pedestal and the statue; steel rods had been cemented into the top of the pedestal, and the statue lowered onto the rods that ran up inside of the statue's legs for at least three feet.

Merton was clearly concerned that rowdy, drunken students, perhaps frustrated by the loss of a football or basketball championship, might take out their resentments against the administration by toppling the statue, so the statue had been designed with a reinforced stainless steel tube running from the feet through the head to prevent snapping or breaking, even if the riotous students managed to get a rope around the head. To give the statue extra stability, the pedestal top had been widened, and the base of the statue was a thirty-inch-diameter circle of bronze turf on which the figure of Joplin stood. Merton had thought of everything. There were no bolts to be loosened; removal would require the thousand-pound statue to be lifted straight up for at least three feet.

Brady finished his lunch just as the crane lowered the statue onto the pedestal. Workers placed a tarp over the statue and erected a temporary chain-link fence around it for the unveiling two days later, on the same afternoon as the opening performance of the junior class production.

"Come on in, Denny," Paul Merton said through the doorway he had just opened into his press spokesman's office.

"I've got the speech ready for the statue dedication," Denny Bowtern said.

"Great. Now we've got a little finessing to do. I want to announce that Chief Clymer is stepping down, but I don't want it to distract too much from the dedication," Merton said.

"Clymer agreed to step down? That's great. That should put an end to the infiltration flap. Is he leaving campus?"

"No, I gave him a job in the criminal justice program. He'll be a full professor of policing science."

"He's getting tenure? That might raise some hackles with the faculty."

"No, I'm giving him a five-year contract. That was his timeline for retiring. He'll have access to my travel budget to jet around to conferences and rub elbows with his old buddies. I promised to use my influence in Washington to get him appointed to some high-profile commission. I've got the lobbyists working on that now. He'll be happy, mostly sitting on his ass, teaching a few courses, being an old war horse."

"You're not worried about some future tell-all exposé of the real story behind the infiltration?" Denny said.

"No, I don't think so. Clymer didn't have a problem with the infiltration; he believed there was a real threat. I didn't really force the idea on him. I laid out the case, and he bought it. I wouldn't have ordered him to do it if he'd had any real objections. I would've found another way. Now he's doing

THE LAST ACT

the honorable thing by taking responsibility for it. And I'm doing my part by making his final years here pleasant ones. It's important that loyal administrators are seen as being taken care of when difficulties like this arise."

"So you want something quick and low-key about Clymer: late-breaking information that you just received, he's stepping down to pursue academic interests, yadda-yadda, he's been an excellent chief with a long and illustrious service to the university, yadda-yadda, and then directly into the dedication speech for Joplin's statue with no questions until the end. You will then deflect questions about Clymer for a future press conference after more information is available—which will never happen."

"Denny, you're a genius."

"I know, sir. I learned from the best."

"I've got to go back to campus," Brady told Sarah. "The junior class production is Friday, dress rehearsal is tomorrow, and we've had a major equipment failure. None of the backdrops are ready. I'll be late. Don't wait up for me."

Sarah gave Brady a puzzled look. "Okay, but try not to be too late."

"Don't worry. I'll be all right," he said, almost grinning.

Brady had left some work to do on the set. He needed an excuse for being in the theater, just in case anyone asked. He had spent much of the morning locating the ancient jacks that had been used even before his time in the department to raise and lower stage platforms. He'd tested the jacks this morning to be sure they were in working order. He had smuggled the largest crowbar he could find into the theater, and he found some reinforced metal piping that he could fit on the end of the crowbar for extra leverage. Together, the bar and the pipe should be enough to raise the statue to get a wedge underneath the edge. Gradually, he would lift and wedge each side of the statue high enough to put the three ancient platform jacks underneath the base. With the jacks he would be able to raise the statue above the stabilizing bars. Then, by releasing one of the jacks, the statue would tip over, and, if planned correctly, the upper torso of the statue should hit the large rock that for decades had been the centerpiece of the garden in front of the administration building into which Joplin's likeness was trespassing.

Brady finished working on the set around 10 p.m. He went backstage to the dressing rooms to rest for a few hours; he set the alarm clock for 2 a.m. He knew campus security would decrease patrols after the bars closed. It was a Wednesday night in mid-April. There were no evening sports or theater events scheduled, and it was still too cold for students to be carousing so late.

Getting the initial wedges under the base of the statue was hard work, but once the statue was wedged up six inches, the jacks slid in easily. Brady came out from underneath the tarp to double-check that no one was around. He had oiled the jacks, but lifting a statue of this size and weight another two and a half feet was going to make some noise and show some movement. With the coast clear, he started cranking the jacks one at a time, raising the statue about one inch on a side, and then switching to the next jack.

By 3:30 the statue had been lifted more than two feet. Brady knew that was close, no more than a couple more rounds to clear the stabilizing bars. He needed a break and some water; he had been sweating profusely, as much from nerves as exertion. He stepped outside of the tarp to look at the concealed statue in the dim light of the quadrangle.

Brady felt a wave of satisfaction wash over him. He was about to do something meaningful again. It was only symbolic and would never have the impact of Dr. King's visit to campus in 1965, but it was the best opportunity open to him.

Finishing his water, Brady heard a high-pitched rushing sound. He ducked down next to the rock, thinking the sound came from a student riding by on a bicycle. Nothing. He turned back to the statue. Through the opening he'd made in the tarp, he could see some kind of dark liquid running down the pedestal.

"What the...? Oh crap!" Brady realized one of the jacks had failed, leaking fluid through a broken seal. He looked up to see Hank Joplin leaning toward him through the opening in the tarp. A creak. Then a loud snap. One of the stabilizing rods had broken.

"Hello?"

"Is this Sarah Mannion?"

"Yes, who is this?"

"Ma'am, this is Officer Rafaela Jimenez. I'm the night-duty officer for campus police. It's about your husband, Brady Mannion."

"What about him? Is he sick?"

"No, ma'am. There's been an accident. He's been taken to the hospital."

"An accident. Is it serious?"

"Yes, ma'am."

"How serious?"

"Ma'am, when the ambulance took him he wasn't breathing."

"Oh, God. No."

"Ma'am, a car will come by to take you to the hospital."

"Thank you. I'll get ready."

A few minutes later a university police car pulled into the Mannion driveway, and Officer Jimenez knocked on the door. "Mrs. Mannion. I'm Officer Jimenez. I called a few minutes ago. I'll take you to the hospital."

"Thank you."

Once the police car was on Central Avenue going toward Finch Hospital, Rafaela asked, "Ma'am, do you have any idea why your husband was working on the statue of President Joplin so late at night."

"What? I don't understand. Brady works in the Theater Department. He was getting the set ready for the junior class production on Friday."

"Your husband was crushed when the statue of President Joplin fell over on him. Some old jacks from the Theater Department were used to lift the statue. We wondered why your husband might have been working on the statue?"

"I don't know. He never said anything to me about the statue."

The police car pulled into the hospital driveway. Rafaela opened the door for Sarah, and they vanished inside the building.

Paul Merton finished his phone call with Clancy Construction and rushed down the corridor to where Porter Davidson and Cecil Jacobs, chair and vice-chair of the board of trustees, waited for him. "Sorry to be late. I was just getting an update on the statue from Clancy. It looks like they might be able to repair the pedestal by early next week."

"Paul, we think the dedication of the statue should be postponed for a while," Davidson said.

"Yes, it's tainted by the tragic death of a long-time employee and former student," Jacobs added.

"By all accounts, Mannion was trying to vandalize the statue," Merton said. "We'll be condoning vandalism if we don't go ahead with the dedication."

"It has been brought to our attention that you had some history with Mannion, history that involved President Joplin and the visit to campus by the Reverend Dr. Martin Luther King," Jacobs said.

"Well, yes. Mannion was a student activist back then. He helped organize the King visit," Merton said.

"And I was an NAACP organizer of that event when I was a student," Jacobs said. "I remember Mannion. I remember that he left town shortly afterwards for Canada, evading the draft."

"Yes, I guess so. I don't really remember."

"Do you remember telling President Joplin that Mannion had dropped his economics class and might be ineligible for a deferment?" Jacobs said.

"No," Merton said. "That was a long time ago."

"Well, the ACLU has a document suggesting that you were spying for Joplin and that you informed on Mannion because he was involved in Dr. King's visit," Jacobs said.

"Now, let's not resurrect a lot of old politics. Those days are long gone, Cecil," Davidson said. Turning to Merton, he said, "Paul, I think you can see that dedicating the statue now will stir up a lot of old and best-forgotten memories. Let's give this some time to settle."

"How long?"

"Let's take a look at this again next fall. Assess the climate as regards the infiltration fuss."

Merton's face was frozen, frosting over the feelings that lay beneath.

"Oh," Jacobs said, "we want to be sure that the university treats Mannion's death as accidental. Mannion's wife should get full workers' compensation benefits, retirement, health insurance, everything."

"Sure," Merton muttered.

"Paul, you asked about your next contract because university policy says administrators must retire at age 65, and you will be over 64 when your current contract expires next year," Davidson said.

"The Board can waive the age limit," Merton said.

"But it won't in this case," Jacobs said. He rose and left the room, followed, after a brief interval, by Davidson.

Souvenir of Miami

Shelly Lynn Fletcher

In the summer of 1937, Gay North was an idealistic twelve-year old. She lived in Pasadena, California, with her mother, her younger sister, and about ten eclectic "boarders." They all lived in the big white house on El Molino Street, a three-story Victorian home that Gay's single mother, Mrs. North, had converted into a boarding house for students at the Pasadena Playhouse. The boarders, all aspiring actors, had migrated to Southern California to fulfill their dreams of stardom. In its huge basement, the El Molino house even sported a small stage, complete with theatre seats. It was a haven for aspiring performers. This was a stimulating location in which to grow up. It was not surprising that Gay, herself a gifted musician, dreamed of a career in the world of entertainment.

That summer, Gay had won a spot as a pianist with a touring group of local "child prodigies." Six young musicians were selected. What an opportunity! Along with their music teacher, the prodigies would travel by train from coast to coast. They would be on the road for the entire summer. To help with expenses, the little troupe stopped off in a variety of small towns along the way, performing their musical recital in local churches or community pavilions across America.

Mrs. North proudly packed up her talented oldest daughter and reminded Gay, "Don't forget to smile, mind your manners, and send us a postcard from Florida!" It was the first time that Gay had ever traveled without her mother. It was a boost to her confidence and an opportunity to experience independence. The adventure had begun, and Gay felt *very* grown up!

By the middle of July, the traveling performers finally made it all the way to Miami, Florida. Gay now felt like a seasoned, globetrotting artist. She was the first in her family to ever make it all the way from the Pacific Ocean to the Atlantic Ocean. This momentous occasion warranted more than a mere postcard. To commemorate the day, Gay perused the tourist shops along the boardwalk in search of the perfect souvenir to send home to her mother and sister.

At last, Gay spied the consummate gift to represent Florida. The sign in the shop's window boasted, *"Live Baby Alligator...Mailed Anywhere in the U.S.A.!"* Instantly, Gay knew this was exactly the thing to send back home to California. She ogled the tank of tiny reptiles as they scurried around. Each was about three inches long, with shiny black eyes and a boundless source of energy. On each alligator's back, the words "Souvenir of Miami" were painted in bright orange script.

According to the shopkeeper, the critter would be fed just prior to shipping, and then it would stay asleep during its journey via the U.S. Postal Service. Traveling safely in its small excelsior-lined, ventilated cardboard box, the pet would arrive, happy and healthy, at its new home. Unbelievably, this marvelous find was sold for the low cost of one dollar, and the Postman would have it in California within a week! Gay gladly paid the dollar to the clerk, and *Alice the Alligator* was on her way!

As promised, a week later Mrs. North received a 4x8-inch package in the mail. The mysterious gift box was stamped "A Souvenir of Miami" and "Handle With Care." Gay's mother was excited to be the recipient of this gift from her adventurous daughter. Could it be a box of candies, a colorful sun-hat, or a delicate glass vase? It goes without saying that never in her wildest dreams did this mother expect to be in possession of a scaly, exotic animal.

"Welcome to your new home, Alice the Alligator!" read the gift card that Gay had enclosed. Her mother was definitely surprised as she peered into the alligator's box. This was truly an unexpected gift, but like all good mothers, Mrs. North was touched by the sentiment behind her daughter's selection. And so the El Molino Street house was now home to a baby alligator, imported all the way from Miami, Florida!

Ever the responsible citizen, the new pet owner swiftly went into action to find an appropriate new home for the gator. Unfortunately, Mrs. North had grown up in the city and hadn't had much experience with the care and feeding of pets. She assumed that a gator, which naturally lived in the Florida swamps, must need to be in a shallow, freshwater environment. Additionally, she reasoned that this critter would need to swim, stay hydrated, and eat whatever water vegetation it could scrounge up. Logically, the bathtub on the second floor was recruited as a temporary cage. Ever the considerate landlady, Mrs. North was aware that, eventually, the boarding house tenants would also need to use the tub. Another location would have to be enlisted for this latest occupant's long term home, but that was a problem that could be solved at a later time.

Early the following morning, while Mrs. North was watering the flower beds, she discovered the solution. The Oriental Garden gracing the front yard boasted a large oval fish pond. The pond was about ten feet around and three feet in depth. The beautiful waterscape was home to several varieties of lovely lily pads and exotic flowering water plants, not to mention a cluster of fifteen or twenty colorful koi fish. Soon Alice was removed from the upstairs bathtub and relocated to the fish pond.

As the days went by, Mrs. North occasionally caught a glimpse of Alice swimming through the murky green waters or sunning herself along the banks. Alice proved to be an agreeable pet, never straying from the pond area, and appropriately growing larger every day. There was, however, one noticeable change in the Oriental Garden's fish pond. The residents of the El Molino Street house observed that the pond, once brimming with large carp in shades of gold, orange, and white, now appeared to have a smaller fish population. Mrs. North dutifully surveyed the inhabitants of the pond. Sure enough, she could now only count eight large fish swimming through the waters. What had happened to all of the other fish? Could it be that Alice was not a vegetarian after all? Perhaps Mrs. North should seek advice from an expert.

The concerned landlady immediately took action. She made a phone call to the folks at the Los Angeles Zoo, who assured her that Alice was *indeed* feasting on a diet of fresh koi!

Horrified, Mrs. North immediately offered up the carnivorous Alice as a donation to the Los Angeles Zoo. The gift was duly noted, and a staffer arranged for someone to pick up the alligator. A truck would be in the Pasadena area on Wednesday, just two days away.

The following day, when a survey of the pond produced only a sighting of three remaining fish, Mrs. North began to worry. Additionally, Alice was feeling more comfortable out of the water. On several occasions that Tuesday, the tenants, while strolling in the California sunshine, had discovered Alice several feet away from the pond. The resourceful residents (all aspiring actors, singers, dancers, or musicians) took up any available weapons (trumpets, canes, silk-fans, or garden rakes) to assist in their new role as temporary reptile-wranglers. The creative thespians took turns shooing

Alice back into the water. Once Alice was in the pond, the residents would go about their daily rehearsals. On the surface, all appeared as it should, but Mrs. North was worried about this precarious situation. What would become of her boarding house business if their neighborhood was now being stalked by a dangerous wild animal?

Wednesday finally arrived. What a relief it was when the truck from the zoo finally pulled up in front of the El Molino Street house. Now things around the boarding house could once again return to normal. From the parlor window Mrs. North watched the two uniformed men use their nets and poles to skim the pond. They also checked under the porch, between the bushes, and alongside the steps. Alas, the search produced no Alice!

The team reported the unsuccessful capture to Mrs. North. "Please call us if she returns," called the man. "The zoo is a better place for an alligator than a boarding house!" The men were laughing and shaking their heads as they drove off.

Disappointed, the residents all swarmed out to the Oriental Garden. All eyes perused the contents of the pond. Just as the men from the Los Angeles zoo had told them, Alice was nowhere to be found. Additionally, the pond, once brimming with lovely large carp, was now completely void of any animal life. What had become of Alice? Where could she be?

Gay returned from her tour at the end of the summer. The aspiring actors who resided at the boarding house went on with their training. A few gained moderate success in show business, but most just moved on with their lives. The El Molino Street house remained a boarding house for the next fifteen years, but the pond never again was home to any fish…or any reptiles. I guess we can assume that, after devouring her *"Last Supper"* of the koi in the pond, Alice the Alligator took off in search of other food sources in the Pasadena area. And now, over seventy years later, whenever I'm near the newsstand at the grocery store, I still search the headlines of trashy tabloids. Maybe someday I'll find a headline reading, "Giant 75 Year Old Alligator Discovered in the Sewers of Pasadena." Hmm, I wonder if it will still have "Souvenir of Miami" painted on its back?

Queen Guinevere

Jean Brier Lusk

I had barely turned fifteen when I won the lead role of Queen Guinevere in our high school production of "Launcelot and Elaine."

The story had intertwined love affairs. Launcelot, a dashing knight in shining armor, loved beautiful Elaine. King Arthur loved his queen, Guinevere. She, however, had her eye on Launcelot, who strung her along for a while to gain favors from the king through her intercession.

At this point in life, I had never had a date, much less kissed a boy. So at the rehearsal for the garden scene, where Guinevere kissed Sir Launcelot, I was totally unprepared.

I was dressed in school clothes, ankle socks, and saddle shoes. We acted out the scene, which ended with a kiss. My lines were perfectly delivered and ended with a peck on Launcelot's cheek. Why was everyone tittering? Launcelot had a stunned look on his face.

Beautiful Elaine came over, pushed me aside and said, "This is how you do it." She then planted an impassioned kiss on Launcelot's lips.

At the opening night production, I was filled with butterflies and excitement. The auditorium was packed. The curtain opened. Dressed in my regal gown and cape, a crown upon my head, I became Queen Guinevere—and she knew how to kiss.

Wilderness Retreat

Janet Kreitz

She was small. I was six two, and the top of her head just reached my chest. Her legs, long and sleek, made men both young and old fantasize about dalliances with her. The slight curve of her belly left over from having babies did not detract, but in a sense made her more appealing. Hers was the voice men wanted to hear first thing in the morning.

Sunday morning she arrived at Wilderness Retreat. I was a guide at the upscale resort that offered camping and fishing along the Snake River in Wyoming. She was alone, but didn't give off the scent of loneliness.

She was one of six in the group: city folks who spent their days in suits behind desks talking with customers they didn't like, now living for the week with nature away from the noise, grime, and crime of urban life.

I wanted to touch her, hear the sound of her voice, and watch her easy, warm, inviting smile light up her face. Enthusiastic, she didn't mind the mosquitoes, followed instructions about casting, laughed as the raft rolled through the current, watched me bone and fillet the catch of the day for the evening meal. I saw her face when my eyes closed at night and opened them in the morning.

Her life story fit thousands of women: married, two kids, and divorced. She had weathered a series of lovers that left her disappointed in men. I didn't share my life story with her: the weeks, months, and years of bad choices. Besides, I knew she wouldn't cotton to a felon. In the rage of youth I had thought a gun and the till at the Gas & Go would solve my problems.

I had known women I met at Cowboys, the bar on Salmon Street. Some stayed awhile, but I don't know how to relate to women. Shoot, I don't know how to relate to myself.

The week ended. I swallowed hard when she hugged me and thanked me for a marvelous week on the river.

Every day I feel her hug.

Almond Eyes

Richard Lampl

It was the almond eyes. Everything had changed except the light brown, almost yellow, almond-shaped eyes. Fred recognized them, the eyes with a slight blemish in the upper right corner of her left eye. He was almost sure he knew the woman holding out the white ceramic cup. He had rushed past her as she sat on the red brick sidewalk in front of the Washington Metrorail station on L Street. She was almost leaning against, but barely touching, one of the round red brick pillars that supported the office building surrounding the station entrance. He remembered her name as he prepared to descend into the Metrorail. Could this be Kerry, his secretary of ten years ago?

What had happened to her? Her hair was stringy, unevenly chopped by dull scissors or a razor. Her hair color was a combination of dirty blonde, dirty brown, and just plain dirty. Her face was gaunt, at least what he could see of it under the frayed rags wrapped around her. Her forehead and cheeks were red and scaly, like a peeling sunburn. Her mouth was hidden behind a faded baby blue quilt that looked like it had been dragged along the ground for months by someone named Linus.

As he stepped on the "Down" escalator, he remembered a different Kerry in Charleston, South Carolina, when she first applied for the job as his secretary. A clean cut, fair-skinned kid who looked like she had misplaced her halo, she had a combination of youthful exuberance and rosy-cheeked candor with long, blonde hair bleached by the southern sun. Her hair cascaded around her in a frenzied state of liquid motion when she walked, and a constant brushing back with one hand or the other was a necessary part of conversation. She wore clear nail polish on well-manicured hands and did not need any colored lipstick. Her full lips, the kind that women of the 1990's would risk the plastic surgeon's knife to duplicate, turned downward at the corners of her smile. She was a trifle heavy for a high school cheering squad, but otherwise looked like the stereotypical cheerleader.

This fresh, giddy enthusiasm is bound to pay off for her in the advertising world, reasoned Fred, when he hired her as a combination secretary and account executive trainee. She was inexperienced, but her eagerness, her liquid exuberance showed so much promise he never hesitated in his decision to bring her aboard.

"What makes you think you would fit into the advertising world?" he had asked as she sat on the green leather chair on the opposite side of his desk.

"Well, gee," she said, as she brushed back wayward strands of hair. She fidgeted in her chair, crossing and re-crossing her tanned legs. "You know, it's a glamorous world, with beautiful people on TV selling things. I want to be part of it."

Her obviously unprepared answer had showed a great lack of understanding of the realities of a career in advertising. Yet there was enthusiasm in the way she said it, and youth and eagerness in her body language. He would teach her.

Her almond eyes widened at the variety of products and the quirkiness of people that came to the office of his struggling five-person ad agency. She quickly learned the over-enthusiastic jargon of the trade, the false confidence and bravado of his account executives, and the cynical, doubting belief of his clients. She took it all in from her desk outside his office, a space she shared with two account executives and a graphic artist. Fred had filled this windowless room with potted plants in an attempt to bring the outdoors inside.

He had just one small, nagging doubt: it would be easy to fall in love with this animated, charming woman. When she was near, was the light buzzing sound in his head a sign of real affection?

"Kerry is so young." he told a friend. "A dozen years younger than me."

Youth and enthusiasm. Rub them together and dormant feelings might catch fire. He had to restrain himself. Two mountain-sized objects held him back: his wife, Karen, and his advertising agency. Fred was trying to hold a shaky marriage together, and the business community of Charleston would frown on a May-December romance. And there was a third thing. He did not believe Kerry would accept his advances if he tried. He had seen what happened when one of his account executives, Walt Shipman, made a verbal pass at her.

Her cheeks bloomed scarlet as she turned and looked directly at him, almond eyes reproachful. "You stay away from me. I'm saving myself for my husband." With that, she spun away, her long blond hair momentarily splaying out almost horizontally to the ground.

It was her first stay in a big city, and her naivete was too good to last. The reservoir of youthful innocence burst like a dam in a subtropical Charleston storm. Fred attributed her incipient, spiraling downfall to an incident in his office about five months after she started. She was sniveling at her desk. Each time he passed, she tried to look away. She did not want him to see her tears, but her anguish was too obvious. He said nothing as he passed her and went into his office, a twelve-by-twelve box whose only redeeming feature was the view of a wavy section of sweetgrass topping a low country marsh on the opposite side of the Ashley River. He could hear the whimpering from inside his office. He stepped out once and asked, "What's wrong?"

Her answer was a shake of the head and more crying. Probably something silly, like a quarrel with a boyfriend, he thought. After an awkward moment and the offer of a handkerchief, which she refused, he left her sniveling at her desk and returned to his office with an ineffectual, "If I can help..."

At six o'clock, after his account executives and graphic artist had gone home, Kerry came into his office, puffy-faced and red-eyed. The reason for her misery came out as she crossed to his desk. In a sentence broken by sobs, sighs, and great intakes of breath, she said, "The doctor said I can't have any children."

That was it. He could see it meant everything to her. Kerry was from Holly Hill, a Bible-belt town on the edge of the South Carolina low country, halfway between Charleston and Columbia. Obviously, one of her prime small town values was the creation and nurturing of a family. She wanted her piece of the American dream, just like her respectable, churchgoing parents and grandparents before her. In her mind that would all be gone now. This was quite a blow to someone who had generations of family values drilled into her.

He murmured something about adoption, but this only raised the decibel level of her moans. He came around his desk to comfort her. He held her in his arms, her head on his shoulder. Her racking sobs went through him. He stroked the back of her hair, rubbed her shoulders and back to quiet her.

The sobs gradually subsided, but neither made an attempt to break away. Instead, she gazed up at him with narrowing, tear-filled almond eyes and something else. A blank look.

Without a word or any other sign she moved her pelvis against his with one swift motion. It was no accident. Almond eyes were now bordered with steely gray around the rims. Youthful exuberance and wonderment were replaced by darkened determination. No smile, no laughter, but there was no mistaking the want in her. Reason left him. Dizziness tilted his brain. The buzzing inside him smothered all rational thought.

He meant to say something practical like, "Are you sure you want to do this?" or "Don't you think we had better stop?" But the words never came out. Raw feelings took over. Gentle stroking grew into sexual aggression, and Kerry was the aggressor. Her body had betrayed her, humiliated her. Now it was her turn for revenge, revenge on her own body.

With a great effort, sanity and good judgment prevailed. He finally managed to say, "Look, we can't do this." He pushed her away and readjusted his shirt and pants. The buzzing in his head slowly dissipated.

"I knew what I was doing." Her voice was steady but flat as she made a perfunctory check of her clothes. She did not look at him. "No sense in saving it. For what?" A tug, a pull on her clothes to straighten them was all she did before walking out.

It was a new Kerry who arrived at the office the next morning, a different Kerry with a different look on her face, one he had not seen before. A grim set to her jaw pulled the soft round cheeks into a hard line. There were no tears today. No chit-chat. It was pointless to talk about it. Maybe they could talk when she got over the shock of her disappointment. Maybe then. But it never happened. He could not get her to relax.

Less than a month later, she told him she was leaving. She was driving to California with Walt Shipman in her Honda. Shipman had found a job in the advertising department of a Hollywood film studio. This was no surprise to Fred. Advertising people moved around a lot. He expected to lose account execs. What did surprise him was the whereabouts of Christina, Walt's wife. How did she fit into this setup?

It all became clear three weeks later. Shipman, a sly womanizer who would say or do anything to make a conquest, had booted Kerry out.

Shipman had merely wanted companionship on the drive across the country and had fully intended to resume his marriage. His wife, Christina, had left Charleston earlier to look for a new house. If Christina knew about Kerry, she never let on.

Fred lost track of Kerry soon after she came back East. She wouldn't stay in California and couldn't come back to Charleston. What the scandal mongers didn't know, the gossipers would fill in. He learned second hand that Kerry had a job in Washington. Fred had often thought about looking her up, but didn't know how to find her. How and why Kerry became what she was when he saw her at the Metro station was a mystery.

Deep down, there was another reason he didn't look for her. He was skeptical about how he would be accepted. Fred could pass for handsome, with straight black hair and a wide-cheek-boned face, except for one thing. He was short, shorter than a lot of women he tried to date. His height had plagued him through the growing years. Doctors in his hometown of Greenville, South Carolina said five-foot-two was not short enough to prescribe growth hormones.

Karen was taller. He lost her and his marriage six months after Kerry's departure, when his ad agency ran out of clients. Karen said directly, without cushioning her words, that he had no business sense and would never amount to anything. Maybe she was right, but he was not convinced. He felt he had some real ability inside; he just needed some incentive, a project and a goal, to bring it out. He had faith in his ultimate ability, but maybe it was not in advertising.

When he was offered a job writing for a whole grain cereal advocacy group in Washington, D.C., he readily agreed. The press releases, advertising blurbs, speeches, and testimony he wrote were not exactly inspirational, but they were a good change of pace for him. His new job was less demanding and gave him the opportunity to wait, he hoped, for his next big soul-satisfying move.

Fred shuddered as the escalator descended. He had a hard time imagining how Kerry could descend to the level of the creature he had seen begging at the subway entrance. Memory was a funny thing. You can stuff something down in your subconscious for years, then a trigger gets pulled, and it all comes back. The almond eyes were the trigger. Years could be condensed in a flash. He decided he had to go back. He traded the "Down" escalator at the bottom for "Up."

His approach was direct. He stood over her in a dark gray business suit, his shiny black loafers almost touching her dirty sneakers. "Hello, Kerry."

No response. She did not look up.

"Hello, Kerry."

An uneasy stirring. She shifted away from his voice without looking up.

"Hello, Kerry Curry," her full name.

That got him a quick turn and a hundredth-of-a-second look of anger. Eyes were still her most beautiful feature, perhaps now her only attribute. No sign of recognition, just annoyance at being disturbed.

"Kerry? It's Fred Campbell. You know, from the advertising agency in Charleston?"

She raised a cracked cup from the folds of her garments. The words "Life's a Bitch" in big red block letters surrounded the cup. Her nails were grimy stumps on pudgy fingers.

He tried again. "Fred Campbell from Charleston?"

He wanted recognition. She wanted no part of him. She held the cup towards him, still not looking up.

"Kerry!" He was more demanding this time.

She extended the cup toward him. The inside was dirty brown from baked-on-something that could have been coffee.

He would play the game. He put in a quarter. A dull "thunk." It was the only coin there. He put in another, then another. "Kerry, I'd like to talk to you."

She shoved the cup out farther, still not looking up.

He had no more change. He put in a dollar bill. "Talk to me."

She did. "I'm not Kerry. Go away."

"Don't you know me?"

"Go away, mister. Stop annoying me." She pulled the cup into her fold of rags.

"Kerry, can I help you?"

No response. She would not look at him.

"Can we go someplace to talk? Have something to eat?"

She sat absolutely still. No rejection this time.

He was encouraged. He said, "Meet me for a drink."

There was a long thoughtful pause, and then she said in a low, almost inaudible voice, "Callahan's. Twenty minutes."

Three words, but they were enough. Callahan's was a bar in an old misfit of a building stuffed in the middle of a downtown block. It had no street face of its own, but was hemmed in by the back side of buildings that fronted on four streets. No view. Access was over a gravel-and-rubble-strewn parking lot. Was it the offer of a drink that enticed her?

He was there with five minutes to spare. She arrived ten minutes late wearing jeans. The rags were gone, left somewhere. She must have been wearing the shirt and jeans beneath them. The jeans were not clean either. Levi blue and smudgy brown fought for dominance, with brown winning. It was the same with her sneakers. Nike would be glad their trademark had been scuffed off years before. A dumpster odor preceded her as she slipped into the shadowy booth he had chosen. She looked down at the polyurethane-covered oak table. Her first words were not ones recognition.

"I'll have vodka, double."

He signaled a waitress and ordered. "Double vodka and a scotch and soda."

She continued to stare at the patterns in the oak.

"Don't you remember me?" He moved to touch her hand, but stopped. "You used to work at my advertising agency in Charleston." He thought he could jog her memory. "Do you remember?"

No answer. She still looked down.

He wasn't about to give up. "Kerry, it is you. I recognize your eyes. Aren't you going to say something?"

The waitress came with their drinks. Kerry snatched the vodka from the coaster in front of Fred, where it had mistakenly been put. With a quick snap back of her head, she swallowed the colorless liquid in one gulp and returned to her down-looking pose, with no word or further acknowledgement.

Fred lifted his glass and quietly sipped his scotch, pondering his next move. "Do you remember anything at all about Charleston? The agency? We worked together. You were my secretary."

Nothing.

"Would you like another drink?"

She nodded.

He called to the waitress. "Another vodka."

"Double," Kerry corrected

"Double," Fred repeated to the waitress. "Or, better still, bring the bottle."

He had returned his attention to the table. "You must recall something. It was your first job when you came from Holly Hill."

She ignored him by shifting her attention to the empty glass. The waitress, slightly distressed by the ragged creature she was serving, slammed the vodka bottle down on the table. It wobbled unsteadily for a second, but before it could topple over, a nail-cracked hand was on it. Kerry filled her glass. She downed the second double vodka without hesitation with the same backward snap of her head. Then she sat back and for the first time looked at him. "I remember you. It was a long time ago, in Charleston." Her eyes were livelier now, more alert. She had no trouble looking directly at him. Her face, still dirty, still red and raspy, had awakened. Was she acting like she knew him because he was buying?

"That's right." Suddenly the world was brighter for him. "Yes, I'm glad you remember. My ad agency and my marriage flopped after you left Charleston. There was nothing left for me there, so I moved up here. And you?"

"I moved here." She was purposely blanking out the Walt Shipman experience. Her finger traced a circle of slightly spilled vodka on the table. Her finger went round and round, faster and faster until the tabletop squeaked as the vodka evaporated.

"I'm getting hungry, aren't you?" said Fred. The drawn face and the frailty of her body beneath the decrepit clothes bothered him. "Suppose I call the waitress."

"No thanks." She grabbed the bottle and started to get up. "I gotta go."

He shrugged. Straight vodka with nothing to eat. "Wait. I can't leave it this way," he said as she got up. "It's been so long."

He put his hand on her arm, but she snatched it away. She looked up at a TV hanging over the bar. She wasn't interested in the volleyball game. She just did not want to talk to him. Trying to draw conversation out of her was not going to work. At least he had made some verbal contact. "Can I offer you something? Some money?"

"No." She paused. "Well, eight ninety-five."

"Why such an odd amount?"

"Bottle of vodka."

"Is that all you want?" Her independent attitude in contrast to her shoddy appearance was annoying. "A bottle of vodka? That's not enough. Surely I can do more." He was getting nowhere, his jaw set in exasperation. "Look, I don't want to lose touch. Too many years. I don't like to see you like this. I can help." Too late, he mentally kicked himself for saying the last words. He was offering pity, and she was not looking for pity.

"All I want," she said as she shuffled toward the door. "A bottle of vodka is all I want."

"Wait." He reached into his pocket as he got up. "Here's my business card. It has my home phone number on it, too." He handed it to her as she reached the door. "You can call me anytime."

She took the card and was gone.

He got up and looked outside. The open doorway framed an artistic arrangement of dumpsters and garbage cans, but no Kerry.

"Did I do the right thing?" he asked himself. He had been generous and giving. She had certainly shown she was emotionally alive and responsive, despite her deadpan expression and shoddy appearance. Perhaps he had been too generous. Perhaps she couldn't handle kindness.

"I should have seen that," Fred murmured to himself. "I'll have to try again. Maybe she'll call. If not, I'll have to find her. There are only so many subway stations on the Metrorail. And I'll do better next time."

First Runner-up: Best Poetry Contest

Apron Song

Bobbie Jean Bishop

Birthing another apron, soon to
be dusted with flour, splattered
by sauce, my machine hums,
needle catching cloth in even
bites—this garment geared for
duty in a kitchen teeming with
cooking sprites and nonstick
skillets—I think of Saint Myrtle,
my grandmother, apron tied like
a second skin around her waist,
how she moved quick as a skater
over scarred linoleum, one eye
on sizzling bacon in a steamy
kitchen, thick with temperature
and chemistry. Her remarkable
victuals stand their ground in
trickle down genes, the way she
starched tablecloths, and made
routines turn into ritual. With
years like rough stones in a
tumble behind me, she comes to
mind as my slipper smoothes this
pedal powering apron seams. I
lift the zipper foot from stitches
tiny as capillaries, blood-red
threads transfusing yesterday.

First Runner-up: Best Fiction Contest

Ed's Halley

Wynn Melton

Halley dried her hands on her apron and pushed open the wooden screen door to step out onto the front porch. Ed, coming in from the back yard, walked slowly around the side of the house. With one hand, he shaded his eyes to peer toward the sound of hoofbeats and the creak of a wagon.

Halley tensed with fear as she watched the dust kicked up by the fast trotting horses. She knew, when the wagon passed the last curve, that it had passed the only other house on their country road. It could only mean they were on their way to see Ed, since his was the last house.

As soon as Ed spied her, he ordered, "Git yourself back in the house until I see what this is about. Keep the kids inside, too."

He leaned his hoe against the side of the weather-beaten clapboard house. With a light kick at his dog's rear, he said, "Shut up, Dude. I see 'em." The dog retreated under the house, where it was cool. Ed posted himself just outside the front gate with his thumbs caught in the bib of his work-worn overalls. He waited and watched. Dude began to slowly creep out, but as soon as Ed saw him he tossed back a small stone. "Damn it, dog. Git back." Tail between his legs, Dude obeyed, returning to his watch from under the house.

Halley obediently went back inside. She sat at the kitchen table and continued to peel the apples she had gathered right after daylight from the two trees out back. Soon, she must decide whether to make apple butter or can them for pies. Sarah, Ed's four-year-old daughter, played with her rag doll on the floor near Halley's feet. Earlier that morning, Halley had brushed Sarah's hair many times before placing handmade ribbons in it. To Halley, Sarah was as pretty or prettier than any doll she'd ever seen. Clint, Ed's son, just past one year old, was asleep on a pallet on the floor. Halley kept a watchful eye to shoo away any flies that might disturb him.

The wagon came around the last bend of the road through a dust cloud that was heavier this year than most because it had been almost three weeks since they had a drop of rain. Ed recognized the horses.

"Sister Nellie," he muttered to himself. "Knew she'd be comin' soon. Can't wait. Well, best we get it all out now and over with. T'ain't a dang thing she can do about it anyways."

Ray, Nellie's husband, pulled the horses to a stop when the wagon was almost even with Ed. He dropped the lines and leaned across Nelly's lap to look at Ed. Sheepishly, he said, "I wanted to wait, but your sister wouldn't."

Ed spit out his chaw of tobacco before replying, "Well, you're here. Git on down. Come see the kids."

Nellie huffed herself up like an old hen protecting her chicks and looked straight ahead. "We'll do no such thing, Ed Kearney. I know you got that woman in there. Yes, I heard what she is. I shore did." She turned directly to scowl at Ed. "How could you have her 'round your childrens? And just a year and three days since their poor mother passed. Poor dear Clara." She shook her head with conviction. "Poor Ed, my brother, you got the devil in you, you have. But we're gonna pray for you. But right now, I just come to tell you, get her out of there and back on that houseboat with all those other husseys. Women making a living like that. And shame on you. Shame… shame." Looking down on him with fire in her eyes, Nellie ordered, "I come to take my niece and nephew back home with me till she's gone. Now go get 'em out here and their clothes too. We'll sit right here and wait."

"Ain't gonna happen, Nelly." Ed was confident as he looked up at Nelly. The words in his mouth spilled out as if they were cut in stone. "She's here to stay. You can't have my children, either. I needed help with my kids and this place. Kids take a likin' to her already. Now you can either come in or git goin'. Whatever your pleasure, but you ain't gettin' my kids. Understand?"

Nelly's eyes never wavered from Ed's. Her words were abrupt and sharp when she said, "Ain't goin' in there where you're livin' in sin. You just brought her in there in front of those little kids and you ain't even married. Our dear mother would just die all over again if she'd knowed about this."

As strong as if he were standing on a Bible, Ed announced, "We're gettin' married and soon. I just gotta get the preacher here. Right now I'm awful busy, and Halley's cannin' every day while stuff is ready. I gave you a choice. What'll it be?"

With a jerk of her head, Nelly said, "Ha! Ain't no preacher gonna marry you to a woman like that. If he did we'd drum him right out of this county."

Ed laughed. "Preacher Porter would do anything for a pint of my white lightnin', and you know it. I might hav'ta throw in a couple ol' hens this time. Now you can either come in or git goin'. We're just wastin' time here in this hot sun. I'm busy gettin' ready to cut a couple pigs."

Solemnly, Ray nodded and said, "Ed's right. What do you want to do?"

Nelly snapped at Ray. "Turn this wagon 'round and head for home. He lost all his senses. Brother…brother. I am so ashamed of you. If you weren't my brother, I'd have nothin' to do with you. Shame!"

When the wagon was headed back, she leaned across in front of Ray and called, "'Cause you're my brother, you're always welcome at my house, but don't you ever bring that ol' alley cat with you. Hear? I ain't havin' her at my place."

True to his nature, Ed accepted everything with little emotion and returned to his work. That evening, he told Halley he would be visiting Preacher Porter to make arrangements for them to marry. Halley's stomach was churning with nerves, but she asked nothing. She wanted a home…this home. At no time did she feel threatened by him, but she knew Ed was strong-headed. His word was the law. He was the boss, and she accepted that.

The next day, with a clean white shirt under his almost new bib overalls, he straddled his horse to ride a few miles to Preacher Porter's house, hoping he would find him at home.

Preacher Porter was sitting on his front porch on a cane bottom chair, leaning back against the house. When Ed got within earshot, he dropped the chair upright with four legs on the floor. He waited until Ed was a few steps closer before he called, "Come on in and sit a spell. Just sittin' here thinkin' about you. You know bad news travels fast in these here parts. Been wonderin' what's up your sleeve, doin' a crazy thing like that."

Ed tied his horse to a fence post, opened the yard gate and sauntered up on the porch before he said a word. The words came smooth out of his mouth, "Kinda 'spectin' me, you say? Guess my sister done told the whole county by now."

Preacher Porter chuckled. "That she shore did. There was a gatherin' outside after church for almost an hour, talkin' about things. She's sure het up about it. Me, I kinda get a kick out of it, but Ed, you know this is downright solid Christian country. A man bringing a woman to just live with ain't right, specially when she's that kind of woman. I understand men, I do, but keeping her…no."

Ed turned his hat in his hands and began slowly, as if he was afraid Preacher Porter might not understand every word. "So. I'm pleased we are about right on the same page. That be the reason for my visit. You see, we're gettin' hitched when you come on Saturday at noon to my place. Be shore and bring your wife and her dumb brother, as I suspect we'll need to be witnessed. We'll be a little late for church Sunday, but when we gets there, you'll stop immediately and introduce us to the people. Mr. Ed and Mrs. Halley Kearney. I'll wear khaki pants and shirt again, and buy her a new dress down at Debow's Store, so we look proper."

Preacher Porter, shaking his head and waving his hands in the air, blurted, "Now…hold on there, mister. I can't marry you to a sportin' woman which everyone knows about. You gotta be out of your mind."

Ed's bent his head toward Preacher Porter and folded his arms as clear words slowly spilled out of his mouth. "I say you will, and you will. Now, I would have offered you a pint of my whte lightnin' and possibly a couple of ol' hens—but I ain't gonna do it now. You've fluffed my feathers. You will be there and do as I say—you will. Understand?"

Preacher Porter was shocked and taken aback a bit. He looked up at Ed and said, "Mister, you don't understand. I'm the preacher in these parts. Can't just do like you want. No, Ed. The Lord would be angry with me, and so would my people. You gotta take her back where you got her. No sir, I can't do that. Won't!"

Ed, assured he had the weapon to make the Preacher do anything, took a couple steps closer to him. He looked down on the short, overweight, bald headed pathetic man and almost laughed. "Oh yes, you will, 'cause you could be horsewhipped and driven right out of this county. Most of the men know your likin' for whiskey, but not about the women…their wives…even one man's daughter." He paused, and a smile of satisfaction creased his poker face when he asked, "Want me to name 'em?"

Preacher Porter's face paled and, almost pleading, he said, "Ed, now go away. You don't know nothin'."

Ed put his strong right hand on the preacher's shoulder and shoved him back till his chair was leaning against the wall again. "I know. I shore do.

When you're alone a lot—offers come your way, and they talk. Mostly I don't know 'em all, but I know plenty enough to get rid of you." He moved his hand from the preacher's shoulder and stood erect. "So, I will see you Saturday at noon. Ya hear?"

His body now free, the chair righted on the floor again, Preacher Porter stood and reached for Ed's right hand to shake. "It'll be my pleasure, Ed. Give my best to your woman. Her name's Halley, you say. I look forward to meetin' her. I'm real pleased you asked my little woman and Brother Boomer. You can count on us bein' there." Knowing Ed as he did, he was not surprised when Ed untied his horse from the fence post, mounted, and rode off without saying another word.

That evening, Ed presented Halley with a large bag from Deboy's Store. Her eyes were wide with surprise. She opened it to find a light blue satin dress, trimmed in fine white lace and pearl buttons. She was silent for a time, then she said, "Ed, it's too expensive for me. Where will I wear it? You must take it back."

He stepped closer to take the dress from her. Holding it up against her with a twinkle in his eyes and a smile of satisfaction, he said, "You'll be very handsome. The preacher will marry us Saturday at noon, and you'll wear it to church every Sunday."

Tears gathered in her eyes and streamed down her face. "Ed, I ain't never been to a church. Never. Won't know what to do. They won't like me. You must go by yourself. Take the dress back."

He took her into his arms and said, "Woman, don't you fret. You will be with me. They can go to hell. Now go see how it fits, and where you may need to take it up a tuck or two."

Faceless Bride
(At age 68, a cousin gave me a complete framed copy of this photo, with all the faces. I don't know if this "trimming" was a custom, or simply due to sadness.)

M. C. Little

Who is the girl?
the one with no face;
in the long, fancy dress of old, white lace;
hands buried in a cluster of flowers and ribbon streamers.

Who was the girl?
whose face was trimmed out,
leaving only a dark brown hairdo—
and borders of a bridal veil.

The gray cardboard, A-frame held this picture for all to see;
it sat on a doily on the living room table,
or sometimes on the console record player
full of music: "I'm sending you a big bouquet of roses…"

Why did this girl have no face? I wondered…
Next to the faceless bride stood a handsome, smiling, young man—
in a suit, with a flower on his coat, looking like one who shared
Double Mint gum; pinched our cheeks and called us "Bella."

The missing face…where did it go? Is this face floating around in our house,
wearing tears and very red lipstick; yelling into the black, daffodil-style phone,
while painting her fingernails on the dining room table?
Was the bride's face trimmed out with those curved toenail scissors?

What happened to the faceless bride?

It Takes Two to Tango

Aris DeNigris

Every year, for as long as I can remember, my husband and I have spent our three-month winters along the southeastern coast of Florida. About six years ago, with the decline in real estate values, we decided to sell the condo we had owned for some thirty-five years and instead traveled to the northwestern part of the state, where we had often been regaled with tales of beaches that had sand like spun white sugar. So hesitantly we began our new adventures in the most northwestern part of the state: Panama City Beach, bordering the state of Alabama. In the following years, we visited Sarasota, then Venice and Naples. After that, we tried a slightly different venue and visited Costa Rica in Central America, at the coaxing of friends who had lived and worked there for several years. It all seemed too wonderful to be scooting around here and there and not be tied down to the same location every year—no state taxes to be paid, no condominium charges every four months, so stress free. Ah, but nothing is as simple as we would like to imagine.

We were a bit indecisive, at first, because of an illness that had plagued me periodically, so by the time we decided to travel, we were a bit hard put to find another location in a spot that would suit our specifications: two bedrooms, two baths, large modern television and DVD, twin beds, comfortable lounge chairs, good lighting, and, most importantly, immaculately clean and near the beach.

For the first time in years, we were almost resigned to spending the winter at our home in the north, but then I had a call from a realtor I had spoken to during the earlier part of the year. She told me about an available property she thought might meet with our approval, with the exception of the location. No beach!

Since it was late in the season and the winter winds were already howling, like little children waiting for the ice cream vendor's bell we chose to believe her and hoped for the best. I won't go into details about just how difficult it was to have our car shipped at a reasonable rate (suddenly increased by $100—"so many cars heading south," they said); make travel plans with the airlines (at an unreasonable rate); rent a car at the airport to drive to our destination (thirty-five miles from the airport, where a light rain had just begun to welcome us); find our way to a new location while I blessed the inventors of the GPS system every mile along the way...and on and on it went until we arrived safely, though weather- and travel-worn. We are no longer young, even though we sometimes forget to factor in this very important detail when making our plans. On reflection, all I can think of at this point is just how much we must have hated the thought of spending a winter in the snow. We still do!

After settling in, getting our car, and returning the rental one, we looked around. Granted, the apartment was immaculate. The kitchen was in good order, but the furniture, while very clean, was old and uncomfortable, vintage 1950's. Everything, including the double bed (we've slept in twin beds for the last forty years of our marriage and had specifically told the realtor how important this was for our comfort) was small and low and difficult to get up from once we were seated or sleeping. The television screen was so small, the picture so faint, the sound so muted that we were almost tempted to go out and rent another. But I must say that the warm, glorious sun continued to shine and never failed to greet us every morning while we had breakfast on the balcony overlooking a beautiful golf course that was home to mama and papa duck and their six little ducklings, who waddled back and forth searching for either ferns or bugs or whatever.

And after a time, we did settle in. We met our neighbors, ordered a weekly newspaper, and began receiving mail from our near-frozen friends up north in what they said was the coldest winter in many years. We were glad to be in the sun. After we found our way around the complex, we discovered many swimming pools, indoor and outdoor. The outdoor olympic-sized pool was the biggest we had ever seen and, together with an enormous hot tub, we found our surroundings to have taken on new energy in spite of all the disappointments when we first arrived.

On Sunday afternoons, people would wander into an area around the pool where a local disc jockey would be "holding court" under an open building with a thatched roof, playing really beautiful nostalgic music that we seniors (80's, 90's, and upwards...no kidding) would enjoy. He also played some salsas, rhumbas, meringues, and tangos, and occasionally sang, accompanying the music in a soft, melodious voice. We were surprised to see so many residents who were all such good dancers. They danced to everything—and, of course, the high ratio of women to men made line dancing very popular for the "girls."

Everything was thoughtfully set up with a seating area under the thatched roof dancing area. Those who couldn't dance, or didn't feel like it, would have some wonderful entertainment just watching. The people splashing and swimming around in the pool enjoyed it just as much, as they exercised and danced to the beat of the music. It was lovely. There were ice cold pitchers of lemonade, with cheese, crackers, and various other "munchies" spread out in platters on a large table for everyone to enjoy.

My husband and I danced a few numbers, but I was not able to do too much because of a knee that was giving me some problems, so we spent a good deal of the time just observing, enjoying the music and the atmosphere: palm trees swaying, beautiful music, a glass of cold lemonade at hand, a spirit of conviviality with new friends…what more could we ask for? We were soon to find out.

Wandering into this idyllic and surreal atmosphere was a tall, elegant-looking older man and a beautifully dressed petite woman with lovely coifed blonde hair. He was nattily dressed with an ascot at his neck, impeccably creased trousers, and a full head of white hair that matched his slim, mustached, tanned face. With her head just about reaching his shoulder, she was enveloped in a lovely, flowery, filmy chiffon dress and colorful sandals. Both wore dark glasses. She had a walker, he used a cane. They came slowly into the dance area under the thatched roof. Just observing them was a treat, but we thought they would surely just "sit it out." Imagine our surprise when, after resting the walker and cane on the backs of their chairs, they moved to the dance floor.

At first they tried the slower dances, but you could see, from watching for just a few minutes into the dance, that they had spent a long time together because of the precision-like moves they were carefully executing. "That's beautiful," we said to each other, and to those seated near us, who agreed.

Shortly after that, the tempo of the music changed. The sensuously haunting rhythms of the tango poured forth from the speakers. This time, we looked at each other with the same thought: that this will separate the "men from the boys." Much to everyone's surprise, this beautiful, graceful couple stayed on the dance floor and assumed the classic positions of tango dancers: she with her left arm just reaching up to his shoulder with upturned limp hand, head turned as she looked to her left side, pretending to pull away from his advances; he, holding her tiny waist, their upper bodies slightly apart as if pulling away from each other, hips fitting closely together in the classic tango stance. In spite of the beautiful music, the pitchers of lemonade, even the tray of "munchies," conversation and laughter grew quieter as everyone looked toward the dance area to watch what we now refer to as "The Tango of All Tangos."

He gently twirled the woman around as she kicked her leg in a backward motion. Slowly at first, but with the grace of a dancer who has known the joys and exciting precision of this dance in earlier times, she brought her leg slowly to the side. He was just as adept in his rhythmic interpretation of pursuit—holding her closely, not an inch of space between them, still the pursuer, and she, the object of his ardent wooing. With their bodies almost writhing in slow motion, the tempo of their dancing increased to follow the music, while the aging group of onlookers sat transfixed, so quiet you could hear their gasps and deep sighs of delight, shock, and amazement. If ever there was a more sensuous looking couple, none of us had ever seen one. (Rumor later had them in their nineties.)

As the music came to a slow ending, they remained very still, entwined in each other's arms for several minutes. For those of us fortunate enough to have witnessed this superb performance, we were still to witness one more tender expression of love and devotion. The pièce de résistance, if you will. Before leaving the dance area filled with a hushed audience of envious observers, still holding his lady close, the man bent his face down to the top of her head and kissed it. Slowly, precisely, seemingly oblivious to all, they proceeded toward the chairs that held the walker and the cane, and then they slowly walked away amidst the loud applause and cheers of the observers. Some were seen to be also wiping their eyes.

By that time, I'd say our vacation had taken on new meaning. As I looked tenderly at my husband and mentioned the Latin dancing lessons we had once begun and then stopped, he grew silent. Later, when we were driving back to our apartment, he said that, since his back had begun to give him some trouble, low furniture and all, perhaps we should think

IT TAKES TWO TO TANGO

about returning home a bit earlier so he could be checked out by his doctor. Funny, I hadn't heard him complain about his back since the time we were at a friend's daughter's wedding, where he danced the night away. I think it was the "chicken dance" that did it—but that was a long, long time ago.

Several months later, after we had returned home, I had a letter from one of the Florida neighbors we met on vacation. She was with us when we witnessed "The Tango of All Tangos." With the letter was an obituary from the Florida newspaper dated a few days before. It read as follows:

> SEVERRA, Senor Pablo and Senora Musee, lately of Madrid, Spain and Palm Beach, Florida, sadly passed away in their ancestral home of Madrid. The couple had no children but left several nieces and nephews, all of Madrid. The cause of their deaths is as yet undetermined. The couple were widely acclaimed professional Flamenco dancers in the early 20th century, performing to packed audiences in all the great and famous concert halls of Europe and even before royalty of the time. Their specialty was a version of the Tango of their own creation. No other dancers were ever able to interpret it with the ardor and artistic vitality they displayed. Their devotion and loyalty to each other was well-known throughout their long lives together, evidenced even at their passing, which found them with their arms around each other as they slept. They were two of the brightest and most talented young performers of their day and will be greatly missed by their many friends and admirers.

My Shadow Dances

Terrie Jacks

I do not dance.
I move about
a veteran of my age.

But my shadow does.
It dances on the wall.
I do wish it would behave.

It dips and stretches,
bends and twirls,
stands tall upon its toes,
gives a skip,
then a swirl,
ouch!
a backward dip,
at the end it hops,
leaps and spins,
then gives an elegant bow.

I do not applaud
for watching it makes me tired.
Why doesn't it behave?

Yet envious
I yearn to dance once more
like the shadow on the wall.

Gutter Ball

Barbara Ostrem

Irma was not the world's greatest bowler. Not even close. But what she may have lacked in skill she made up for in determination. Sort of short and a little stout, she was a calculated force of energy whom her husband Ernie called his "little fireplug."

They were a matched pair who enjoyed doing things together, so joining friends in a bowling league was a new adventure they took to with gusto. Ernie liked keeping score because it put him in the front line of action.

Irma's delivery was something to see. She took precisely measured steps as she swung the ball smoothly backward in a graceful arc precariously high for her stature, then let it gain momentum as it came forward to be released, while her arm continued forward and upward like a ballerina on stage. Contrary to initial panic of those who first witnessed her style and were afraid of the approaching missile, she never dropped the ball on that backswing.

Excitement was high this Friday because it was tournament time. Irma was flushed with happiness because she was having a good night and the team was doing well. She was in position to pick up an easy spare when it happened. Eager to knock down the three pins left standing, she muffed the release somehow, and the ball rolled into the gutter. But it didn't quit there. It jumped into the adjacent lane's gutter before continuing its wobbly journey in foreign territory.

Irma was red-faced with embarrassment. Ernie leaned back in his chair, looked thoughtfully at the progress of the errant ball, then drawled, "Irma, hon, ah don't think changin' lanes in the middle of a line like that is allowed in tournament play!"

In the Beginning, the Word

Nancy Sandweiss

I search for my sharp tongue in old photos; by what age was it honed?
Not in babyhood, toddlerhood – not with that sweet face, all-seeing eyes.
Somewhere in childhood the label was affixed, a fact solid as blood type.

I came to believe my words were arrows, irretrievable; wrote a poem
begging forgiveness for my *vile tongue*. I hid it from my parents, slogged
on silent with my burden.

One Yom Kippur the chanted litany of sins flooded me with guilt. After
services I cowered in the backseat of our car, choked out *I'm sorry*.
Did they hear me? Did I speak at all?

Now when Yom Kippur rolls around my grandsons go to temple
with their parents; I stay away from the keening rituals of atonement.
Next year I'll tell them my story, urge them to treat themselves gently.

What's Luck Got To Do with It?

Elisa Drachenberg

Halfway through pulling up the honeycomb blinds, Timothy Hawthorne saw them—their ears pricked for the slightest sound, but motionless, their heads turned toward him. Eyes large and unflinching, even unstartled. He could see three of them. They now began moving slowly between the mountain mahogany and prickly-pear cacti, neither paying attention to him nor completely ignoring him. Then, after just a few seconds, he saw a smaller shape crouching in from the right, down the hill, cautiously heading in the direction of the threesome. Timothy waited. It was absurd to expect a massacre before breakfast, unlikely even to witness a clumsy chase. The bobcat looked much too young and inexperienced, and the mule deer were veterans in the terrain.

Nevertheless, Timothy could not stop himself from tapping his fingernails on the glass, just loud enough to warn the deer. But they hardly lifted their heads, hoping to be mistaken for sculptures or out-of-season Christmas decorations if they simply remained immobile. Timothy didn't know what deer thought or if they thought at all. Still, there they were, halos of sunlight around their bodies, making his heart skip a beat—yes, that was a cliche but nonetheless true.

The tapping sound had startled the bobcat enough to make it saunter up the hill again to the neighbor's swimming pool, and the mule deer began picking their way around the cacti; cautiously their hooves moved them out of his picture frame. Timothy craned his neck, but they were gone, if not from the terrain, then from his view.

These unexpected moments of wildlife—observed solely because he happened to open the blinds at precisely the time he did—always reminded him of the way luck had determined most of his life. Sure, like most human beings he often liked to claim that hard work, determination, creativity, tenacity, talent, and a whole series of other self-promoting qualities—all of which had come into play in the past—were the reason for his success. But in the privacy of his brain he was not arrogant enough to believe he would have gotten this far without the incredible amount of luck in his life.

Timothy did not consider himself blessed. In his thinking the tricky business of blessings would exclude some who had not fared so well, actually far less than well. You didn't have to look far to realize that blessings were apparently bestowed on some and withheld from others, which would or could or should lead to the question of why. Why was there such unevenness in the blessings being handed out? Which then led to the issue of merits. Did those "blessed" individuals actually deserve their wealth, success, fame, or love more than the wretched losers? Were they worthy of blessings, while others were not?

So luck it was. Luck or good timing had let him open the blinds to the mini-wildlife show this morning. A moment later, and he would have seen nothing more than sun-haloed bushes and shrubs. The does and bobcats and javelinas and foxes and mountain lions and all the other desert animals he had spotted at one time or another were still out on his land, though no longer visible to him. Because luck, not ingenuity, had shaped most of his life, Christina, his wife, called him Lucky Tim, paraphrasing the Kingsley Amis novel. And since he had not read *Lucky Jim*, he believed that this was a label he deserved more than any other.

He felt the cold tiles under his bare feet, a reminder that the nights were still too chilly to be making breakfast without putting on his wool-lined slippers, which were practical but far from stylish. He was fifty-three, in good shape, his body still strong from working in the garden, but there was what Christina called his beer belly, even though he loathed the yeasty smell of beer. In restaurants she never ordered anything but German beer. "Germany is the only country that still brews according to the *Reinheitsgebot*. No preservatives, no colors, no additives," she claimed, clearly trying to tempt him into sampling the piss-golden liquid on the table. "Take a sip. It's like with olives; you have to develop a taste for the good things in life."

Unconvinced, he would take one swallow of German beer or one garlic-drenched Spanish olive just to humor her. His gestures of consent would make her happy, and her lopsided smile would again invoke the mantra in his head: Lucky Tim, lucky, lucky Tim.

If he thought about it—and he thought about it often—had it not been for fortuitous circumstances bringing them together, he could have missed her and never realized his loss, just as he could have missed the deer this morning. It was quite unlikely they would ever meet, and even more unlikely that she would be interested in him. She was one of those intellectuals who had no use for men like him, who were smart enough, but not smart enough for her. When they did meet—before the premiere of one of his industrial films—she was surrounded by at least ten of the company men who were calculating their chances of getting her into their beds, or into a bed in a hotel if they were married, as most of them were. She was standing in the middle of the circle, arms hanging loosely at her sides, hands curled back as if in some bizarre yoga position. Now she dipped slightly lower until he could no longer see her, and then, slowly, came up with an odd guttural roar that seemed to remind him of something, something he knew quite well and should easily recognize, but couldn't in the moment.

Again she dipped down, the men clapped and laughed, forming a slightly tighter circle around her. And again she came up roaring, her hands and arms now bent backwards as if she had been resting on them, as if someone had forced her up from someplace more peaceful. Suddenly he remembered the sound: the annoyed voice of an animal shoved and prodded to obey a command. He had lived with those very same irritated roars for the past ten months, filming and editing his film for this insurance company. They had invested heavily by inviting more than a thousand guests to this Performance Hall for the pre-opening party. His documentaries and other films were far from forgettable and this one, if not magnificent, per se, had several elements that would stay with you for its calculated, surprising effect: the vast, empty desert of the Sahara stretching out calm, peaceful, seemingly endless. And abruptly there it was, a horrid screeching sound, again and again as the camera, in achingly slow motion, veered to the place of action.

Apparently she worked for this company. Somehow, during the six months of filming, he had never even glimpsed her. Or was she the partner of one of those men who were encircling her? He shook his head, refusing to think that she could be someone's wife. She raised her empty glass now in a film star way, a bit affected, a bit flushed, a bit innocent, yet fully aware of the effect she had on the men. "I need more champagne," she said, her hair the color of camels in the desert. And as easily as she had mesmerized them, she walked out of the ring of wanting men and headed toward the bar.

Timothy Hawthorne somehow managed to stand next to her. To steady his trembling fingers, he picked up a glass. No words formed. A mere introduction seemed quaint. Had it not been for his increasingly shaking hands, he could have offered to fill her empty glass. As it turned out, she did not want more alcohol. She reached for a pitcher of water. "Would you like some?"

He nodded.

She poured and, by the time she had finished filling her own glass, he had formulated a somewhat unusual question. "Have you ever seen them?"

"Seen what?"

"Weren't you mimicking a camel? Over there? For those guys?" He tried to keep any kind of jealousy out of his voice.

"Yes." Her voice was pleasant, but aloof.

"Why a camel?"

"Who wants to know?"

And just when he thought he was annoying her, she gave him an opening. He explained that he, Timothy Hawthorne, was the filmmaker who had spent the past ten months filming and editing the film they were about to watch. "It features camels lying in the desert, laden down with goods, and therefore livid when their keepers force them to get up."

"Christina Walters," she said, shaking his hand. "It seems I already know you. I watched your film 138 times."

It turned out that Christina had just returned from a tradeshow in Munich, where, for ten days, his film was shown in a loop from morning until closing. So she knew all about the caravan in the desert, about the camels and their outrageous screams, which she had imitated so perfectly. The camel imitation led to dinner, which led to a movie, which led to her confession that she had divorced her philandering husband, an English professor who seemed so certain of her love that he shared his freely with a wide range of female students. This, Christina claimed, was the reason why she was absolutely not in the least bit interested in any kind of relationship. Timothy heard her words, but refused to believe them. Actually, for the first time since his wife had deserted him two years earlier—yes, for his best friend—Timothy perceived this departure as good timing and good fortune, in short: a stroke of luck.

In October, shortly after her divorce, Christina had moved to Tucson and found a job with the very corporation that had contracted Timothy a year earlier to produce an "inspiring" film about *Insurance Done Right*. Coincidence…

Christina, pale, freckled Christina, initially welcomed the warmth of the Southwest after the frigid winters of Minnesota, but her skin and eyes, always dry and itchy, kept urging her to find a halfway place, warmer than Minneapolis and cooler than Tucson. Her grandparent's winter retreat, a Mediterranean-style house in the foothills, proved too large for her alone. She had been grateful for their offer to stay there until she could find something more suitable. But after months of fierce, unrelenting heat, her thirsty brain could only think of leaving. Timothy, on the other hand, was a native of Arizona and couldn't imagine a better place for a man keen on sunshine.

He showed her the city. He introduced her to friends. He took her to galleries. Slowly, she let herself ease into a routine of shared activities. They saw plays and movies. They went to musicals and concerts. They had dinners and lunches. She began to trust him, even like him. But the heat issue could not be solved.

On a Saturday in June, she had agreed to an early hike, but by the time they left Saguaro National Monument two hours later, the temperature had reached a miserable 115 degrees. At the car, Timothy handed her a bottle of ice-cold water from the cooler. Then, before taking a sip from his own bottle, he gently wiped the sweat off her face with a wet paper towel. Since she had clearly and emphatically stated from the start that she was not interested in a "relationship," and since Timothy never seemed to expect more from her than the friendship she offered, she was shocked to find herself feeling fonder of him than she had thought possible. If she now found him adorable, that did not necessarily mean she adored him—or did it? Wasn't adoration simply a synonym for love?

She needed a rest from the heat and from her bewildering thoughts and feelings. She fantasized about a getaway to someplace where it was warm, but not hot. Timothy suggested Flagstaff, where she rented a cabin at Lake Mary. And there, during this solitary week, Christina—aloof, rational, cynical Christina—realized she was falling in love with the man who might have been waiting for this moment all along. When she called him—she could not possibly face him to reveal her startling "emotional reversal"—he seemed preoccupied, thrilled and euphoric but.... Yes, there was an unexpected *but*.

It turned out that Christina's confession could not have come at a worse moment. Timothy's production company found itself in a remarkable position: seemingly overnight, a large amount of vague prospects became actual commitments. Flooded with new orders, he needed to hire additional staff; put together crews; several screenplays needed reworking; there were meetings and location scouts planned in Cameroon. Tension oozed from every word. "Oh, Christina," he said, almost close to tears, "I've been hoping for you to...for such a long time...and now...God, I'm so happy. No, that sounds so trite...I'm, I'm, oh yes, I'm so incredibly happy...and what absolutely horrible timing...no, not you, just this whole explosion of contracts, this work overload...Will you wait for me? Please?"

So what did all this mean? If she was serious about being with him, and she was, then she needed to stay in Tucson in the unbearable heat. She needed to accept that, at this moment of Timothy's life, his work required a significant amount of his efforts. She needed to be patient and grant him time: a more precious gift than she'd realized.

"Of course, I will," she promised.

In mid-July clouds were building, practicing for the big monsoon that usually brought the long-awaited rains, though this year it brought mostly humidity. Christina was drenched before she took a shower, and equally drenched shortly after, her body sticky, clothes clinging to her skin. The air-conditioning in her grandparent's house could not keep up. She moved to the basement, which, unsurprisingly, turned out to be a bit cooler but also harbored a strangely putrid smell that inspired nightmares of dead rodents and flesh-eating mold.

During the day, she designed software for the company that, in a peculiar way, had brought her together with Timothy Hawthorne. At night, she lay on her uncomfortable pullout bed, vexed by the "adoration" she still felt for the man who had accepted her terms for all these months and who now—when she had finally been tamed by this curious horse whisperer—slaved in some other desert in Kuwait, or Israel, or Egypt. Apparently this, his homegrown Arizona desert, was not enough for him. There were repeated, unexpected complications that prolonged his stay away from her. She struggled to be patient, even understanding, by no means natural qualities for her. When August finally brought the first rains, the violent downpours washed away part of the front yard. She was exhausted from lack of sleep, from the tedious, uninspiring work she had to finish before September and from her inability to reconcile her independent nature with her craving for the body of that desert-man who skyped regularly, but parked his flesh thousands of miles away from her. How could he assume she would cheerfully wait for his return?

She had always considered feminists, at least some of them, to be theatrical. Why burn your bra if what you wanted was the same salary as a man? Why preach and write and demonstrate about discrimination against women, about men's sexist behavior, about the whole laundry list of completely justified grievances, if that somehow led to wearing earth-mother clothing and frumpy sandals, but little improvement? When Christina Walters applied for a job, she asked what the men in her position earned and simply expected the same salary. Perhaps it was her confident approach, perhaps her winning smile, and surely the crucial fact that there were just not enough first-rate software specialists in her field must have played a role. Whatever the reasons, Christina usually got what she wanted. At the time of her divorce—convinced she would never trust another man—she had talked herself into believing that lovers, just like jobs, needed to be and stay stimulating. If those demands were no longer met, she'd simply leave. She was her own woman, whatever that meant, and men were—well, they were easily exchangeable if you kept yourself from becoming attached, or let's say it: falling in love. Because love, she realized, was an emotion that only the cynical would consider a four-letter word in equal standing with fuck.

September came. The much-awaited monsoon turned out to be a lackluster imitation of the rainstorms she had grown up with in the Midwest. Her assignment came to an end, and her growing irritation at forcing herself into the unfamiliar role of the selfless and tolerant partner caught up with her. She locked her grandparent's house, left her job, left Tucson and Arizona. Then she drove to Los Angeles to visit a college friend who had been inviting her to spend some time with her and her "eclectic collection of low-maintenance friends."

How could she have expected "low maintenance" to entail pleasure? During a night of bland, almost dreary sex with someone she'd met at a party in Beverly Hills, she envisioned clawing her nails into Timothy's back, drawing blood for having wound up between the incredibly soft and silky, 1000-thread-count satin sheets of a man so handsome, yet so obtuse and erotically uninspired.

The next morning, she put on makeup, eager to avoid meeting her own eyes in the mirror. Bastard. Why should she feel guilty about having sex with someone else? She would never accept infidelities in a marriage. But this was different; she and Timothy were not even a couple. Anyway, how long was she supposed to wait? Bastard. His absence clearly inspired her foolish choices, drove her to decisions she did not want to make. Because once you decided to love someone, if after all this time you found yourself, against your will, falling in love with someone, wasn't it the other's responsibility to be there, physically? To be there and keep you fulfilled? Was it fair to remove himself from her life for whatever good reason? She found her own questions childish and unworthy of herself, yet she kept thinking them.

"If you can't be with the one you love, love the one you're with," her friend sang when she got home. Christina rolled her eyes.

That day, she actually wrote a break-up email to Timothy, who was somewhere en route to Kenya. But the thought of him rushing around in some African country or other, concentrating on filming and producing, getting permits and props and actors and all the myriad things that demanded all his focus, kept her from actually hitting "send." This was not a mature way to end a relationship, even if the word "relationship" hardly applied. Despite her rage, Christina somehow mustered the strength to suppress her spiteful and unkind words. She was not a woman scorned, simply a woman neglected, disused really. Did that warrant a hurtful retaliation?

For a couple of days, she considered going back to Minneapolis, but shuddered at the prospect of blizzards, ice, and cold. Instead, Christina—miserable after two weeks of dinners with men who mostly bored her by bragging about their exotic cars, sprawling designer-decorated mansions, or anything else money could buy, and realizing that this was not the kind of distraction she needed or wanted—booked a flight to Rarotonga, an island in the South Pacific, which, according to Internet promises, was still largely untouched by tourism.

In a small hotel, a few miles from the airport, she sat under the canopy on one of the cerulean-blue wooden chairs, sipping coffee and eating such large amounts of passion fruit and papayas that she expected to come down with the Cook Island's equivalent of Montezuma's revenge.

Surrounded by wafting palm trees, she watched waves crash against the reef, never tiring of the slightly changing configurations. She walked the incredibly white beach of the lagoon, gathering shells, turquoise and pink, and smooth pieces of orange-red corral. In these days of chosen solitude at the Tangaroa Hotel, she strived to erase all love for Timothy. She even convinced herself she was experiencing—if not happiness—then at least contentment.

The best part about this paradise—complete with breathtaking sunsets that reminded her of the kitschy postcards she'd received as a little girl from an aunt—was her unreachability. As a rule, the Internet was "down" and telephone calls to or from foreign countries somehow seemed impossible to relay to the lobby, let alone to private rooms. The last time Christina had heard from Timothy was while she was staying with her friend in Los Angeles. And then she had neglected to tell him about her island plans.

She had left her friend, Terry, with strict instructions not to disclose her whereabouts, which proved to be quite difficult, since Timothy kept calling her. He had returned to Tucson, inundated with post-production work, with feverish attempts to get things finished, yet incapable of concentrating. His Christina was gone, vanished, without so much as a message, and her friend, Terry, seemed sympathetic, but claimed that her loyalty to Christina was stronger than her concern for his woes. Timothy listened to Terry's descriptions of Christina, which actually increased the ache in the throbbing nuisance his heart had become. Hearing Terry talk about Christina, and they talked about little else, would not bring her back and only led to missing her more.

"I marvel at the way she dresses, doesn't she look stunning with those impossibly high heels, those figure-hugging clothes, that amazing ginger hair. And doesn't she have the most dramatic, inquisitive eyes?" Was Terry deliberately tormenting him? He sighed. Terry droned on. "She's far too attractive to have a brain, yet she does; in fact, she's so bright, it makes you cringe. She makes you feel inferior without meaning to. Sometimes, I detest her for no good reason at all. She's such an impossible mixture, don't you agree?" Terry didn't wait for a response. "Thank God, her teeth are not as white or straight as they could be, and perhaps her lips could be fuller, but…" Terry giggled. Timothy despaired.

And then, about three weeks after Christina's disappearance, on Terry's stay-at-home-with-amovie night, Timothy rang her doorbell, disheveled and unshaven. Terry hardly recognized him with those purplish-blue rings under his eyes and strangely twitching fingers. A few glasses of wine quickly led to Timothy's tearful plea for help. Terry—still not revealing, not directly at least, Christina's whereabouts—told him that the next flight to Rarotonga would leave on Sunday and there was a delightful little hotel a few yards from the ocean. Timothy booked the flight and got through to the hotel, unaware that there was only one seat left on the plane and that the hotel, mere moments earlier, had received a cancellation. Lucky people are seldom aware of the accomplishments of the universe.

His encounter with Christina turned out to be less lucky, despite the cerulean-blue chairs facing the turquoise Pacific Ocean, despite the exotic fish with iridescent colors, despite all the trappings people look for in vacation paradises. "But I am here now!" he repeated, adding clumsily that on the island it was equally as hot as Tucson and, with the added humidity, absolutely dreadful. Was this all about climate or heat or weather or what?

They were not growing any closer. Had it not been for his father's sudden death, they would have gone on dodging the issue: equal pay in the relationship. Apparently, it all came down to two things: who loves whom more—as if that were a measurable quantity—and to the willingness to sacrifice. Sacrifice? Wasn't love all about not having to sa-cri-fice, but to give up gladly, freely, and with a smile, without remorse or reluctance?

Luck sometimes masquerades as tragedy. Can one talk about luck in the face of someone's death? Of one's own father's death? Only if this death meant finally breaking free of the anguish and agony caused by cancer's thrust to victory. Faced with battles and losses of such magnitude, and realizing that their own war did not merit to be called anything close to that, they flew back to Tucson to bury Timothy's father. Then, slowly, they began the never-ending process of growing to be and staying as a couple.

If all's well that ends well, then this tale should end here. Timothy Hawthorne was a man smart enough to spot and cherish moments of bliss without expecting the world to become a fuzzy ball of happiness. He was also a pragmatist and had exchanged Tucson for Prescott and filming for painting. Gradually, he and Christina settled into married life. Here, in the mile-high city, in the mountains of Arizona, with its much cooler temperatures, Timothy spent his not-painting time with deer-watching and gardening, with hiking and "antiquing." One day, while leisurely sipping coffee in the library cafe, he pondered a gym membership to work off what Christina had incorrectly labeled his beer belly. All was still well.

But life eagerly presents temptations, fluctuations, and instabilities coupled with anxieties or—on its more perilous flipside—blandness and the eternal boredom caused by an unchallenging existence. Wasn't it possible that he and Christina could grow apart? Or do difficult beginnings inevitably lead to good endings?

Let us say that, sometimes, when life lures us into believing nothing can go wrong, we become careless. Going to the gym started out as a twice-a-week, two-hour session with Kimberly, a cute personal trainer whose lean, tanned body left nothing to be desired. Slowly, Timothy increased his workouts, eventually exercising more than four hours every day. Initially, Christina praised him for his efforts. His body thinned, his muscles grew toned, his confidence increased to the point where he felt it necessary to replace his entire wardrobe with smarter-looking, trendier clothes. He bought silk underwear and a lingering aftershave. He told Christina he was considering a facelift. After all, why should he spend the last decades of his life with a creased face and a sagging turkey neck? He bought and applied facial serums that promised the miracles aging people wanted to believe.

His paintings increasingly exuded an air of something that was difficult to describe, yet easily perceived: even the negative space oozed some erotic quality. It would be unfair to assume that Timothy took his proverbial good fortune for granted. He pondered the dangers and decided on prudence. He didn't hesitate to renew his club membership, despite the increased price.

One afternoon in May, Timothy was unloading trays of lavender and rosemary, eager to replace the plants that had not survived last winter's snow, when he realized that Christina's car was gone. He paused. She worked from home, and it was unusual for her to be out in the afternoon. Until then he had not noticed the large box on his workbench, wrapped in shiny black paper. He could make out Christina's curvy handwriting on the post-it note stuck to the top. *For Tim from Christina, the creature that roars*, he read. The bright cerulean-blue color of the bow reminded him of something he couldn't recall at this moment, but figured it would come to him later. He detected a hint of Christina's perfume and wondered what he had done right to deserve this surprise package.

Inside the box, sheets of turquoise tissue paper, printed with exotic fish, formed a lining. The bottom was covered with a layer of fine white sand, and partially embedded in the sand were a few shells and pieces of coral. But Timothy's eyes first settled on a heavy gold necklace, the one he had given Christina only three days earlier. He'd invited her to Giovanni's for lunch, arranging beforehand that their waiter would deliver a small black gift bag together with the menus. Christina had unwrapped the gold necklace and studied the engraving: *For Christina from Timothy, the luckiest man*. She'd let her fingertips move over the words and for a brief moment seemed overwhelmed.

"What's the occasion?" she finally asked without looking at him. And then, almost as an afterthought, she added, "You *have* been very lucky."

Now he found half of this necklace wrapped like a chain around the leg of a camel, an exquisitely well-crafted camel with large long-lashed eyes. Just a week ago, he had admired a camel like this in one of the antique stores downtown. He'd told Christina about it. "Far too expensive, but gorgeous," he'd said. And now he held it in his hands. It was made of soft tan leather, with a brown harness, its mouth open, yellowed teeth showing. But in the store he had not noticed its insolent face, twisted in rage, as if it were screaming curses. Its entire body posture was that of defiance, as if it had just been forced into doing something it loathed doing.

Timothy, not sure what to make of this gift, raked his fingers through the sand for a note. What he found was a thin case that contained Christina's smart phone. Puzzled, he switched it on and recognized what seemed to be a selfie video that Christina had taken in their bedroom. She was kneeling on their Persian rug, arms limp, hands folded backwards, as if in some strange yoga position. Her face was turned away, hidden from view. He made out the sound of a wailing guitar, and then Janis Joplin's raw voice. As if that were her cue, Christina calmly raised her head, her arms unfolded from her sides, and she staggered to her feet with an unbearably painful roar. Her ginger hair still hid part of her face, but Timothy could make out her long lashes, the smudged mascara and her tear-streaked cheek.

Changes in Cove, Utah

Kathleen Elliott Gilroy

I remember you driving slowly, along the winding dirt and gravel road.
Down past the field of wild turkeys, clustered randomly,
strutting, plump-bellied, bobbing wattles, charming, naive, innocents.
On past the stripped mountain, broken down for gravel,
past the fallow farm that once housed calves and dairy cows.
Past the tall and narrow wood-built granary, in decline.
All around us, autumn leaves were pitched asunder, scents of dampness
and decay rode cold, snapping bites of air…warning us of winter's coming,
as bare limbs snapped and fell like brittle bones.
A split rail fence, off to the right, near my passenger window.
A camera in my lap. Our conversation stalled, caught on webs
of your approaching Death. Not the heart, the failing kidneys,
but that nemesis called cancer. Mountains between us and Idaho,
clots of clouds draped in wet woolen outer garments. A comfortable,
melancholy silence of acceptance. And then, heroically, a wall-eyed,
five point buck leaped across the road! Head held high, antlers scraping
overhanging boughs of trees and bushes…the graceful ballet leap
cleared the road, the hood of car…while the camera, brought for
taking memorable pictures, slid onto the floor mat by my feet.
The magnificent buck, readied for rut with an unseen doe,
saw us from the corner of his eye, !ost momentum, caught
his right back hoofs on near-invisible strung wire atop the fence.
A stumble, with his forelegs buckled, then he rose again,
up in seconds, maintaining his stride of elegance. Perhaps, we too,
learn to move on, past unexpected glitches in our lives, and
stride again in undefined pastures, somewhere on the other side.

Empty

Steven Snyder

I do not understand the how or why
of the ever-multiplication of cells
that hollows me out empty,
a vacuousness vaster than
                any sentoric trance.

A very famous person once said
anybody can quit smoking,
it takes a real man to face cancer.

That's the crux.
Do I want to face a long battle
with chemo, hair loss, exhaustion
or let it take me?

I'm losing my memory
and the ability to remember.
I'm losing my dreams
and the ability to dream.
There is little here to hold me.
I want to go on to the other side
while everyone is urging me to stay.

Ode to a Winter Night

Wilfred F. Mossman

From my doorstep I gazed wondering at the moon, white and shining high in the icy heavens where a few stars lay like a tiny fire kindling in the mighty hearth. It was clear and cold and I gazed at a mighty cottonwood, barren, until black raised its mighty arm between the moon and I.

A slanting house top gleamed its snowy sides down on the whitened earth beneath. A darkened figure of night crept like a gigantic mammal across my path, casting a cold fleeting shadow. The wind raised a low melancholy howl, which sent tinkling creepy shivers up my back as it brought flitting into my mind pictures of an ancient ancestor, the wolf, and went howling on its way.

The bluffs—stony, cold, white, projecting—stood like mighty sentinels guarding the cold flattened earth below. I felt the cold silently slip into my still body as paralysis might creep into the frame of an aged man.

A wracking shiver shook my body and my teeth clicked involuntarily, much against my will. The moon and the romantic beauty of the scene crept away. What once was something I could gaze at forever turned into something black, hideous, and terrifying. My fingers grew numb and my shivering stopped. Only the cold merciless night remained.

I took one last look, hoping to bring again the memory of the scene so beautiful, but could not. Only the emptiness remained. The moon stared back at me like some dreadful monster. I turned away and crept into my room, where darkness and warmth replaced the pain of my half frozen body.

Falls

Joan T. Doran

He is cute, adorable, this baby taking
his first wobbly steps to coos and claps
from his doting throng. When he falls
startled not knowing if he'll laugh or cry
he's swept up in a rush of arms, the darling.

In the background, looking for his cane
stands Grandpa who decides to take a wobbly
cane-less step before his dead weight
crashes to the floor. Puddled in chagrin
he blinks up trembling at blank faces blinking down.

Grandpa earns no coos and claps
no doting words or saving arms—
just embarrassment, stunned silence—
Should we call the ambulance this time?
Whatever else this latest fall may be
it's not adorable.

Winner: Best Poetry Contest

Dyad

Lynda Riese

All your children grown up and gone,
it's your turn to be rocked
in the shade of the elm
that grew tall before you were born,
whose leaves return more sparse
with each new spring.
Now winter's here, folding you in,
lulling you, and you dream of sleep,
your arms weighed down,
your breasts still spilling milk.
You have a new baby who tugs at your skirt;
he clings like a nursling,
this man you've lived with for fifty years,
diapered, incontinent, his bald head bowed
as you change him the second time today.
When you bathe his frail body,
leaning over the clawfoot tub,
he grasps your soapy hands
to pull himself up, his lips quivering,
a child forming his first word,
the sibilant "s" hissing
as steam clouds the bathroom mirror,
the round vowel in "sorry"
drawn out mournfully.
You scrub him, soothe him,
rinsing his thighs, buttocks,
his pale sex that floats aimlessly.
As sweat beads your brow,
you think of damp nights and fireflies,
the white clapboard house along the Rock River,
your husband's sure hand in the summer dark.

Leaving

Linda Klein

Let the night fall,
casting leafy shadows as we wait.
I will cradle you in my arms,
as if you were my own child.

Your skin is pale and thin,
hanging from your bones
like a worn baby blanket,
as if it were a cover to protect you.

You drift helplessly in and out of sleep,
returning to tell me of relatives long gone.
I listen and nod,
as if I am sure you have seen them.

Time is in the room with us,
that cheat who comes too soon
to take what is most precious,
as if he had a perfect right to do so.

Let the moon eclipse the sun, little brother.
My tears must not startle you.
I will hold you close,
as if to keep a part of you when you leave and
      cannot return to me.

A Sack Of Potatoes

Mary R. Durfee

My friend, Bill, picked me up on this particular night after he lost the bet we made and had to spring for a dinner treat at the beach. I made a joke of it.

"Ha, ha!" I said. "I told you the Yankees were going to win." We were going over a bridge at the north end of Oneida, New York when suddenly I saw a huge sign advertising a free clinic opening that night. "Oh, Bill! Did you see that sign? Would you mind turning around so we can go take a look?"

Bill managed to find a place to park. Sure enough, we saw a sign advertising a free health clinic dedicated to providing health care services to low income, uninsured adults.

"Bill, do you mind if I go in for a minute to see what's going on?"

"No, of course not. I want to go in, too. This must be something new I haven't heard about."

We were cordially greeted at the door and shown around to satisfy our curiosity. On our way out, we stopped at the exit desk to pick up some brochures. I watched a short, stooped man put a sack of potatoes on the desk. The nurse thanked him, and then noticed the inquisitive look on my face.

"Oh, that's Ernie," she said. "He's not able to work, but he raised a new patch of potatoes that he sells at the Farmer's Market. He felt he had to pay us something until he gets back on his feet. They go in that box over there, where we collect food for the food pantry. Some folks are just too embarrassed or ashamed at not being able to pay their medical bills. But it's okay. That's what we're here for, and that sack of potatoes will go a long way to feed some hungry family."

We left the clinic quite well informed about its charitable purpose.

"Let's go home, Bill," I said. "It's too late for dinner. Forget about our bet. Maybe some other time. We can stop and pick up some limburger cheese and beer. I'm sort of excited about what we discovered tonight. I want to find out more. It brings back so many memories of my childhood."

I remembered eating bowls of potato soup, and I just loved it. In fact, we always had a lot of soup. Turnip soup, beet soup, all kinds of vegetable soups. Maybe that's why we kids grew up so healthy. All five of us. My parents took care of any health issues we encountered. Yes, we had all the childhood diseases and medications to take care of them. But when we needed a real doctor, Father hitched up one of the horses to a buggy, drove into the village where the doctor lived, and brought him back to the farm to administer his services. Then Father drove him all the way back to his home. We had no money to pay him, but he always accepted a dozen eggs and a gallon of hard cider.

"Remember, Bill, that was a long time ago before cars and paved roads, no electricity, phones, or televisions. I know I'm getting on in age, but I still remember. Right now, I'm interested in this 'new age' I'm living in. I've never heard of 'free clinics,' and I'm going to check this one out."

The next week turned out to be very interesting, as I researched free health clinics. It all began with a "dream" by a Doctor Martyn, who is on the staff of Oneida City Hospital. She spent some time overseas as a relief volunteer for the millions of victims of the tsunami disaster. She successfully established free health clinics for the sick and needy. When she returned home she met up with one Amanda Larson, who had also just returned from Europe after having served a stint with the "Heifer Foundation," an organization that donated animals to poor farmers, who then shared the offspring with neighbors or relatives. Getting their lives back together after devastating wars took everything they owned.

Amanda Larson is president of the Gorman Foundation, a charitable foundation. In subsequent talks, she and Doctor Martyn became fast friends. They decided the thing to do was to create a free medical clinic over here, a payback for our own needs. They partnered with the "Community Action Partnership" (CAP) and opened the clinic in December 2010. It was named the Mary Rose Center after Larson's 96-year-old grandmother, who never had any health insurance. Fortunately, Mary Rose is living a long healthy life. Was it potato soup or just healthy genes?

The health clinic is totally free and dedicated to providing health care to over 7,000 uninsured people in Madison County and surrounding areas. It is entirely staffed by volunteers, retired doctors, and nurses. Clerical volunteers do all the paperwork. Patients are treated for varying needs based upon their individual profiles. Primary services include physical exams, disease prevention and screening, vaccinations, education (medical), and prescription assistance. The clinic also offers counseling, smoking cessation programs, plus laboratory and radiology services.

The clinic is for low income, uninsured people who are sixteen years of age and older. There is no state or government involvement. Everything is volunteer, even janitorial services, plumbing, and carpentry. Each patient at the center is treated with dignity and respect. Good quality service is administered regardless of income or lack of insurance. A "motto" for the clinic may very well be: "High quality health care is a basic human right, regardless of social or economic status."

And the sack of potatoes? A symbol of appreciation offered by a grateful human being.

I will be there
(Marion's Theme)

Bob Schurr

If you put my ashes in the sea, you will always be close to me.
For there is water everywhere, if you look I will be there.

The water goes up, to the sky, and along with it will always go I.
So when the clouds come, and bring the rain, I will be there to ease your pain.

We are always together, you and I, in the morning sun and evening sky.
As the tide goes in, and the tide goes out, I will, always, be about.

You don't have to think about it, you will just know,
When it is quiet, or when the winds blow.

As the years go by, it won't dim the light, tho stormy sea or darkest night.
For love is stronger than anything, and to it, you can always cling.

Don't dwell on it, or take the time, it will always give you peace of mind.
So live your life, without a care, and just know that I will be there.

I'll see all the good things in your life. I'll help you through pain and strife.
Just throw my ashes in the sea, and you will always be close to me.

Second Runner-up: Best Non-fiction Contest

Calvin

Jean Brier Lusk

My daughter, Cheryl, has severe diabetes. She lives alone in a small apartment in Tigard and has assistants five days a week. They provide light cooking, housecleaning, and companionship.

During the time Calvin was with Cheryl, he was invaluable. He had an instinct as to her health needs. While cleaning and cooking were not his talents, he was a great companion. He was entertaining and loved to play. He was able to make her laugh—a great quality.

In addition, however, he had a sixth sense that let him know when her condition would worsen. Before she was about to have a hypoglycemic attack, he would alert her. She would eat some fruit or sip juice, and thus avert the debilitating situation. If an asthma attack was imminent, she would quickly use her inhaler after Calvin alerted her to do so. Calvin also seemed ahead of the situation when her general health was in a slump, and he would stay with her for comfort.

For this, Cheryl and the family were deeply grateful. We all grieved when Calvin passed away. He was the most wonderful caregiver a cat could ever be. The memory of his love, loyalty, and skill still warms our hearts. His methods of alerting her were:

> Hypoglycemia – lick the inside of her elbow
> Asthma – sit on her chest and purr loudly
> General ill health – stay close, touching her

Thank you, dear Calvin, and rest in peace—you earned it! We love you forever.

The Rose Tree

Albert Russo

Shelly and Minica brought me a gift
oh, not a beautifully wrapped present
as they are wont to gratify me with
tokens of their sisterly love

No, this time, they gave me
something that can only be defined
as otherworldly, magical, straight out of a fairy tale
yet at the same time, that thing, call it miraculous,
was palpable and spread a subtle perfume
around their inclined heads

When visiting my parents' last abode
outside Brussels, in a tranquil Flemish village
they felt suddenly overwhelmed
no more bleeding, no more tears—
one or two maybe—but a feeling
of nostalgia and longing,
mixed with a touch of ineffable joy

A rose tree had grown, all abloom
as if it were bending to kiss the beloved couple
now reunited in eternity, wishing them a new start
in the afterlife, with boundless merriment and happiness.

The Garden

Sherry Stoneback

I wake up in the morning and pull the blinds up, look out the window over the back yard, and it makes me smile, starting my day on a happy note. The Southern Magnolia from this perspective shows shiny green leaves with backs of soft brown suede; this time of year its ovoid-shaped snow-white buds are pointed to the sky, like candles on a Christmas tree. Viewed from the ground, the buds are hidden in the leaves. Only from above do they look like this, as though I have a secret view from the second floor. They open to huge flowers with few petals and are gone faster than they came.

The roses this year were glorious; the warm, early spring caused them all to begin blooming at the same time. Dozens are open, large and robust. I find beauty in the variety of roses: different colors and shapes, some with few petals and some with almost 100 on each flower. Sometimes the many petals make the stems bend down with heaviness, causing the stems to start growing upwards again.

The roses' fragrance is evident from a few feet away. Up on a terrace at the left side of the yard, one bush sends out branches that support dozens of four-petal hot pink blooms in a circle resembling fireworks; this makes me smile and holds my attention for quite some time. The image makes my heart happy and is the gift I give myself on what I know will be long, tedious days. I never cut these flowers to take inside; it would spoil the show.

The rhodys are mostly hot pink and very showy now. I watch two rhodys on the right side of the yard, having forgotten over the winter what color to expect; they turn out to be pristine white with a tongue of lemon yellow inside—a delight!

There's a dahlia garden in a raised bed at the top of the garden; those are pretty from the house, but are meant for cutting. Once they start blooming, they are unique and colorful, fun to cut and bring inside.

I have to say I love roses the best. Some years they bloom from spring to almost Christmas. They attract all my senses: for the eye, a variety of shapes and colors – petals on some bushes start as one color and become another as they open; for the nose, their fragrance, like sweet tea; for the touch, petals soft and fleshy – I love to pull one off, feel it and smell. Roses are the most sensual flowers in the garden.

I always have a private debate whether to cut my flowers and bring them inside or leave them outside, where they last longer. If I leave them outside, they delight my eye; even as they fade, they look beautiful from a distance. If I get greedy and cut them to bring the beauty inside, they fade fast and don't last as long.

We sit on the patio swing in the evenings to look at the garden. This is my view of what heaven will be like, at least for me. Vern and I are quiet for the most part, only commenting on the plants, frogs, and birds we see and hear, and our occasional interaction with the dogs.

HONORABLE MENTION

OVER THE RIDGE FROM PARADISE

Susan Cummins Miller

Tonight, at 10:03, Wynne sent me word that Salazar had died.

I confess, I'd rarely thought of the old Arabian in the last three years, knowing he was feeding quietly in a Chiricahua Mountains pasture. But his sudden passing brought it all back... Wynne's e-mail request. My response: Sixteen days ranch-sitting for two llamas, three cats, one dog, three horses, and assorted wildlife? Sixteen days alone (more or less) in the fullness of summer? Sure. Why not?

Privately I'd said to myself, *What could go wrong?*

"Never volunteer," my father used to say. Good advice. He lived to be ninety. He also said to me, "Hubris was the Achilles heel of Alexander the Great."

"I thought he died of sepsis or malaria or poison."

"Yes, but hubris led him to believe he was invincible."

I ignored both Dad's advice and Alexander's precedent when I accepted the gig in the Chiricahua Mountains of southeastern Arizona. I needed a quiet place to finish my novel. Wynne needed two-legged supervision for her menagerie.

Easy enough, I thought. I'd cared for the small ranch a couple of years earlier—*sans* livestock—and even set a novel nearby. The ranch was smaller than Alexander's empire. Surely I could manage for a couple of weeks.

At the time Wynne extended the invitation, my father had been gone three years. Not even an echo of advice floated on the Tucson air. Or I wasn't listening. He would have said I got what I deserved.

What follows are my notes of that sojourn...

June 18, Day 1. Whitetail Canyon, Chiricahua Mountains.

I arrive a day early so that Wynne can show me the routine. Horses first. They're her dearest loves. Wynne's an endurance rider—or was, before one horse became too old, a replacement contracted equine meningitis, and *his* replacement injured a leg in a trailer accident, delaying training.

Horses and I have a turbulent history. I took English-saddle riding lessons as a Girl Scout. I was tossed out of the saddle the first day, as the instructor adjusted the stirrups. Not an auspicious start.

I haven't ridden a horse in twenty-two years. And that last time followed a dry spell of twenty-five years. Both events were catastrophes. The first took place on my cousin's ranch near St. Maries, Idaho, aboard an Arabian-Morgan that hadn't seen a saddle since the Charge of San Juan Hill. Everything was dandy till Mo spied the barn and broke into a gallop. He jumped a ditch. I didn't. My mother put my arms into slings, and my cousin insisted I get back on the horse. So I steered Mo around the pasture with my knees for half an hour.

Fast-forward a quarter century. My husband and I took our two sons camping in Maryland. My younger sister and her little boys were with us. It rained every day. When the storm finally passed, Peggy suggested we take the boys riding at a nearby stable. Everything went smoothly until she asked permission to gallop her gelding. Our guide, a teenage girl, thought about it for all of two seconds before giving the green light.

I pulled off the narrow trail to give Sis room to pass me. Unfortunately, when her horse took off, my mare bolted, galloping through the brush and between trees, refusing to respond to my dragging on the reins. Ducking under branches, I shouted in her ear. I cursed. She went faster. I lost the reins and clung to the saddle horn.

Behind me, the guide yelled instructions. My sons watched, silent with awe. I didn't want them to grow up afraid of horses, so my mind repeated *Don't fall off, don't fall off, don't fall off* to the rhythm of the hoofbeats. We stopped only when my sister did. She turned, grinning with exhilaration. I contemplated killing her with my bare hands. Too many witnesses. I gathered the reins and my few remaining shreds of dignity, and plodded back to the others as if nothing had happened.

But now I'm babysitting three high-spirited Arabians.

Wynne assures me that I won't have to saddle and ride them, just feed them, and give one his meds. This is not as easy as it sounds, I discover. All are not equal in *Equus-land*. Horses run in herds led by a dominant male. Kheegan's a gray-speckled white gelding. They're all geldings. He's the alpha male, the *capo di tutti capi,* and will steal food from either of the other two. He must be fed first, to distract him. Control him, and I control the two further down in the pecking order.

The middle-ranking horse, Wasabi, a gray-white horse who requires medicine for equine meningitis and a swelling on his neck, will snatch food from the horse at the bottom of the pecking order, Salazar. Hence, the bay must be fed in a separate pen. Simple, in theory. But Wynne's demonstration reveals that each horse is jealous of the attention paid to the others.

Wynne asks if I've got the gist of it. No problem, I say. They're in good hands.

She seems reassured. I don't spoil the mood by reminding her I'm allergic to hay—to grasses of all kinds.

June 19, Day 2.

Wynne takes off at five a.m. I'm on my own. I hum "I Will Survive" as she drives away.

In the feed shed, I review the instructions. Kheegan gets one scoop of horse feed and a small leaf of alfalfa. The alfalfa's to keep him occupied while Wasabi receives his horse pellets laced with medicine. Mustn't dose the wrong horse. Complication: Wasabi's neck is so sore he can't lower his muzzle to the ground. He also has a habit of turning over his bowl, which means the medicine drains into the soil. Must hold the bowl under his nose till he finishes.

So the procedure comes down to this: Get all the food bowls ready. Lure Kheegan to one side of the yard with a leaf of alfalfa. Run back around the hay shed and hand-feed Wasabi as Salazar watches hungrily. Run back to the other side of the shed to give Kheegan his bowl, then give a handful of alfalfa to Wasabi to keep him busy while I lure Salazar into his pen. Only then can I check the water troughs and barrels to make sure they're full and clean.

I'm exhausted, and it's only 6 a.m.

I bring another leaf of alfalfa to the fence that separates the llamas from the horses. The llamas, attuned to human schedules, wait patiently. I scatter the alfalfa in two lines inside the fence, so the male, Spud, doesn't claim most of it. While they're munching, I check their hay bales and water trough. Tadpoles in the trough. I'm mesmerized by their movement. When the llamas finish breakfast, they follow me back to the house for a handful of pellets. Their lips are soft against my palm, their eyelashes obscenely long. Chisel-like teeth resurrect memories of 18-million-year-old fossil camels I collected in the Mojave Desert thirty-five years ago. I ask the female llama, Azteca, to open her mouth far enough so I can see the chevron folds of the molars. She ignores me. I'm not about to press the matter and risk losing a finger. Or two.

Wasps are building a nest in the alcove outside the kitchen door. They dive-bomb me as I pass. One stings my shoulder. I discover three more nests under the patio eaves. I wait till evening to take a broom to the nests. They're built to last, so each takes a few whacks. I sweep them up and dump them in the yard for the ants.

June 20, Day 3.

In the afternoon, I take a long walk with Sneezle, the part-terrier mutt. We hike up the ridge through basement gneiss and tilted layers of Paleozoic sedimentary rock. Limestone, dolomite, sandstone. Underfoot are limestone cobbles dotted with fusulinids, tiny football-shaped fossils that lived in the seas here three hundred million years ago.

Wild grasses obscure the ground on the lower slopes. Wary of rattlesnakes, I pick my way up trails weaving through piñon pine, alligator juniper, prickly pear, blooming claret-cup cactus, staghorn cholla, and agave. The air is dry and sharp as flaked obsidian. I'm in the homeland of Juh and Cochise, the country of the Chiricahua Apache. Geronimo and his band traveled these hills on the way to and from raids in Mexico, and while escaping U.S. soldiers. Geronimo surrendered in Skeleton Canyon, which cuts the Peloncillo Mountains to the east. Now that canyon, the Chiricahuas, and the San Simon Valley lying in between are traversed by illegals—those coming for work, those bringing drugs.

My older son, twenty-six, calls while I'm in the shower. Wrapped in a towel, dripping on the saltillo tile floor, I listen as he asks how I make sauce for tortelloni. He is Asperger's Syndrome, the highest-functioning form of Autism, so it's important that he be given the exact steps. Aspies rarely improvise. Theirs is a structured, orderly world. I'll be away for another two weeks. I refuse to think about all the things that could go wrong.

Did I mention I'm allergic to cats? I was rooming with Scout, Topaz, and Squeak. For some mysterious or perverse reason, cats love me. These three are lap-warmers and shoulder-drapers, so I have to keep the door to my bedroom closed. Even smoky-gray Squeak, fourteen, who was feral until a winter storm and a coyote chased her into Wynne's house six months ago, wants to wrap herself around me. She has the color of a Russian Blue, the jumping ability of a Siberian, and the vocalizations of a Siamese. She talks, especially at night. I put her outdoors when I go to bed.

Before I turn out the light, I catch two assassin beetles in and around my bed and release them outside. Assassin beetles, relatives of a poisonous beetle in South America, breed in packrat nests. If you're sensitive, the beetle's bite can trigger anaphylactic shock. So far, I haven't been sensitive. There's always tomorrow.

Sneezle barks, facing the rear yard. Might be raccoons. They can't get to the front feeder, the branches aren't strong enough. I bring in the back hummingbird feeder. Around 3 a.m. Squeak calls through the screen door, asking to come in. I make the mistake of opening the door. She yowls till first light. Earplugs don't work.

June 21, Day 4.

Packrats are nesting in the old pine bureau on the outdoor walkway. The drawers overflow with collected mesquite pods. Rock squirrels use it as a Circle K. I suspect it's the breeding area of the assassin beetles.

Canyon towhees, indigo buntings, cardinals, Mexican jays, Gambel's quail, and mourning doves devour grain from the feeders. The animals I tend are surviving. I haven't driven them crazy yet, nor they me. Wasabi's chest and neck look better, but he still can't reach the ground. Or he's faking it. I think he likes being hand-fed.

Today's the solstice, the first day of summer, the longest day of the year. The summer after he published *Lolita*, Vladimir Nabokov's wife, Vera, drove him to Paradise, a former mining town on the other side of the ridge behind Wynne's ranch house. Nabokov was a renowned butterfly expert. He spent the summer collecting and describing specimens. Some of his tiny Marina Blues are fluttering about the soil under the tomato plants. Others are mating, tail to tail, like dragonflies. I take photos, feeling like a voyeur.

I'm also in charge of the vegetable garden and assorted potted plants? Slugs have found the tomatoes. The basil's going to seed. So's the spinach. I can't eat them fast enough. I'm grateful I haven't killed anything. Wynne knows I have a black thumb. She gave me the job anyway. She must have been desperate.

Coyotes run through the yard at dusk. Sneezle chases them. She's half their size. I'm not sure what she'll do if she catches one, but it won't be pretty. The defender-of-ranch-virtue returns, dusty and hungry and satisfied. Tail wagging. No wounds. Mission accomplished.

June 22, Day 5.

Being in the outback, I haven't missed being emotionally caught up in the national or familial catastrophe-of-the-day. The small problems of this ranch are enough for me to handle as I strive to follow my novel to its climax and resolution.

I think Salazar, the oldest horse, is putting on a bit of weight. Or perhaps I'm imagining that his ribs aren't showing quite as much. I feed Wasabi, *el segundo,* from the top of the salt block this morning. The medicine I give him in his feed seems to be working, allowing his head to reach a little lower each day.

Sneezle again chases a coyote off the property late in the afternoon. He's quite the ferocious beast. And he guards my door at night.

I tangle with Tango the cat at dinnertime—he slips out with Squeak (the once-feral cat), as the dog's coming in. I'd been warned that Tango's a lot more eager to get out since he lost weight and became energetic. Lost weight? He's heavy as bushel of potatoes, I discover, when I pick him up. Lucky I don't slip a disk. Wynne also said that Tango's very forgiving when you drag him back in. *An contraire, mon amie.* He sulks for the rest of the evening.

June 23, Day 6.

I find the front birdfeeder catawampus on the branch and three-quarters empty this morning. Perhaps a dove or other heavy bird landed to feed? I refill it and determine to solve the mystery.

I think a packrat has made a nest in the air conditioner. Lots of twigs collected at the back and base. So I refuse to turn it on unless I have to. It's 90 degrees in the shade, but I write on the porch, fan blades churning overhead. River cobbles weigh down my pages.

The final chapters are finding their way into print. Should have them done tomorrow. Then I'll go back to the beginning and start revising.

I make scrambled eggs with spinach, mushrooms, and herbs for lunch. Marinate tonight's chicken in basil, dill, garlic, EVOO, and wine vinegar. A brief thunderstorm hits at six when I go down to get the mail. Gorgeous quintuple rainbow. Four color sequences together, another one high up. This is why I'm here—rainbows and silence and solitude.

The gas grill doesn't have a starter, and I'd been warned that it has a tendency to set hand and hair afire. I manage to light it at first flick of my butane wand, without holding my hand over the grill. A minor triumph.

Over dinner and a glass of cabernet, I contemplate my "state," as in Milton's "Sonnet on His Blindness," one of my father's favorite poems. He would have enjoyed this adventure. My state may not be kingly, but I have four-footed and winged minions—if I include the wild birds. Because I dispense food with largesse, they tolerate my temporary dominion. But I must watch for a palace coup at any moment. Chaos waits in the wings.

Scout, the gray-striped cat, escapes as I'm letting Sneezle out at bedtime. I leave the door open and chase her back into the house. I'm beginning to get the hang of this. Another thunderstorm during the night. Squeak cries to come in from the dry back porch. I take pity on her. Again. But close my door against her yowls.

June 24, Day 7.

I step on Squeak as I come out of the bathroom this morning. She's in the shadows and I don't have my glasses on. Turn my ankle. It begins to swell. Find a bandage in the bathroom cupboard. Squeak's unhurt, and wraps herself around my good ankle. Not an apology. Just leaving her scent, staking her claim before the other cats can. Next time it rains, she can stay out in the alcove.

I discover cat feces on the armchair cushion in the living room. Of course it happened while I was washing the dinosaur-patterned sheet that covered the chair. I take the cushion out to the deck, hose it off, and leave it to dry in the sun. I call Wynne to tell her. Might as well share the good news.

Wynne seems to be running an assisted-living center for elderly animals. She took in the llamas after their Tucson owner couldn't deal with them anymore (his camels went to the cattle ranch at the mouth of the canyon). Over breakfast, I ponder how to fit llamas into a story set on the San Francisco Peninsula. Can't make it work.

Muggy today. One cat loses her dinner in Wynne's office. Another has diarrhea. Probably Squeak. She feeds on field mice, grass, and insects every night. I clean up the messes and barricade the office door. Establish new pecking order. Only Sneezle's allowed into the office. I'm allergic to dogs, too, but not as violently—at least, not short-haired terrier mutts.

A neighbor calls to report a "cinnamon bruin, about 115-120 pounds," up-canyon. I'd heard two shots Sunday afternoon. He put the second shot near the bear's nose, he says, to scare it away. But it was "dumb as a box of rocks"—to which I take exception. Being a geologist, I'm overly fond of rocks. I'm also not allergic to them. And they don't vomit on the floor and poop on the cushions. Next time, I'll volunteer to house-sit a rock shop or geology field camp.

June 25, Day 8.

The spring on the new screen door is broken. I've ignored it thus far, but finally engage. We tussle. I can't disentangle the frigging inner spring, but I jerry-rig a connection. Fingers crossed it'll hold till Wynne can figure out a better solution.

There's a gap under the screen door that's large enough for snakes to come through. And scorpions. Found one under the bed last night. I tuck a bath towel into the space and resolve to wear sandals at all times.

June 26, Day 9.

I find one of the llamas munching away at birdseed on the ground, and banging the feeder with his head each time he comes up for air. I shoo Spud away and refill the feeder.

The back hummingbird feeder's empty. Might be bats. They can suck one dry in under twenty minutes. But I suspect bats would go for the front one as well, and that remains untouched.

Thunderstorm at 11:30 a.m. The power goes out. Could be out for days. No backup generator. My computer's only got a few hours of battery life. Might have to resort to pen and paper.

June 27, Day 10.

The novel's rolling along, although more slowly than I anticipate. As usual. Squeak and I battle wills daily, but it's a contest of equals. I'm not sure what that says about me.

An immature Lesser Blue Heron lands noisily on the roof, then perches on the edge for five minutes or so. Magical and unexpected in this desert ranch, so far from water. I can't get my camera without scaring him. Instead, we watch each other.

The llamas have a new trick. This morning both of them are munching on fallen birdseed, and the feeder is nearly empty. Haven't caught them purposefully dumping out the seed, but the same situation occurs under the back yard feeder this afternoon. And then they have the gall to beg for pellets. The birds are foraging on the ground at the moment. I make an executive decision: rope-and tape-off the front and rear seed feeders.

I think the monsoon's with us. Afternoon storms for the last three days, and I hear thunder in the distance. Squeak's the only house animal not bothered by the thunder. Wasabi finishes his medicine this morning. He still wants to be hand-fed, though I can't see any swelling.

Squeak doesn't like the Senior cat food. She'll eat a few pieces as a snack, but turns up her nose otherwise. I try some on Tango. She eats a little, as does Scout. At dinner, I try giving Squeak a spoonful of moist cat food on some Senior feed. She eats the moist food and leaves the other. For some reason I'm worried that she'll starve, despite her hunting capabilities. Go figure.

The last straw: The llamas have beheaded the tomato plant under the hackberry tree. They know no shame. Or boundaries, either.

June 28, Day 11.

Squeak caught a field mouse during the night. Apparently she doesn't go in for entrails and heads. She left them by the laundry room door for me. They were still warm. This diet might explain the diarrhea, and why she's not interested in dry cat food.

The llamas are at it again this morning. They slipped under my barriers. I add another row of tape. There's a certain ludicrous irony in a mystery writer stringing crime-scene tape (all I could find, once the rope was gone) around her environs.

Today Wasabi gets his nose all the way to the ground when he thinks I'm not looking. Definitely responding to the meds.

Squeak sits outside the gate barring my office, yowling so loudly that I expect Wynne can hear her in D.C. I'm a poor substitute for Squeak's mistress.

June 30, Day 13.

Wasabi doesn't want to, or can't, eat his food off the ground, so I give it to him on the salt block. I put my coffee mug too near Scout's dish and spend the next ten minutes cleaning up pottery fragments. At least it wasn't Wedgwood.

At day's end, the irrigation system blows up. Well-water's shooting everywhere. I start turning off outside faucets. Water's now coursing down the wash beside the house. Wynne didn't tell me where the shut-off valve is. I call the ranch at the mouth of the canyon.

The rancher—I'll call her Toni—shows up thirty minutes later. She got home from her teaching job just after I called. It's dusk. She heads out into the dirt yard to a hole in the ground covered by a wooden lid. I remove the lid, saying, "Let me get a flashlight. There might be scorpions in there."

She's tired after a two-hour commute. Just shakes her head and reaches in. Twists. The water shuts off. "Wynne should have told you about this."

We walk over to the irrigation panel, reattach the hose. Add some duct tape. Don't have a clue how to reprogram the panel—or even if I *need* to reprogram the panel. I decide to water by hand.

After Toni leaves, I take a flashlight with me to check the hole enclosing the shutoff valve. At the bottom a scorpion, the length of my middle finger, scuttles under the pipe. Holy shit.

I bring in the rear hummingbird feeder at bedtime. We had a visitor last night. No tracks, but it might have been a coatimundi. Or bats.

July 1, Day 14.

Wasabi again unable to eat his food off the ground, so I give him a Bute. When I let Salazar out of his pen after breakfast, I notice Wasabi has some swelling again on his neck. Same general area as before, maybe a little farther back. That explains why he can't lower his head as he could over the weekend. I call Toni again. Her brother's a veterinarian, and the owner of the ranch. He'll be returning to the ranch in a few days.

I remove a loose upper string from the horse hay bale, per Wynne's instructions, so the horses don't entangle their hooves. Instead they scatter hay with great abandon. Toni says she leaves her strings in place for that reason, and her horses have no problems. Too late to put the spilled soup back in the pot, but I'll know better next time. Oh. Right. There won't be a next time.

Squeak gives me another present this morning—a lovely little kidney in front of the chair I like to sit in. No other remains of the day. She spits up her morning treat almost as soon as she scarfs it down. I decide I'm not a cat person.

The llamas are staying out of the bird-feeder zones. For now. Making good progress on the novel, though I polish off half a bag of Hershey's Nuggets when I'm particularly frustrated. More thundershowers.

July 2, Day 15.

Wasabi's neck is still swollen. I try to touch it, to see if it's hot, but he shies away. Per Toni's instructions, I give him two Butes this morning with his feed. He cleans the dish. I've created an addict.

Salazar may be deciding he likes me. Kheegan's not so sure. Haven't a clue about Wasabi. But they all tolerate my coming and going because I am the goddess of sustenance. Demeter. Ceres. The Giver of Grain. I'm good with that. Toleration beats hostility, hands down.

Raccoon prints in the damp earth under the hummingbird feeder. Heavy showers last night, so I forgot to bring in the feeder. It's empty. Mystery solved.

Haven't a clue how to discourage the masked robbers, other than to continue bringing in the feeder each night. Sneezle didn't even bark. Some watchdog she is. Saves her favors for the coyotes.

I discover Squeak will eat the Senior feed if it's put on the floor as a snack—they *all* will. I feel like I just solved the conundrum of cold fusion.

I finish the first draft. It feels anticlimactic.

July 3, Day 16

Kheegan lets me pat his neck, but only because he thinks I bring treats. Salazar nuzzles my hand. Wasabi's untouchable.

Toni arrives to look at Wasabi so she can describe the swelling to her brother by phone. Takes us forever to catch Wasabi and halter him. He hurts, and is skittish on the best of days. Toni thinks the swelling's abscessing. She tries to insert a needle to drain it and give him some relief, but he'll have none of it. Can't get a needle in anywhere to deliver penicillin, either. So she gives him a syringe full of sulfa orally. She'll call her brother and see what he recommends. In the meantime, I'm to give Wasabi a sulfa dose with an evening feeding. I hope he'll take it in his pellets if I hold the pan. I'm not about to put a syringe near his mouth.

Hubris is draining away. I can hear my father chuckling.

This evening I dissolve sulfa in water to make a paste, then squirt it on Wasabi's feed. He eats some of the foul-tasting pellets, shakes his head and whole body, and takes another mouthful. Finishes the entire bowl. It's as if he's apologizing for being so fretful earlier today. But it's a good thing I've been hand-feeding him off and on for two weeks—he knows what to expect and trusts me not to do anything stupid, such as take away his food before he's finished.

Wynne would be so proud of him. Hell, *I'm* proud of him. Clearly, I prefer horses to cats.

July 4, Day 17.

I'm up at five-thirty, cleaning the house. Don't have time to vacuum, but I figure the cats will just shed more, so what's the point? Toni arrives at eight to check on Wasabi and help give him his medicine. Salazar nudges my shoulder. I turn and give him a farewell kiss on the nose.

I'm on the road at nine. Sneezle's riding shotgun. I'm dropping her off at Toni's ranch. It's dog heaven—cattle, camels, horses, dogs, chickens, and cats. Enough new smells for a lifetime. Sneezle jumps out of the Jeep without a backward glance. Clearly not big on good-byes.

I drive down the road singing the "Ode to Joy" in German. Tears blur my eyes.

Wynne's flight gets in at 1:30. She calls from her cell phone as she drives to the Chiricahuas, asking if I had a "soft landing" in Tucson. Her cell dies before I can answer. She follows it up with an e-mail the next day. Wasabi wasn't happy about letting Wynne near his abscess either. Somehow that makes me feel better. Then she relates the gory details of the lancing. I tell her I'm eternally grateful I missed it.

When the news about Salazar came tonight, I thought back to my time on the ranch. He was the rock—steadfast, gentle, patient. Like my father, who lived gracefully and with humor, but without complaint, during the four years after my mother's passing. Both man and horse lived to extreme old age, yet had good health until the end. And their endings were blessedly quick and peaceful. Dad drifted off with a mystery open on his lap. Salazar lay down in his pasture. Both died alone.

They left behind life lessons I've yet to decipher, much less assimilate. "In Greek," my father used to say, "the opposite of hubris is *arete*."

"Didn't you flunk Greek?" I asked him.

"That's neither here nor there."

Neither here nor there. As in, *somewhere unspecified.*

Over the ridge from Paradise, somewhere under a quintuple rainbow, the energies that once were Dad and Salazar roam free.

Nevermore

Maurice Hirsch

Waist-high wild sunflowers
left powdery yellow streaks on my legs
as the bay stallion shoved through,
head enveloped by thick green stems.
At the bank of the Huzzah, we broke free, splashed
across its gravel bottom. Water
rose up to his belly, pushed at my boots.
Emerging on the other side, sweat
and the river dripped, breathing slowed,
as we walked into the forest trail's shade.

Now, the sunflowers are gone, the field plowed,
planted with wheat and beans. Fording the Huzzah,
its cold water, the trail's spider webs tangled in my hair
are only memories as I ride manicured park paths
where puddles barely wet a fetlock.

This Little Piggy

Mitzie Skrbin

I grew up on a farm in Mars PA, a rural area in southwestern Pennsylvania. The summer I was about ten years old, my sisters and I went out to play after breakfast. Around noon, my mother realized she had neither seen nor heard us for some time. She went out on the porch and called us in for lunch, but got no response. Mom checked out the barn, the wagon shed, and the spring house, but we were nowhere to be found. She became a little concerned because we usually told her if we were going elsewhere than the yard to play. Mom decided to ask my grandfather, who lived in one wing of the old farmhouse, if he had seen us.

Mom opened the door to Granpap's kitchen, then stood in the doorway and burst out laughing. Grandpap and the four of us sat in the ladder-backed chairs around his kitchen table. We each had an old towel draped over our shoulder and a tiny pink piglet cradled in one arm, noisily and greedily drinking the warm milk that we dropped from the tip of a bent teaspoon into each eager little mouth. From time to time, we had to stop to burp them.

My grandfather had been tending a pregnant sow for a neighboring farmer. A few days earlier, she'd had her first litter. Now, pigs aren't always good first time parents. She was resisting the piglets attempts to suckle and did not seem to know what to do with the little pink creatures that had appeared in her pen. Grandpap was afraid she might trample them or worse. There had been six piglets; now there were only five. Of course, animals sometimes sense when a runt won't survive. So he gathered them into a market basket and was taking them home to try hand feeding them. When he saw us playing in the yard, he enlisted our aid. We were only too happy to comply, but we forgot to tell Mom.

After a day or two of hand feeding, the piglets were noticeably stronger. A couple had opened their eyes and were standing, so my grandfather decided to re-introduce them to their mother. She was lying in the clean straw in the corner of the pen, her teats engorged. He knelt beside her and, holding her down firmly with one hand, he placed the little ones at the dinner table, one by one. After a minute or two, she stopped struggling and relaxed. She looked down at her babies, laid down her head, closed her eyes and, with a contented sigh, accepted the role of motherhood.

Messages in the Sand

Dorothy Parcel

…Women's Essentials

One day after lunch, my friend picked up the bill and added a bit for the waitress. Then he took out a thin wallet and extracted a card. After signing the bill, he took off his glasses and put them in his shirt pocket. I heaved my overstuffed purse onto my shoulder and hated him. Silently.

A time before that, I had bought a small purse, promising myself I would carry only the essentials. The essentials turned out to be a wallet for my driver's license and other important cards. I also needed three pairs of glasses: sunglasses, driving glasses, and reading glasses for the footnotes at the library. I have an epi pin in case I'm attacked by an allergy, stuff for a shiny nose, and even some money. Men don't have to carry all these things, and it isn't fair.

Finally, I gave up and bought a reasonably sized purse that looks like a small suitcase. And I don't care!

…Toes

Long ago, toes were probably useful for climbing trees to get away from predators who wanted us for lunch. Toes were longer then, of course. But even the stubby things we have now help us walk without stumbling too much.

After toes got shorter because the ancients spent more time on the ground, they found that thorns and sharp stones hurt, so they began wrapping their feet with the hides of animals they managed to kill. The leaders, of course, got the favored parts of the hide, and then the old men, and finally the females. The old women brought up the rear. Well, if a lion was going to eat someone, it might as well be an old woman.

Later, humans ended up in places like Siberia, and they found they needed something more sturdy, so they invented boots. That worked until modern times, when shoes came into fashion. They discovered that only the rare grownup climbed trees, and few of us have visited Siberia.

Then they invented more styles for shoes. Men's shoes have stayed about the same since 1880. Not women's shoes. No. Men decided that high heels made women look great. Besides, women can't run fast in high heels.

Finally, they cut the front out of high heels, and toes again came into fashion. Only today the toenails are painted red, blue, or gold. The more things change, the more...

...Mysteries

Lately, I've been losing things. This week I lost a big black notebook, the house keys, a dog license that came in the mail, and my brown shoes. In the last few weeks, I've lost a ream of computer paper, six bananas, a sack of potato chips, and two boxes of facial tissue. But the biggest thing I lost was my car in the grocer's parking lot.

I didn't actually lose the car. I only parked it in a different part of the lot than I usually do. Then I couldn't find it. I didn't cry, but I muttered a lot under my breath as I pushed a loaded cart what seemed about four miles until I found the car.

I guess losing things is better than what I did a couple of months ago. Then I was breaking things. I broke the dishwasher, the handle of my favorite shovel, and the door of the shed. Losing things is cheaper than breaking them, but just as maddening.

...To Sleep, Or Not

I have insomnia. Or rather, I enjoy insomnia. Some of my first memories are of staring at the snow or rain or moonlight out the windows in the dead of night. I slept in the same room as my sisters, so I listened to them snoring away. In the olden days, rural electrification hadn't come our way, so I couldn't read the hours away, as I do now.

Then, a couple of months ago, I read an article about sleep. The writer's point was that the idea of people needing eight hours of sleep a night was a modern idea, with no basis in historical fact. His theme was that at no time in the past did people sleep straight through the night. They slept a few hours, then got up and did a few chores, checked the animals, and tended the fire. Then they went back to bed for a while.

Reading that was a great relief to me, for I didn't know anyone who admitted to my kind of sleep habits. I heard people say they had insomnia, but what they meant was they didn't sleep well last night.

I was happy to read the article, for I always assumed that my habit was because I was the middle child. Everyone knows that middle children are strange and often dangerous people.

Someone Else's Shoes

Shirley Shatsky

Across the aisle
shiny
tasseled loafers
black
trimmed in
saddle brown

not a style
for you, yet
they carried me
to a time of love.

You always chose
laced shoes
to mold
your wide feet,
sneakers closed
with Velcro.

How faithfully
you shined
the leather
neatly lined
them up
in rows
like soldiers
at attention.

That stranger's
footwear
made me
wonder
who wears
my reluctant
donation.

Do caring hands
dust and
polish them;
are they
lined up in rows?

Ritual

Bonnie Papenfuss

I ponder momentarily,
close the bedroom door,
turn on the overhead,
punch in the numbers,
and wait:
eight rings, nine.
A weak voice answers.
Mine rises in volume.
She greets me by name.
We chat for a time,
her morning activities
told over and over.
She grows weary.
We say our goodbyes
punctuated with
I love you's.
I breath a deep sigh,
give thanks,
and wonder silently;
how many more
Sunday rituals
before my voice
is that of a stranger?

Stolen

Tilya Gallay Helfield

"Our car's been stolen." He usually forgets to call me from the office unless it's bad news.

"Our old car? Are you sure? Who would want it?"

"I'm sure. I parked it on Elm Street, and when I went out to get it, it was gone."

"I can't believe anyone would steal it! There's a big dent in the front fender where you had that accident last month."

"They don't make the parking spaces big enough. You can't fit a normal size car into one anymore. I called the police and gave them a description. I'll let you know what happens."

He calls me back an hour later. "The police found the car parked on Atwater just below Sainte-Catherine. They said the thieves parked it there so it would be ready to be picked up and driven down to the docks, where they can ship it to Russia to sell on the black market."

I call him back a half hour later. His secretary tells me, "He's gone out to lunch."

"He was pretty upset about the car being stolen. It's a good thing the police found it so quickly."

"The car wasn't stolen. He forgot where he parked it. The police found it on Atwater, just where he left it when he drove in to work this morning."

"Has this happened before?"

"Oh, yes. Several times. More often lately. But this is the first time he's called the police." She's laughing, but it isn't funny.

I recall previous forebodings—misplaced files, unrecognized acquaintances, forgotten names, dates, routes to once-familiar places. The same questions asked over and over.

He tells the kids all about it when he gets home from work. "My car was stolen today. The police found it parked on Atwater, ready for transport down to the docks and off to the black market in Russia."

We go out to dinner with friends the next night and he tells them the stolen car story.

He tells it again and again whenever the subject of car theft comes up in conversation. Or even if it doesn't. "Those car thieves nearly got away with it. I have to give the police credit. They didn't waste any time finding my car and returning it to me."

I know that, when the time comes, all the policemen in the world won't be able to find him and return him to me.

Friends from the Senior Center

Anita Curran Guenin

Saturday, we walk across the parking lot after dinner at Joe's cafe. Between spaces in our chatter, footsteps behind us stop. We look over our shoulders, don't see Phil. He is gone, along with his stripey tie and hairy ears. We posit that he must have parked on the other side of the building. The darker side.

Five of us meet a few days later to play gin, sip decaf. We kid each other about knee replacements, high blood pressure. Phil doesn't come. As Muriel asks if we know his last name, someone calls out "Rummy."

Wasn't Hilda behind me, carrying her yoga roll? Where did she get to, I wonder. Was she wearing pink or blue sweats? Can't recall, but she is not in her regular space in the yoga room. Pads are realigned to fill the gap. Groans begin along with stretches.

Time to have dinner at Joe's again. Muriel picks me up and we go into the bright light of the diner. "Where's Harry," I muse, studying the pattern in the formica table. "Are you going to have the special?" Muriel points at a picture of food on the plastic menu.

Harry comes in, has someone with him. "This is…" He pauses unhappily, doesn't finish. "Mind if I sit down," she asks.

Not at all, we nod in agreement. She looks a little like Hilda, I think. Or does she. Hilda's hair was white, or maybe gray. I don't remember.

BODY MEMORY

Carol Christian

getting older
doesn't mean
i don't
remember
when i could run
so fast
with my eyes
half closed
the east wind
smacking my face
keeping me on course
my arms straight out
from my side
plowing through
the air
almost
but not quite
taking flight

getting older
doesn't mean
i don't
remember
clamoring up
and down
rocky cliffs
the sun tempering
my skin
my body
sweaty
and strong
and satisfied

getting older doesn't mean i don't remember

The Adventures of Flight Attendants

Mary Margaret Baker

Patti and Jenny are sisters who work as Flight Attendants. Each of the girls works for a different airline. The sisters love their occupations.

Anyone applying to work on a plane must have a college education. He or she must be attractive, a neat dresser, and not overweight.

When Patti applied for an attendant job, she competed with two hundred people wanting to be hired. Patti and another person were chosen. At the time, Patti was twenty-two years old.

Each airline has its own place where they train future flight attendants. The trainees face a vigorous course of studies. The trainee has to prove that she can handle every situation on the airplane. The attendant must be drug free and alcohol free. If a worker is drunk or found with illegal drugs in her possession, she will be fired immediately.

One of the scariest parts of the training was jumping from a high platform into a lake.

A new trainee must take a difficult written test. Every year the flight attendant must return to the training area to see if she is still capable of doing her job.

Patti was a good example to her sister, who wished to have the same occupation as Patti. Jenny applied at a different airline and was hired at age thirty. Jenny went through vigorous training and has to be retested every year. She has been a flight attendant for over ten years. Both girls could write a book about their travels.

Both girls get to take care of the rich and famous. Some are nice to take care of, and others have bad manners. On one trip, Patti got to serve a gracious princess.

Patti flies to Europe or other far-off places. The Airlines reserves hotel rooms for their workers to rest after a long trip.

Jen usually has day trips within the U.S., and she is glad to get home to her husband, two cats, and dog.

Patti is married and has two children. She sees to it that her children are always being cared for by a responsible adult.

Each of the girls has experienced bad weather on a flight. Two ladies on Jen's flight were scared and started screaming. I might have been screaming right along with them, as I am afraid in storms.

During one storm, Patti was sitting in a jump seat and hanging on to the curtain that separates first class from coach. The plane was going up and down, and even sideways. At the end of the storm, she could not stand up because her legs were firmly wrapped up in the first class curtain.

One of Patti's funniest and most embarrassing moments came when the plane hit turbulence, knocking her off balance and landing her on a Mideastern man's lap.

On anothers of Patti's trips, a man not obeying rules got up before the plane came to a complete stop and retrieved his luggage from the overhead bin. His suitcase knocked Patti to the floor. The man did not apologize. He stepped over her and made his way to the plane's exit.

On a flight to Europe, Patti had to deal with a very rude couple, who decided they wanted to sit in first class, even though they had only paid for seats in coach. It took a long time to get them moved to their new seats. Once they were in first class, the couple resorted to obnoxious behavior. People all around them began complaining about them. Patti was called on to tell the couple to behave. The couple was arrested as they exited the plane.

Three people on Jen's flight had too much to drink before they boarded the flight. When the men began fighting, both men were put in restraints and arrested as they exited the plane.

One Christmas Day, Jen had a fun day at work. The lady pilot was dressed as Santa, and she greeted every one getting on the plane. A man in first class was holding his five-month-old kangaroo, named Jose. Jose was wrapped in a royal blue blanket. Everyone in first class got to hold Jose and have their picture taken with him. One man was fascinated with Jose and hated to give him up. Jose's owner invited all the workers on the plane to take a tour of his kangaroo farm. The man also showed Jose to the people in coach.

The flight attendants always enjoyed a visit to Egypt. After a rest at the hotel, they would dress in Egyptian clothes and rent camels to go see the ancient Pyramids. Inside one of the Pyramids, the walls looked as if they had been recently painted, despite the fact that they were painted thousands and thousands of years ago.

THE ADVENTURES OF FLIGHT ATTENDANTS

Flights to Egypt were stopped when terrorist attacks began to happen.

Besides passing out beverages and food, the flight attendants have a lot of other duties, like keeping things clean on the plane. On one trip, it seemed like everyone had the flu. A lot of people were throwing up, putting Jen on clean-up duty for almost the entire trip.

The airlines give the flight attendants' families free flying privileges. This includes their mothers and fathers, plus in-laws. With flying privileges the girls can visit their Mom and Dad, and other friends and cousins in different states.

As long as these two sisters have the stamina to work on a plane, they will continue to be flight attendants. Perhaps you will meet Patti or Jenny on one of your flights.

Happy flying, Patti and Jenny!

Honorable Mention

A Study of Small Days

Bernadette Blue

Yesterdays slip before the kitchen window,
like slides beneath a microscope revealing life
in the single cells of moments lived,
while I peer over the sink, adjusting passing years
to eke some knowing from the study of small days.

Like scientists, who isolate the parts to unify the whole,
I separate the memories now, clatter dirty dishes in a pan,
and seek design in the relevance of random bits recalled:

Father, stamping out a cigarette beneath the golden ash.
A child, racing across the yard the day he died,
and falling from the tree like a baby bird
in a reckless tumble, tears and breaking bones.

A thousand cells, they multiply as I stand in stasis
following the flux of cruelty and beauty in the
season I have viewed – exclaiming sunsets, and
worrying over droughts – waiting for the rain,
then hoping it would stop.

And all the while the children raced the years across the yard,
I charted hummingbird returns, and collected slides of birthday
parties on the lawn, and barbeques with friends.
And summer storms that chased the children's squeals
to the safety of the house.

Where I watched, exhilarated – the vicarious observer
preparing slides for changing seasons, teenage courtships on a swing,
and college holiday returns.

Memories turn to years and lifetimes lived.
Breezes move a lonely swing today – sway the cells of single moments lived—
while I stand at the kitchen window seeking knowing in a study of small days.

Moveable Feast

Phylis Warady

I'm five when we move to a small beach town hugging the Chesapeake Bay. It's the height of the great depression, circa 1929 through the mid-1940's. My stepfather is a Chief Petty Officer in the U.S. Coast Guard. I'm learning to read from billboards I see from the train on the way to Baltimore on shopping trips with my mother and from the funny papers. I know that Annie Rooney's dog is named Zero, but since the country school where I start first grade at age six doesn't teach phonetics, it's years before I know how to pronounce a 'Z'.

I'm nine and my brother is six when my stepfather is transferred to the Boston Lighthouse. We live in an apartment in Chelsea. At least twice a week my mother takes us after school to see a double feature—which, more often that not, gives me nightmares, chiefly triggered by my mind's insistence on playing the "what if?" game, thus making mincemeat of the happiest of happy endings.

A year later—yet another transfer. This time to Wood's Hole, Massachusetts. By now I'm inured to yearly upheavals for seemingly neither rhyme nor reason. I hesitate to make new friends, knowing I'm destined to lose touch once we move on. I'm fast becoming a cynic when I stumble across the local library. Its exterior is stone; its interior gives off the musty smell of mildew that causes my nose to twitch. Much I care. Books cram the shelves in the children's section. Each Monday, I check out an entire series. I tie them to the shelf behind the seat of the bike I earned babysitting and pedal home. At my mom's nightly call of "Lights out," I retreat under the covers with my treasured flashlight. By Wednesday, I return the entire series and check out another dozen.

World War II rages. Blackout curtains shroud every window. Now eleven, I've devoured the entire children's section and pester the librarian for permission to read books shelved in other sections. In short order, I discover Daniel Webster, Nathaniel Hawthorne, and Abigail Adams, plus a cache of historical novels that feature seafaring whalers with spouses haunting widow walks.

Even better, for the next three years we stay put. Best of all, each of those years the librarian hands me the list of current children's books and lets me choose which ones to order. Thanks to her mentoring, I consider the local library my best friend ever. Just the same, at age twelve, I'm only dimly aware that I've formed a lifelong bond with all public libraries.

Fast-forward two decades. In my mid-thirties, I challenge myself to write a novel and choose Regency England as my setting. Such a decision requires tons of research. I soon consider diaries, letters, autobiographies, and well-researched biographies the most useful resources. Unearthing these treasures requires the assistance of countless librarians.

At my local library, I fill out the form requesting the diaries of Elizabeth Robinson, the original bluestocking. For a modest fee, a helpful librarian initiates the search.

Given today's electronic search engines, my request would have been processed in a day or two. But at the time I sought background material for my "work-in-progress," the World Wide Web was in its infancy and there wasn't yet a convenient Google. Consequently, it took several months to locate diaries written in the 18th century. Yet, once found and in my hands, I'm allowed to keep them several weeks before being obliged to return them to their "home" library.

To paraphrase Dr. Johnson, it may well take over a half a library of research material to write a single historical novel. Happily for me, after several rewrites a publisher bought my first novel, resulting in copies on library shelves over the entire country. More recently, this same novel has been reissued in large print and now graces the shelves of my local library, as well as countless others.

Given my ongoing love affair with public libraries, insuring me as a child that I'd always have a friend waiting to be checked out—no matter how often my stepfather was transferred—it's easy to see why, as an adult, I continue to hold each and every library, great or small, in the highest esteem.

Still Life

Bill Alewyn

I've heard those whispered rumors and so have you. Alzheimer's. The first (or second or even third) onset signs of pre-senile dementia. Who among us over sixty with even a hint of self-awareness doesn't think from time to time about the dreaded dementia and the devastating havoc it would wreak upon our loved ones?

It makes a difference, I suppose, not that it should, when the victim in question turns out to be a former U.S. President, one you didn't vote for, twice, the same former U.S. President who made an ignominious exit from office while our nation simultaneously hemorrhaged from a three hundred million dollar a day war in Iraq and the opening throes of the Great Recession, the same former U.S. President who had the highest disapproval rating since—well, since they started polling presidential approval ratings in the first place. The crusading Christian who started a Middle Eastern war for no better reason than he could get away with it, mission accomplished, and because "They tried to kill my daddy!" The same one with the suspect moral intelligence, the one everyone called "Junior," who couldn't pronounce the word "nuclear," who originally squeaked into office by a questionable 5 to 4 Supreme Court vote, screw the populace, *that* former U.S. President. The disengaged one who, frankly, it's no state secret, wasn't all that bright to begin with, but, like I say, I didn't vote for him, even though I live in Texas, in a county where there are more registered sex offenders than Democrats, though I happen to be one of them—Democrat, that is, not a sex offender—although there are a few good old boys around here with rifle racks in their Cadillacs that absolutely refuse to distinguish between the two.

My name is Madeline Stouffer. I'm 63, a widow, and a vituperative old sourpuss (just ask anyone around). I'm also a librarian, an honorable and historically subversive profession, the director of a small public library here in Valley Mills, Texas, a little wart of a town outside Waco, not too far from that other wart of a town called Crawford, where Junior, the alleged

Alzheimer's victim, now resides in semi-reclusion, painting nude self-portraits, or so the rumors go.

Far as I can see, Junior's doing just fine. He's actually been to our library…twice. The first time he came in asking for directions, all by his lonesome; we're a very small town and so that should tell you something about his orienteering skills, if nothing else. One day he just shows up out of the Texas blue, no assistants or Secret Service escorts to guide him, maybe it was the hired help's day off. And so, I'm here to tell you, he was alone, very personable, a little self-deprecating (which usually goes a long way with me), and only slightly disengaged and disoriented, not what you'd call overtly dysfunctional by anyone's stretch of the imagination—and, believe you me, I'd have been the first woman in this town, or in this state for that matter, to tell you whether all eight of his cognitive pistons were lighting up his cylinders.

"I hate to be a bother to you," he said, knowing all the time he knew that I knew who he was, and hoping like hell our little chance encounter would become the highlight of my postmenopausal month, which it clearly wasn't. "Excuse me, but are you the director of this library?"

"Yes, I am."

"Then could you please direct me to the nearest florist in town?"

"This is a public library, not the corner Quick-Stop," I said, mustering more civility than I thought myself capable of. "I'm sure the Super Wal-Mart in Waco will have exactly what you're looking for, Mr. President."

"Oh, thank you very much." He seemed a little taken aback, not so much by my words, perhaps, but because I hadn't fawned all over his snakeskin Tony Lamas and his faux Texas charm.

It's no secret I've never liked the man, or his family, or their politics, but that's neither here nor there, not in this town where I'm whispered to be something of a bitter old woman, and maybe I am. They tell us elephants never forget, and maybe they don't, but neither do ill-tempered old librarians with their full memories intact. I'm not talking about last month's overdue fines or who put the goldfish in the water cooler back in 1997, I'm talking about the 4,486 young Americans who were lost in that crusader's misguided mission accomplished—small town patriotic boys, and big city patriotic boys, and some patriotic boys who couldn't find Iraq with a GPS, but all of them gone now, sanctified by presidential decree, not to mention all the legless, armless, sightless, traumatized brain-damaged ones lucky enough to have made it out of that country alive. No, some of us don't forget, and now it's our job to guide to informational sites those who one day might become overly curious about our military foray into Iraq. 4,486. Yes, I'm still bitter, angry, too. Don't go jumping to any moral conclusions here. I did not lose a husband or a son or a father or a sweetheart in that particular fracas, but, as you can see, I do carry my anger and my bitterness with me, every single day. Why? Some of us who live in this country don't forget. Maybe that's part of our job, too.

The second time Junior came into my library—yes, I did say *my* library, I'm as proprietary as a brindled pit bull bitch with a litter of pups—was about a year after he graced us with his first accidental visit. It appears Junior had taken up painting by then—you know, portraits of the family dog and those now famous nude self-portraits, which I believe is how those ugly rumors of dementia got started in the first place. But, personally, I have no juicy heretofore empirical evidence of any mental deterioration in that man (then again, as the old joke goes, in Junior's case, how could you tell?). What I did see for myself the second time I met him was that famous good old boy sense of entitlement that living here in Texas seems to artificially inseminate into the very worst of our male populace. And so, on that second and what I hope will be our final intercourse together, I saw in his pale blue eyes what I can only describe as a kind of unearned and all too easy acceptance of his historical whereabouts in the grand design.

Strangely enough, Junior wanted to know the titles of a few books on "perspective" and did we have a "couple really good ones on the shelf" he could take home with him.

"Yes," I said, "we have a few books on perspective, but you might try the V.A. hospital in Fort Worth/Dallas for some real eye-popping points of view." I was *born* in Texas, you see, unlike some presidential poseurs I could mention, and we are famous for not suffering damn fools too lightly, and maybe that's why we still have the death penalty in this contentious state.

But bless what passes for that man's enlightened heart; he never did step back into *my* library.

They say that dementia is a disease of the mind—but I think for some it's a disease of the heart. Maybe as we grow older some of us in this world have the universal need to forget. Memories can be painful, perhaps too painful at times, and so Alzheimer's becomes in many cases a kind of defense mechanism. Now, in reality I'm willing to concede not all that many cases feel this need to forget, not in McLennan County, Texas, where there are still more registered sex offenders than Democrats, so maybe, just maybe, I'm projecting a greater sense of humanity onto some people than they're morally capable of.

I do know what I've seen for myself, and it's amazing, absolutely amazing, the amount of physical shock and wholesale violence the average human being can withstand, and yet, thanks in part to advances made in medical science, still manage to survive. Maybe, for some, memories are like that, too. But if that's true (and I said *if*), then I know of one man's memories, at least (and his conscience, maybe), that must be on some kind of permanent artificial life support. And, if that's the case, wouldn't it be more humane if the rest of us considered euthanasia at the onset?

Only, like it or not, this is not how we do business in America. Not with former presidents, self-appointed vigilantes, bald-faced liars, mass murderers, counter terrorist terrorists, men who by all evidentiary experience to the contrary never developed a social conscience, let alone any kind of memory of that alleged conscience.

It's an inexplicable country we live in, sometimes. It seems to me we would rather impeach our presidents for deliberately lying about the extramarital blowjobs they receive than the ones who would deliberately perjure themselves about their reasons for invading entire countries—Al Qaeda terrorists, WMDs, enriched "yellow cake" uranium—when, in reality, the only yellow cake that administration ever saw was the one they served on gilt-edged plates to their high dollar campaign contributors.

Oh, yes, I'm bitter, bitter to the tired old marrow. And I still have my selective memory, thank you very much, just like that smug nude-painting dilettante responsible for starting yet another uniquely American war (one of many in the memory of this acrimonious baby boomer), one that, today—4,486—nobody feels the need to talk about. But I want you to know, and it's important to me that you understand: I believe and I support a multiple-party system in this country, a system of Democrats and—yes, dare I say it—Republicans, a system of checks and balances designed to keep us all honest. But I also believe we need to be more vigilant when it comes to electing those who seek a responsible public office. I'm a realist, too, or call it perspective, when it comes to the big picture. And we are all too fallible and all too human; I get that part of the equation. I'm not asking for miracles here; I realize at times one or two less than capable types will fall between the cracks, but isn't that all the more reason we must hold those who seek public office accountable, just as we are accountable for electing them? Maybe if we can all do that, then maybe, just maybe, I won't be quite so acrimonious in my encroaching old age.

Instead, I saw just last month where they ceremoniously opened Junior's Presidential Library over in Dallas—where all the former presidents, and even one disappointing current one, spoke in radiant hypocrisies for all the world to hear. Like it or not, *this* is how we do business in America—and for a man who can't pronounce the word "nuclear" and who, with the exception of *My Pet Goat*, probably never read a book from cover to cover in his entitled life. But I'm not a former U.S. president, a living American institution who once wielded the unseasonable power to wage total war on millions because someone allegedly tried to kill his daddy. I'm just an embittered old sourpuss whose own father once lost his legs in a war (no, not *that* war, our lives are never as neatly packaged as all that). This was a man who, all reasons for living expended, one day rolled himself out a sixth floor Veteran's Hospital window, and who was later posthumously billed by the federal government for the replacement of a wheelchair that happened to be on loan from that government.

So, yes, I am a bitter old sourpuss, and the mean-spirited rumors of Junior's rising dementia continue to persist, despite an occasional public appearance, or maybe because of them, but at this point they're still only rumors, perpetuated no doubt by bitter old women not unlike myself. But if these rumors are true, then the Days of Irony are returning. Irony, maybe, but not, unfortunately, Old Testament justice; that type of irony would require a kind of inverse dementia that does not exist. The kind where in partial payment for our sins we are granted not a failing memory, but an enhanced one, along with an enhanced social conscience, for as long as medical science can perversely keep that enhanced memory and enhanced conscience alive; that's the kind of Old Testament justice I'd like to see. Instead, this particular transgressor was given a presidential library, compliments of the American taxpayer, plus an honorable seat at the table. Why it's enough to give an old librarian an overdue…aneurysm.

Instead, in rebuttal to my own personal animosities perhaps, and to the best of my knowledge, I'd like to go on record and say those rumors of dementia simply aren't true. And so, I'll say this again: as much as I despise that man, not once in our limited contact with each other did he exhibit a single symptom of early dementia.

Yet, sadly, many of us in this country now do.

Of Politics and Pins

Joan E. Zekas

The plush gray carpet was soft under foot as I padded my way through the Hillman Hall of Minerals and Gems. Our Carnegie Museum of Natural History in Pittsburgh, Pennsylvania was hosting a traveling exhibit of lapel pins belonging to our first woman Secretary of State, Madeline Albright.

There were 50 shadow boxes in all: some with a single pin; some with large clusters of pins—a total of several hundred. Many pins were gifts from Albright's friends. These were arranged in themes such as: "Sealife" (including a 6-inch lobster), "The Heavens" (shooting stars, UFO's and balloons), "Flowers" (two partnered dandelions—one in full bloom and one about to be blown away, frothed with a spray of tiny diamonds). But the significant pins were the ones Albright bought for herself. They were weighted and freighted with political meaning as Albright tried to make her point when she met with various world leaders. *These* pins were not simply to enhance a lady's couture. These were pins with a job to do.

Saddam Hussein, the Iraqi dictator, was a particular thorn. Hussein had his poet-in-residence call Albright an "unparalleled serpent." Fighting fire with fire, she decided to wear a snake pin at her meeting with him. Her message: "Don't Tread on Me," referencing the American Revolution.

One pin was a small, sharp-angled replica of an interceptor missile. Albright wore it in some testy meetings with the Russians, when they balked at changing the anti-ballistic missile treaty. Her remark: "…as you can see, we *know* how to make them *very small*, so you'd better be ready to negotiate." When the Russians bugged a State Department Conference room in 1999, Albright came to a subsequent meeting wearing a giant bug pin on her shoulder.

Showing her personal struggles in a man's world was Albright's pin titled "Breaking the Glass Ceiling." There were shards of rainbow-colored glass with one linear shaft of gold. The one pin that, for me, summed up Albright's effort at political impact was a large pin worn only at very important meetings. It was made of silver with a ball of rough-cut quartz. It depicted Atlas holding the weight of the world on his shoulders.

It was clear that Albright had certainly found a unique way to insert her political will into world affairs. Did it help? Did it change the tone or direction of the political dialogue? I can't know. But it was worth a try, and it sure was gutsy.

A Loner's Plea

Jean Marie Purcell

Slicing a rib roast, most often I tend
to choose as my cut the crusty end.
And almost always what has most appeal
on a loaf of French bread is the heel.
I try, at a movie or Broadway show,
to find an aisle seat in any row.
I listen; hear what others *say* they think.
Little I learn pushes me to some brink.

If we marry we should seek our own kind.
I try hard to believe 'justice is blind'
yet, wince when I overhear it said,
"…the suspect was a loner." And I dread
when people conflate 'losers' with 'loners.'
Few of us waste our time as atoners.
We're somewhat inclined to stuff our bookshelves
and, much of the time, we like ourselves.

In High Gear

Kathleen O'Brien

> *And you cannot go on indefinitely being just an ordinary, decent egg.*
> *We must be hatched or go bad.* —C.S. Lewis

Enough of bulls and bears and zippered minds.
She penny-pinched a hefty bank account,
brown-bagged it, skipped Starbucks
half-caf lattes, clipped coupons.
On her fifty-fifth birthday, Dawn saw the light.

To the dealership for her dream of going topless.
"Lipstick Red," tan canvas, V8.
She pushed buttons and the top came down.
The option of heated seats, Dawn declined,
saying, "I already have hot pants."
She read between the lines, signed,
the left hand not knowing it was right, then
out the show-off room, proud as a one-armed bandit.

Friends packed the car like cigarettes.
With horses unharnessed under the hood,
the Mustang took off like a bat from a belfry.
"Hold on to your hats!" Dawn shouted,
as she pedaled metal with Gucci sandals.
Over hills that rose to the occasion,
beneath summer skies shocked white as sheets,
five ladies sped past amber waves of grain,
past fruited plains that pushed up daisies,
past silos rigid as rules for good girls.

Thrown Rod

Mo Weathers

As car problems go, it was neither grand nor magnificent. But to a high school senior, it was catastrophic. During a miserably cold November, our family had moved to Lakeview, Oregon, but I was still in Springfield, putting a "new" radiator in my rusted-out 1940 Ford coupe so I could drive it the 240 miles to our new home. The job completed, I was ready to travel. I filled up the Ford with gas, water, and oil and headed southeast, a route that would take me across the snowy Cascades to Lakeview. The Ford's heater wasn't working, so I knew it would be a cold trip.

Sixty miles out of Springfield, at McCredie Springs, I stopped for gas and to check the oil. The oil was down about three quarts—a *really* bad sign. I filled it up, bought more oil and went on my way thinking, "I'll stop another sixty miles down the road and put in three more quarts of oil," not realizing that, as I headed up into the Cascades, the engine would be under more strain and would use more oil.

About forty miles farther up into the snow I heard a loud "BANG!" and then "WHACKEDY WHACKEDY WHACKEDY..." Panicked, I quickly pulled over and stopped. The engine sat there idling, quietly going "*whackedy whackedy whackedy...*" The Ford's old engine had used up all its oil and had thrown a rod (car-speak for a ruined engine bearing). What to do? I was in the middle of nowhere, next to a snowdrift, with a bad engine. Sitting there, shivering with cold and thinking, "This can't get any worse," I shut the engine off, dug out three quarts of oil from the trunk, and poured them into the engine. When I started it up it still went "*whackedy whackedy whackedy...*" but wishful thinking made it seem a bit quieter.

Not knowing what else to do, I pulled back onto the highway and continued on toward Lakeview. By this time it was getting dark—and colder—and there was scant traffic on the highway. On through the night I drove, babying the engine at about 35 miles per hour, while it continued whacking away and I kept hoping it wouldn't seize up and stop completely. I stopped another fifty miles or so down the road to pour in more oil, and continued my freezing, white-knuckle drive through the snow toward Lakeview. As I drove, I tried to think of something else besides the *whackedy whackedy whackedy* of the bad rod, like how long it would take me to freeze to death if the Ford's engine seized up and I found myself stranded in the snow.

After about two-and-a-half hours of this, I finally came to a house beside the road in the little town of Ely, about forty-five miles from Lakeview. It was late, but there were still lights on inside the house. Somebody was home. Maybe they could help me. I pulled the Ford into a snowdrift next to the house, got out, walked up the path and knocked on the door.

The family inside took pity on me and let me use their phone to call my dad in Lakeview. About an hour later, Dad and Uncle Gordon showed up with Dad's pickup and a tow rope. After thanking the residents profusely, Dad hooked up my Ford behind his pickup and Gordon climbed into the Ford, while I got into the pickup with Dad. With Dad towing, Gordon keeping the tow rope taut, and me soaking up the heat from the pickup's heater, it was close to midnight when we pulled into Lakeview. Finally, a long, freezing, harrowing day was over, thanks in large measure to Dad and Uncle Gordon—and to a stubborn Ford engine that refused to die. I was home.

I learned a valuable lesson from this experience—check your engine often and always keep it full of oil. And water. And any other thing it needs to operate reliably and safely. The broader lesson here is "maintain your equipment." And this can apply to other things besides equipment—family, friendships, and marriages, for example.

In over sixty more years of driving I've never let another engine run out of oil. And I'm still on my first—and only—marriage.

Maintenance works.

Going Home to Kill

William Killian

He was on his way home to kill,
got caught in traffic,
and his car died—

got out, slammed the door,
laughing, said,
don't care if the whole 49'ers team

is with her. To hell with it.
He never saw her
or his car again.

From that day to this,
nothing, no one
has ever had power over me, he bragged.

He remembered throwing his gun in the river,
walking all night to the next town,
never looking back.

He never looked back until today
as he retold his story
for god knows how many times.

I Would Have Been a Hero If...

Michael B. Mossman

It was all about my last year of high school at Bluff City High. Bluff City is a small town overlooking the bluffs on the Mississippi River. I went out for the football team because it was my last chance to play high school football.

When I was a freshman, I played for a small high school and wasn't very good. After that, I transferred across town to a bigger school. Bluff City High was a large school with many good players. I would not have a chance to make the team. That's why I didn't go out during my sophomore and junior years. I thought that, if I couldn't play well for the smaller school, I wouldn't be able to make the team at the larger school.

One day in gym class, one of the coaches was watching me run. He thought I had developed good speed, and he encouraged me to go out for the football team. I decided to give it a try. I'd always wanted one of the beautiful red and gray uniforms worn by the Bluff City Redbirds. In those days, a kid could return to the game after sitting out for a couple of years.

The best thing that happened was that I made third string halfback on the varsity. I wasn't very big but I had fairly good speed, and that's what the coaches liked. I sat on the bench most of that senior season and only got to play in a couple of games. But I didn't do too badly when I was sent in. We had a good team and won eight of our nine games. We were headed for a play-off.

The final game was to be for the conference championship against East Central. It was scheduled to be played on our home field. We were picked to win by seven points. The game was played on a cold and wet evening in late November. The stands were packed full of people huddled together in order to keep warm. On the very opening play we experienced bad luck. Our starting left halfback had to leave the game because of a shoulder injury. That really hurt our offensive efforts, and we struggled to stay in the game.

We found ourselves behind by six points late in the fourth quarter. Our second string halfback got sick and had to leave the field. The coach was left no choice. He had to send me into the game. "Give it all you've got!" he yelled.

East Central had the ball on our forty-yard line with one minute left to play when I entered the game. Their quarterback dropped back in order to throw a deep pass. I rushed in hard and tackled him for a ten-yard loss. The crowd went wild! We had the ball at mid-field with fifty seconds left to play. A touchdown and an extra point would be enough to assure a win for the Bluff City Redbirds.

On the first play our fullback took the handoff and was tackled at the line of scrimmage. The next two plays resulted in failed pass attempts. It was now our last play with ten seconds left to go in the game. My number was called in the huddle. The play was to be a fake pass and a handoff. Our quarterback would drop back to pass, and then hand the ball off to me. This was going to be my big chance and our last chance to win the game.

Jim Hunter got the ball after the snap. He dropped back to pass. All of the defenders rushed him as planned. Then he handed me the ball! I spotted a huge opening on the left side of their line. I raced through it as fast as my legs would carry me. One defender wasn't fooled. He came on fast in order to bring me down. I shifted my hips and left him sprawling on the ground. There was nothing but clear daylight ahead of me!

My legs were churning, and I was only ten yards away from the winning touchdown. I could smell gridiron glory! Suddenly, I felt a hard slap at my back heel. I began to stumble. Much to my horror, I lost my balance and fell to the ground. I was only one yard short of the goal line! The gun went off, and we had lost the game. The crowd that had been so excited was now hushed. I would have been a hero if I had scored that touchdown. Instead, my half-frozen body rested alone on the cold, hard ground!

The other players weren't mad at me after the game. They knew it was a team effort, and I had given it my best shot. After graduation, I played two years of football for a small college. I was even able to catch several long passes. However, I will always remember that high school game against East Central. I would have been a hero if I could have scored that winning touchdown.

The Kick Is Up and It's Good

Barbara Nuxall Isom

I love to hear the announcer when he says with enthusiasm, "The kick is up, and it's good!"

I didn't have any ponies in this race, so to speak, but I really enjoy high school sports, and tonight it was the Homecoming football game. My friend had inquired earlier as to what was on my schedule for the weekend, and when I named a Friday night local high school football game, she failed to appreciate my anticipation. It's been 56 years since I was in high school, but watching young people compete is very exciting. I had a high school advanced math teacher who stated that math disciplined your brain to think; I feel sports competition teaches you to perform under pressure, and now it's an experience that girls too can benefit from due to Title IX.

It is also a great family night, as we arrive early enough to buy a fundraiser hamburger to eat in the stands. We sit in our usual section and recognize others in the crowd. You can find a whole new group of friends, which has been good for me, as I'm a transplant these past five years. I became acquainted with Karla, who was always there. I learned her young son was on the team and aspiring to one day be quarterback, but I wondered about that, as he was rather small.

In the next couple years he took a real spurt and grew, so it was his dream come true and the team's expectation that he would be the starting quarterback his senior year. I saw Karla at the spring track meet, and she was planning a trip to meet her brand new granddaughter. When she returned, Timmy was scheduled for open heart surgery. I was shocked to learn that an athletic physical had led to the discovery of a heart defect. Surgery was imminent, his dream of being quarterback next fall was dashed.

Now fall is here and Timmy is listed as #1 on the football program, but he is on the sidelines. However, as the local paper wrote, he is helping the team in every way possible. This team plays a different, more complex formation, and the plays are difficult to learn quickly. Since he couldn't play, they had to transform a back fielder into a quarterback. Now Timmy is helping him learn the plays and also throwing passes for receivers to practice catching.

At the start of the second half, the band members, cheerleaders, and students form a tunnel that the players run through after breaking through a painted slogan banner. The last player to run through was a "cape-draped" Timmy, who jumped on top of the team huddle to lead a cheer.

Sadly, one of our players seriously injured his ankle tonight. It wasn't dirty play, it was just what happens sometimes. The opposing team and our team all knelt on one knee while paramedics tended to him and finally took him from the field on a stretcher while the students chanted his name. I remembered how, when I was in high school, they would quickly remove the injured. The manly thing (though also foolish) was to hop off the field.

I enjoy more than the game. I see families together—dads, mothers, grandparents, and young people. Tonight they introduced the Homecoming court and, since some of the escorts were football players, dads and grandfathers proudly escorted the formally dressed girls onto the field. The dance team performed, and tonight was father/daughter performing teams. They all seemed to be having a blast. The marching band gave their usual outstanding performance, and many parents helped to get equipment on the field. I recalled that my brother had been the quarterback in high school; I was a majorette, twirling fire batons (lighter fluid splashed on cotton stuffed in the ends of the baton and lit with a match).

Our parents never came to a game. I believe our mother attended some basketball games when my brother was the point guard on a championship team his senior year. I guess since our dad never attended high school, he couldn't appreciate the significance. I would never place athletics over academia, but it can be a great binder for a community from the beginning, when everyone stands and sings "The Star Spangled Banner" and the fireworks are lit, to the stomping and cheering in the stands. Like tonight, it can be a nail-biting event from start to finish. As we finally ended this time as the victor, it was an evening to enjoy. I have often expressed my view that even the losing team should score some points, as each of those young people also have parents, siblings, and grandparents who are hoping for their success. This opinion is not always popular, but is accepted.

THE KICK IS UP AND IT'S GOOD!

Our players always seem to be smaller physically. Could it be the water? When small players on the program are listed at 5 feet 7 inches and weigh 170 pounds, I wonder if they fudge a little to make it appear they are bigger (to foster intimidation). I don't say they've lied, just stretched the truth. However quick and fast thay might be, it is still hard to intercept a pass from a 6 foot 3 inch receiver, as you can only jump so high. This team is well coached and disciplined, which helps to win games and build character.

You can go to professional and college games, but who can afford them nowadays? I sometimes watch them on television, but it's a plus to attend and be with the crowd. I'm glad I enjoy high school sports. As years go by, very few will remember who won and who lost, much less the score, but they will remember that they got to participate.

Oh, by the way, they won over a tough opponent this night. After the game, one of the players was quoted as saying, "That game was totally for Sam (the injured player). Losing Sam hurts, but we still think we're a good team." He also had the players sign the football and took it to Sam at the hospital, where he was recuperating.

Sophomore Year

Una Nichols Hynum

Girls' school was very proper.
We were not allowed to wear slacks
even when the snow was three feet deep
and were addressed Miss Nichols,
Miss Quimby, Miss Levinson,
not Una, Carol, Mindy.

Every morning we attended chapel
reading from the Old Testament
in deference to our Jewish students.
On Ash Wednesday half the girls
wore a gray smudge on their forehead.

Our favorite teacher, Miss Cavendish,
who taught Sophomore English,
was young and quietly irreverent.
One day she looked out at our young
heads bent over our desks,
pen and paper fiercely in hand.

"Girls" she said. We all looked up—
teachers never interrupt a test.
"I want you to know you cannot get
pregnant kissing a boy." The silence
filled with a collective sigh.

Honorable Mention

My Unibrow: Post-traumatic Tweezer Disorder

Teresa Civello

I'm obsessed with my eyebrows.

There's a quarter-inch gap of bare skin where each brow should begin. But, sadly, that hair will never sprout again. Why all the fuss? Because our eyebrows convey emotion, and thinning brows are one of the first visible signs of aging.

My eyebrow fixation began when I was a Sophomore at All Souls High School in Brooklyn. Rumor had it our Principal, Sister Mary Gertrude, had been an Army WAC during World War II before she entered the convent. True or not, she ran the all-girl school like a military boot camp. With 1,200 recruits.

Upon enrollment, each of us received a booklet with dozens of regulations, beginning with *Absence* and ending with *Work-Study*. Plus we each received an addendum entitled *Lady-like Comportment*. Hemlines, three inches below the knee. Saddle shoes, black and white only. Polished daily. And Sister Gertrude's favorite rule: No makeup, which covered every cosmetic. Eyebrow pencil included.

Back then, the very thin, penciled-in-Greta-Garbo-eyebrow of the 1930s had once again become all the rage among teenage girls. Each of my fifty-three classmates had followed suit and shaved every hair from above her eyes to draw in a thin, high-arched brow. Unfortunately, I inherited my father's unibrow, which gave me the Groucho Marx look. I wanted to be like the other girls. So, on the sly, I stole my mother's tweezers and trimmed the thick hairs from above the bridge of my nose to give the appearance of two distinct brows.

Mom noticed my botched barber skills and spent an hour reshaping my brows until her arms grew tired. "Teresa," she said with a sigh. "Plucking your eyebrows is like mowing the lawn with scissors."

My unibrow returned. School began each morning with announcements over the public address system. Teachers and students sprang to attention when Sister Gertrude's gravelly voice trumpeted like reveille throughout the building. Our sophomore classroom, with its two windowed doors, front and back, was diagonally across from Sister Gertrude's office. All the better for her to spy on us. Sister Gertrude was Omniscient, Omnipotent and Omnipresent. She patrolled the hallways from morning inspection until dismissal. Her sniper vision and acute hearing were always on alert, especially for those violations against lady-like comportment.

I'll never forget that Thursday morning back in April 1958. I stood at the blackboard leading morning prayers when Sister Gertrude burst in. Her face was blood red. Her rosary beads, dangling from her black leather belt, rattled like a snake. We stood and greeted her. "Good morning, Sister Gertrude." She ordered us to sit. As I moved toward my desk, she grabbed my arm and told me to stay put. My stomach began gyrating to *Jailhouse Rock*. She waited until everyone was seated before she spoke.

"I just caught a girl with painted eyebrows, arched so high she looked like a lunatic." Sister Gertrude eyeballed every pencil-browed face in the room. I could see her jaw clenching. "I see that girl wasn't the only crazy-looking student." Her voice lowered. "Is there a rule forbidding makeup?"

"Yes, Sister Gertrude."

"So why are you all wearing eyebrow pencil?"

My classmates froze in their seats.

"You will wash that junk off," she ordered.

Nobody moved.

"Now," she barked. "First row. Go into the bathroom. Scrub your faces. When they come back, next row, you do the same." Sister Gertrude turned and stared at my unibrow. Her eyes squeezed into narrow slits. "You. You're the Class President. Make sure every face is clean before second bell. And I'll be back to check."

With that, Sister Gertrude marched out.

Class was scheduled to begin in ten minutes. There was no way fifty-three girls could get in and out of the bathroom that fast. So, while Sister Gertrude bellowed into the loud speaker about eyebrows and lunatics, almost in unison each girl in my class took out a hankie, spit on it and wiped off her eyebrow pencil.

Our shorthand teacher, Sister Mary Joseph, a hip, freckle-faced young nun, sprinted into our room from the rear door up toward the front desk. With her back to us, she opened her shorthand book and announced a quickie speed test.

We groaned.

Her blue eyes widened as she turned around. She erupted into a belly laugh, covered her mouth and dashed out. She reappeared with Sister de Sales, who took one look at us and cracked up. We just sat there and watched as the two nuns huddled together and spoke quietly. Even though they whispered, we heard the word "Martians." A commotion in the hallway interrupted their conversation. They bolted from the room. I stood and peeked out of the front door window.

A dozen nuns, arms gesturing as they spoke, surrounded Sister Gertrude. Their white habits and black veils fluttered like a flock of cranes. Finally, Sister Gertrude dispersed them. Sister Joseph returned. She said nothing. She walked to the back of the room and gave us dictation until the bell rang. As she packed her briefcase, she motioned me to her desk and spoke in a soft voice. "Teresa. We have to teach standing from the back wall until all the eyebrows grow back. The faculty will speak with Sister Gertrude after school about this. But we're not optimistic." Sister Joseph then pulled me so close that I could count the freckles on her nose. "Your parents pay tuition."

I nodded.

"I would think they'd be upset about this. Right?"

Before I had a chance to speak, Sister Joseph winked and left the room.

The school auditorium, which served as our lunchroom, was filled with 1,200 poofy-haired, light-bulb-looking faces. I sat with the other class presidents to hatch a plan of attack. We recruited the student monitors to spread the word to every table. The plan was simple. Our parents were to call the principal's office early the next morning to complain about the new rule.

During that Friday morning's announcements, Sister Gertrude said not one word about eyebrows or phone calls. We had a looming sense of defeat as our teachers continued instructing us from the back of the classroom. Then, right before we were about to leave for the weekend, Sister Gertrude blared over the public address system.

"Attention students. Monday morning, you will enter the school without eyebrow pencil. You may draw in your brows before class begins. But you must wipe them off before leaving school. You will do this every day until your eyebrows grow back. And they'd better be bushy!"

We smiled at Sister Gertrude's concession. Together, the teachers and students had won a small victory against the Drill Sergeant.

After graduation, I was hell-bent on having two eyebrows. I plucked. Scissored. Razored. Waxed. And burned off my unibrow with Nair™ Depilatory Cream. By age forty, my tortured brows got their revenge. That quarter-inch of hair missing from the beginning of each brow disappeared forever. But I'll have the last laugh. I'm getting my eyebrows tattooed.

The Bat

Robert Pouriea

My sister, Betty, and I went to school in a small town. In our high school it was mandatory that you study biology in the 10th grade, chemistry in the 11th grade, and optional to study physics in the 12th grade. These were our only science classes.

Betty went though high school in three years, so she could go to nursing school with her best friend, Audrey. For extra credits Betty made a butterfly collection. To help her I would catch a butterfly and take it to her. She would pin it to a board with a straight pin.

We lived a couple miles out of town, so in the late summer, when the nights were clear and warm, we would get together with the neighbor kids to look at the stars. Sometimes, bats would fly near us. We could see them against the sky, so we knew they were coming from a cave or old mine nearby.

I found the cave up on the side of a hill. Going into a cave was nothing to me, but this one had a bunch of bats hanging from the roof of the cave. Even in the dark I could see them hanging upside down. I quietly looked around and saw how easy it would be for me to reach them. I went home and told Betty what I had found.

"Betty, I found where the Bats are are coming from. I'll get one of Mom's jars and catch one."

Betty was thrilled with the idea and said, "Good, get one and I'll take it to Biology."

The hardest part was stealing a jar from my mother, but I did it. I punched a hole in the lid with a hammer and nail, and then went back to the cave. Entering the cave carefully so as not to disturb the bats, I raised the jar until it was under a bat. He fit right inside the jar. As I slid the jar to one side, the bat fell inside, and I quickly put the lid on. Once outside the cave, I ran home to show Betty our prize.

Betty took the bat to school and gave it to the biology teacher, who killed it and put it in a jar of liquid to preserve it. I never knew how much credit Betty got, but she did make it through school in three years.

Years later, I went into the service and was home on leave. When I visited the school and the biology lab, I saw the Bat was still there. I was surprised to find he was in good shape after all those years.

Since I don't live there anymore, I often wonder if that bat is still in a jar for the biology class.

A Life Imagined

Alan Dennis

1. Miles is Born

After all these years I never expected that I would be the one to tell this story. Andy was supposed to do it. Andy, the writer. Andy, with the gift of words. Not me. But Andy is dead. And so is Lew. Fred is in the nursing home. So, if you have a little time and a lot of patience, sit with me, and I will start at the beginning.

Miles Quentin Swoboda was born on the Fourth of July, 1962. He was sixteen years old at the time. If you think that sounds a little odd, let me add that Miles had four fathers, too. And no mother. Miles was an idea. He came to me first, but his flesh and bones would not have been possible without Andy, Lew and Fred.

It was Calculus. We were sitting in my room in East House (AKA Toad Hall) and I was in the middle of a Calculus meltdown. I was heading for a C- in Calc 103, which wouldn't do my GPA any favors, when Lew, the math genius, offered to tutor me.

"I thought you'd never ask," I replied. Then it hit me. What if the four of us enrolled an imaginary kid in Calculus, then had Lew take his exams and score an A+!

"You guys are always thinking small," said Andy. "Why not register him in the liberal arts curriculum, see how many courses we can take for him, and get him on the Dean's List by next trimester?"

Now, if you think that sounds impossible, keep in mind that we didn't have any compulsory class attendance in those days. We just had to show up for the final exam and pass it. Naturally, we were supposed to study, you know, like good college material, but many of the gods, like Lew, could cram the night before the final and ace the course.

Fred had a part-time job as a janitor in the Administration building. Not very glamorous work, cleaning out wastebaskets in the evening, but he earned a few dollars to supplement his scholarship and the little bit of money his parents could afford to send him each month. The big perk of the job, which Fred would never divulge to anyone but us, was the buried treasure he found in those wastebaskets. Fred was famous for showing up with the carbon paper originals of answer sheets for tests that had been crumpled up and tossed away. Recopied, these sold for considerably more than Fred's meager hourly wage and made him a highly sought-after person around exam time. Another thing Fred could find was stationery. The official kind, with University letterhead from the Dean's office, or any office we thought we might need to create a backstory for Miles. How we did it, without fancy computers and printers, is a story best saved for tomorrow. So, if you can make it, I'll be here; a lot of it is coming back to me now.

2. Miles Arrives

Miles Q. Swoboda, age 16, from Mays Township, Iowa (don't bother looking it up), was admitted to the University right after his sophomore year at Mays High School, so good were his grades and so glowing the letters of praise from his teachers, counselors, coaches, minister, and former employer at the Mays Drive-Up and Eat-In Diner. Fred collected all this information in an official University admissions file and, while emptying the trash from the Admissions Office, slipped the file into its proper place in the Dean's cabinet. Andy was a skilled calligrapher and, if I may say so, I wasn't too bad at forging signatures either, so between the two of us we managed to produce some very credible documents.

You may be skeptical that we could have pulled this off, but you know how some organizations thrive on paperwork, none more so than a University. We figured it was unlikely that anyone would actually do any fact-checking, what with the hiring freeze and the overworked staff. Fred kept the file up to date, adding copies of bulletins and requests for information sent out to the student community. And we must have been very lucky, because not once did the authorities get wise to us that Fall.

Thanks to Fred, Miles was assigned to a dorm room and a mailbox that happened to be right next to mine. I could reach into my mailbox, twist my wrist and hand around, and grab Miles' mail. Fred also made sure that Miles was paired up with Dr. Gene Prentiss as his faculty advisor. Dr. Prentiss was an anthropologist who was rarely on campus, and who took a much greater interest in the sex life of Samoan teenagers than in middle class Midwestern college students. Dr. Prentiss did very little advising, which suited us just fine.

Classes began in late August. Miles enrolled in English Lit, History of Western Civ, Earth Science, and Calculus. Not an overwhelming schedule for a 16-year old tyro, but not a slam-dunk either. Andy handled the English course; I took care of History; Fred had Science; and Lew, of course, Calculus.

So far, none of this scheming had cost us a dime. We figured it was only a matter of time before some bean-counter in the bursar's office would begin to ask questions about the account of one Miles Q. Swoboda, so we made sure that Fred slipped some very official-looking receipts for payment into Miles' file at the appropriate times.

I'm sure you'll have questions, but in a nutshell, this is how we brought Miles to the University for his freshman year and inaugurated his brilliant career as a young man of mystery. He kept the four of us together as a tight-knit team that year, until other events caused his disappearance and the consequences that followed.

3. Miles Aces English

August 1962 marked the beginning of our little production. By the end of September we had established a modus operandi. Each trimester was ten weeks long. One of us was assigned to each course, as you know, so we occasionally audited one of the classes, seated quietly in the very back row, to stay abreast of any news, announcements, or surprises. If there was a test, we didn't worry, because none of them counted anyway. Only the final. All except English Literature 101.

English Lit required at least one essay a week, although that didn't kick in until the middle of September. Andy wrote eleven papers for Miles that trimester. Some of them were gems. That guy was so gifted. I wish I had saved them. Andy turned them in to the Teaching Assistant, a bearded poet named Booster Puce, who was working on his dissertation and was such a shy person that he kept a drop-box in his tiny office for his students to deposit their work, always when he was not there. He made no appointments unless absolutely necessary, which in Miles' case, was never.

Miles won several awards for writing. His essay on Kafka's "The Metamorphosis," titled "Symbolism, Gregor Samsa, and America's Vietnam Debacle," which attempted to explain the government's compulsion to intervene in the civil war in Southeast Asia, not only earned an A+ in his English Lit class, but also a letter of commendation from the campus chapter of the SDS, which made many copies for distribution around the campus. (Students for a Democratic Society, in case you forgot.)

I found an old volume of The Lumen, the literary magazine, from the Spring Quarter of 1963. "How're You Goin' To Keep Them Down on the Farm," by M. Swoboda, described as an "hilarious account of growing up in small-town Iowa," was voted the Best Light Fiction of the Year. Miles received an invitation to the Editorial Board. He wrote back, thanking them, but cited his busy schedule and heavy workload in his refusal.

We were putting Miles' name out there, spreading it around the campus, getting him known. It was a turbulent time. In most colleges and universities there were almost weekly protests against The Draft. Miles wrote letters to the papers. He published several pamphlets that even appeared downtown, in bookstores and supermarkets.

I wish I could show you an old picture I found of Miles at a demonstration. There he is, back to the camera, between two other guys, holding up a gigantic peace sign.

Does it surprise you that we often had our pictures taken at rallies? As long as we turned our faces away, or moved enough to blur the picture, or wore a hat with a big brim that we could tilt over our eyes as soon as the shutter snapped, we were always "Miles Swoboda" to the photographers, who never once asked for an I.D.

4. MILES MOVES ON

On November 23, the Friday before Thanksgiving, academic honors were posted on the Administration's bulletin board, marking the end of the first trimester. As we crowded around in the cramped corridor, hearing the whoops and congratulations for the best students, we felt rather smug and at the same time incredulous, as there, near the bottom of the page, the very last name under the S's, was "Miles Q. Swoboda 3.96. Dean's List." Andy and Lew found their own names there as well. We had all worked hard on the "Miles Project," which occupied more of our time than we had planned, but for college juniors repeating first-year classes, there was no great academic challenge. We were smug and incredulous and also relieved.

We hurried over to the Rathskeller for a beer and burger special. "Where do we go from here?" was on each of our minds. And I don't just mean about Miles. President Kennedy had blockaded Cuba, there were Russian ships with missiles aboard heading into the Caribbean, and the threat of a major war permeated our quiet halls of ivy.

"Okay," I said, "we won. Why don't we ease up a little for the rest of the year? We don't have to kill Miles off, but we don't have to sign him up for any more classes either."

"Yeah, we could just have him appear in print and win a few more prizes," said Fred. "Problem is, I'm losing my job over in Admin at the end of next trimester. I've applied for the Spring in Italy Program, if things quiet down."

"Think big, boys!" Andy chimed in, his voice rising as he lifted his stein. "In Fred's honor I nominate Miles for Student Senate! I will be his campaign manager. You will be his lackeys. The election is in March. That gives us ten or eleven weeks!"

"One question, please," asked Lew. "What do we do if he wins?"

After Thanksgiving break, Fred slipped a letter into Miles' master file that confirmed his appointment for the next three months off-campus, studying in the laboratory of Dr. Chris Bernard, an obscure South African heart researcher at the Health Sciences Center downtown. Miles would not have to take any classes, but his student status remained secure. By the time Miles and his mentor had to submit their report for Miles to receive academic credit, we would have other plans for him. The nice thing about this was that any active student could run for a campus-wide elective office.

The hot-button issues in late 1962 concerned Vietnam. The "Domino Theory," which had to do with the spread of Communism, the deployment of nearly 12,000 U.S. "advisers" overseas, and The Draft made headlines every day. We wanted to kick the ROTC off our campus and ban military recruiters. But the biggest issues of all were Alcohol and Sex. We could not even have beer in our rooms. And we could not invite members of the opposite sex above the first-floor reception areas of our dorms. Patriotism and vice made potent bedfellows.

5. A New Face

By now you must think that none of us had much of a social life, what with my rambling on about Miles. But we had our flings. I admit I had been "between girlfriends" for the past six months, having been unceremoniously dumped by the lovely Mindy, who was now engaged to the son of our former mayor. I'll take you on a little detour, and we'll return to Miles in a few minutes.

So here I am, seated alone in the Rathskeller, after Lew, Andy, and Fred left me to ponder the next "big idea" to arrive out of Andy's perverse brain and to drown my increasing anxiety about wanting, or being able, to pull it off. I nurse the dregs of my beer and burger and look around the gloom. The Rat, in the basement of the Old Student Union, is one of those dark, dingy, noisy student hangouts I'm sure you've seen, but despite the chatter and churning of hordes of humanity, it's a good place to sit and think. I'm comforted by low beamed ceilings and hanging chandeliers shaped like wagon wheels with little bulbs around the circumference, half of them burned out, that cast a yellow glow on the heavy oak tables flanked by long wooden benches set up picnic-style. It smells of cigarettes, grease, sweat, and old beer, but to us it's home.

I'd seen her before, crossing the Quad with several of her friends: tall, hugging a heavy stack of books and papers to her chest. Something about her walk, the way she held herself, the easy way she tossed her head with that long, shiny black Joan Baez hair when she laughed; for a moment she was the only girl on the Quad. Then she was gone. Now she's at the far end of my table, not twenty feet from me, and I can see she's the most beautiful girl I have ever laid my starved eyes upon. A perfect oval face. Slightly olive skin. Light reflecting off her straight hair. And from this distance I know she's been crying.

I do what any sensitive, empathetic young male would do; I pick up my things and slide down the bench to her end of the table.

"Not having the best day, are you?" I say in my most sincere voice. I have to resist the urge to take the tip of my finger and wipe away a tear by her left eye. Instead, I hand her my slightly used napkin.

"You wouldn't understand," she murmurs, a little catch in her throat.

I'm thinking I've just seen a face I can't forget, and that someone should make a song lyric out of someday. I know that yes, yes, I could understand, if only you would let me. Wednesday, December 19, 1962, 2:15 p.m., The Rathskeller. I am in love.

6. Her Name Is Tanya

If you think love at first sight is just something you read about, let me reassure you that it kayoed me that afternoon in December. Who was she? And why the tears?

The first part is easiest. Her name was Tanya. Tanya Piriak. Russian background. Ukrainian, actually. She came from Monessen, then a smoky steel town in Western Pennsylvania. Her father emigrated just before WWII. It was "get out or wind up in one of Stalin's gulags in Siberia." He found work on a blastfurnace and over the years became a foreman. Tanya was the oldest of seven children. She was like a second mother. They lived in a little house with one bathroom and two bedrooms, plus an attic with mattresses on the floor. There was one school in the town and from the first day her teachers knew Tanya was gifted.

She taught herself to read by age three; by first grade she was well ahead of her class. She skipped a grade somewhere along the way and graduated from high school at sixteen as valedictorian. She was also Miss Monongahela Valley, 1960. She sang solos in the choir and played flute in the orchestra. She was the first in her family to go to college and was a brilliant student. Her eyes were focused on law school, a career in international law.

I knew none of this at the time. All I knew right then, as I sat beside her on the bench in the Rat and watched her try to stop crying, was that it felt as if I were falling headfirst into a deep pool of warm, sweet liquid. Swimming in it. I was hooked. And I didn't know what to do.

"Hey, look at me," I said. I climbed up on the table, stuck a French Fry in each nostril, and did a little tap dance, ending upon one knee, with my arms flung out to each side. "Ta-daa!"

To my amazement, her eyes opened wide, and I saw a little smile at the corners of her mouth. Slowly, the smile grew wider, and I heard a laugh. And what a beautiful laugh, like music filling the hall.

"You're funny," were her fourth and fifth words to me, and I knew I was going to keep on being funny to this beautiful sad girl with the shiny black hair. As I walked her back to her apartment, I kept making stupid jokes. She giggled at most of them, until she just said, "Oh, stop it," and took my hand in hers. We walked the rest of the way in near silence, the only sound our footfalls on the dark pavement.

What troubled Tanya so deeply, in December 1962, was a sign of things to come, for all of us, including Miles.

7. The Trouble with Tanya

Tanya's first words to me had been "You wouldn't understand," and she was right. But I tried. I wanted to know her sorrow. As we sat in her tiny apartment that night in December, she told me the story, which involved her "twin" brother. You remember that she was the oldest of seven children. Well, to her mother's surprise, she became pregnant again about six weeks after Tanya's birth. Mikhail was exactly nine months and twenty-six days younger, but the two of them were known as "the twins." They were inseparable, almost able to read each other's minds. They spoke a secret twin language. Tanya and Mike even looked alike and, as they grew older, most people thought they were real twins.

In 1962 Mike was one of the 100,000-plus young men drafted into the armed services of the good ol' USA, if you'll pardon the cliche. A few of these, including Mike, woke up to find themselves in Southeast Asia, as "advisers" to the government of South Vietnam, fighting in a little civil war. Sad to say, on October 15 in a miserable hamlet named Buon Enao, his helicopter was shot down by the Viet Cong, exploding on impact, killing the pilot and several crew, who were among the thirty Americans who died in Vietnam that year, a ripple in what would become a tsunami. Mike was not one of them. He was listed as "Missing In Action."

Tanya's family received the telegram and phone call from the Army in December. Tanya rushed home to be with her grieving parents and siblings and to await further news. She had just returned to campus the afternoon I saw her, alone and crying, at the far end of my table in the Rathskeller.

"You wouldn't understand" (you, the clown, the peacenik, the draft resister, comfortable with your deferment, your safety assured, as you stage your feeble protests against a war you know so little about).

What a naive fool I was. Weren't we all, in a way, innocent children going about our business while events far away assembled, piece by piece, the makings of a great tragedy that changed everything, even to this day? Here was my first brush with the war, the first person I knew with a family member involved. Mike, given slightly different circumstances, could just as well have been me.

I introduced Tanya to Miles. Naturally, she thought our brain-child was the most ridiculous frat-boy-type stunt and waste of time. She was headed for some very serious times, and I knew that I was too. I realized then that Miles would have to fade away, for there would not be room for him any longer. I felt like a repentant mobster, promising "one more job, and then it's over."

8. Miles Sneaks In

It's early January and the campaign for Student Senate is heating up. We have had time to think about strategy and logistics over the holiday break. There are twenty-three candidates for the sixteen one-year terms, with two consecutive terms allowed. Of the twenty-three, eight are incumbents, who rarely lose, so Miles is, for all practical purposes, running against fourteen other first-timers. Our job is to give him enough exposure to win the few hundred votes that will be enough. I hope I made that clear enough!

While home in upstate New York, Andy wrote ten "position papers" to use for letters to the editor, flyers, and other publications over the next two months. Subjects range from the onerous military presence on our campus to the lack of freedom in our dorms (no alcohol), and to our retrogressive policy of single-sex living, with no members of the opposite sex allowed upstairs. We end all of our promotions with "Miles Ahead with Miles: Swoboda For Senate!" We do all the printing after hours in the basement of the Admin Building, using paper that Fred steals from the offices he cleans.

January is very cold. On the twenty-third it's eighteen below zero, with snow. The arctic snap continues for a month, making life very difficult, confining us indoors most of the time, and the short days and long nights make campaigning about the last thing we want to do, when it strikes us that adversity could create a great opportunity for Miles.

We invent the "Miles Says:" poster. Trees, bulletin boards, and lampposts all over campus sprout bright yellow placards that announce, "Miles Says: Huddle with a Friend!" Within days, we began to see groups of students walking together, arms linked or around each other, in twos and threes and sometimes fours, trudging through the wind and snow, keeping warm. Soon, everyone seems to be doing it. Try it! It works!

Next we post "Miles Says: Next Year, Shower with a Friend!" which slightly exaggerated our co-ed dorm and opposite sex visitor theme, but everybody got the message. I was most proud of "Miles Says: Please Please Me!" which, in case you don't remember, was the title of a popular song that came out that frigid February by a new band from England named, you guessed it, the Beatles. It didn't seem so strange that no one ever actually saw Miles Q. Swoboda.

March arrived, and with it election day. After all the votes were counted. Miles won his seat in the Student Senate. He was sixteenth out of twenty-three, by the narrowest margin edging out a fifth-year junior with the ironic name of Joe Book, famous for earning a prodigious number of credits, just not enough in any single course of study to get close to a college degree.

If the story seems anticlimactic, that's exactly the cloud that enveloped me, as I brought the news to Tanya, with "What do we do if he wins?" in my thoughts. Oh, the gorgeous Springtime of 1963! After the record-setting winter, an explosion of color and fragrance reinforced the fresh breezes off The Lake and Tanya's fingers intertwined with mine. We were in for a surprise.

9. MILES WRITES A LETTER

THE DAILY COLLEGIAN
Friday, April 19, 1963

Letter To The Editor:

Dear Sir: I announce my resignation of my seat in next year's Student Senate for personal reasons. Mr. Book, who will fill the vacancy, has ample experience and capability. He will make an excellent representative. I want to thank my supporters for their recent votes. I have enlisted in the United States Marine Corps. It has been my long-time dream. After completing my basic training, I will volunteer for duty in Vietnam in order to improve the plight of people who suffer under a repressive government and to protect the peace. Good-bye, Semper Fi!
Miles Q. Swoboda, Senator-at-large.

"Oh, that is so-o lame! Who do you think will buy it?" said Lew, in agony.

"Maybe, the more unbelievable, the better. At least, that's what I figured."

"So you did this all on your own. Nice. And where were *we*?"

"Don't tell me you want to continue this farce. Remember whose idea it was in the first place."

It was my decision to send Miles away. We could not keep up the ruse much longer. I sensed exposure getting closer every day. Our little quartet had played well for nearly a year and no one wanted to end on a discordant note, so we celebrated with champagne, seated around a little bonfire in the fireplace in Tanya's living room, but not before Fred made sure to collect all of Miles' official files from the Dean's cabinet. We toasted each other as we fed the flames to guarantee nothing remained of Miles Swoboda, at least as far as the Administration was concerned, except ash. When they came looking on Monday morning, as we knew they should, where would they go?

That is exactly what happened. There was no way to associate any one of us with Miles. No one came forward to report that Lew or I had nailed up all those posters. No one remembered when Miles' essays and other homework assignments appeared in the professors' boxes. In truth, we never learned whether the appearance or disappearance of our boy wonder caused anyone in our Administration to lose sleep. If there was an investigation, it was internal. Perhaps something good came out of it, in terms of better record keeping. I don't want to speculate.

Tanya read every report on the deteriorating situation in Vietnam; she began to know officials in the Defense Department on a first name basis because of her steady stream of letters inquiring about Mike. No one knew anything more. Meanwhile, Buddhist nuns and monks, some of them teenagers, were setting themselves on fire on the evening news. At the same time, freedom marchers ran into fire hoses and police dogs down South. Medgar Evers was murdered. Martin Luther King was jailed. Many of our classmates got on buses and drove into harm's way. All this on TV, all the time.

10. AFTERSHOCKS

1963 did not get better. I know how you and your friends are struggling. I don't minimize what's happening in the world today. But 1963! The March On Washington. I Have A Dream. Then JFK. Oswald. Ruby. I could cry. I am crying! If we didn't have Miles, and if Tanya hadn't been with me, '62-'63 would have been a total catastrophe. Thank God for them! Of course, I tell your grandmother that Tanya was my second most passionate love! Let me go on.

I moved back home for the summer. Your great-uncle Charlie had saved a good job for me in his fortune cookie bakery. I made about $1000 during the break! Fred went to Italy. Lew and Andy went home also; I didn't hear from either of them until the Fall. Tanya stayed in the city, where she worked as a clerk in a big law firm. I came to town a few times to see her, not as often as I wanted, but each time we took up where we left off, as if we had never been separated at all.

I rented an apartment off-campus in August. One of the first things I did was go to the college post office to check for mail from school. There was one letter in my box. This is the strange part, the really strange part: it was postmarked the month before, July 10. And it came from: "MCRD Parris Island, South Carolina," followed by the numbers 29905.

> Dear Mickey,
> Well, it's July Fourth and I am officially 17, although I tell everyone here I'm a year older. Basic is TOUGH, but you would be surprised to see me now. I have muscles! My DI, Gunny Hechler, expected me to wash out, but I guess I showed him. Perseverance! Plus a little help from my buddies. Anyway, just wanted to tell you that I'll likely be sent out West to Pendleton, and I hope soon after that to a post in Vietnam. I know that surprises you. Good luck to the guys back home. And how's that Tanya? I'll try to write again soon.
> Semper Fi,
> Miles (Ret Swoboda 1332990456)

I'm glad I was sitting down, because I nearly fell off my chair. I know what you're thinking. But who? I tracked down Lew and Andy. From the looks on their faces, I knew they were innocent. Fred? Not likely. Tanya had nothing to do with it. She was busy packing! She was leaving! Her family needed her to be closer to home, and she wanted to transfer to Pitt, which had a good law school. Would there be a third shock on my first day back in school?

Over the next three months our long distance love affair slowly starved. I made the difficult journey to Pittsburgh several times and felt deflated. By the end of November we admitted that we must move on. One last kiss, one last clasp of her fingers in mine, and I returned to the city. As if I didn't feel bad enough, there was a second letter in my mailbox from MCB Camp Pendleton, California.

11. Two Unsolved Mysteries

> Dear Mickey!
> Well, I'm here. Sunny California. I made Lance Corporal! They think I'm officer material, except for my age. That's not for me! I'm

studying Vietnamese! What a language! We're going to be in some small villages. I can't say more. I haven't spoken to my parents or written them. They kind of slammed the door on me when I told them I was enlisting. If anything happens to me, I want you to take some things of mine to them in Mays. Would you? I know you will. You're a good friend.
Semper Fi,
Miles

I ran to the bathroom and vomited into the toilet. What in the hell was going on? Who was doing this? We didn't know what to do. There was nobody to ask or tell. No way to track the source. We suspected everyone, but we never found out. Fortunately, the letters stopped. We went on with our lives. We graduated. And we went our own very different ways.

Lew, our mathematician, loved sports and lettered in baseball and basketball. He had a growth spurt in his early twenties, reaching 6 feet 6 inches tall. He was a walk-on for the Kentucky Colonels of the old American Basketball Association, playing for them during their heyday from 1967 to 1976, when they were the winningest team in the ABA, but then he tore up his knee and retired to become a coach. Lew roomed with Bill Bradley. Senator Bill Bradley. He married and quickly fathered two girls. Lucky Lew avoided the war. He died three years ago.

Andy got a Master's at the writing program at Iowa and scored a job with The New Yorker magazine. He married a girl in the circulation department and lived in SoHo. He had one of those "innocent" heart murmurs from childhood and escaped the draft, but he stepped off a curb on 42nd street on his way to the Library, right in front of a cross-town bus. Sad.

Fred went to Dental School in Chicago. After his deferment ran out he got sent to a medical battalion near Da Nang. He survived the war, came home to a lucrative practice, and married his office manager 43 years ago. They're still together, but poor Fred had to go to a nursing home last year when he started wandering off, sometimes in the middle of the night.

Tanya practiced law in Pittsburgh, rising to Assistant District Attorney of Allegheny County. She married, then divorced, married again, divorced that guy too, and raised one beautiful daughter, who is now in college. Tanya is an important figure in The American-Ukrainian Commission, which gives her a chance to travel over there to teach in their law schools and advise their government. Despite all her efforts, her family never learned any more about the fate of their MIA, Mike.

12. The Clinic

"Excuse me, Dr. Wing, but you wanted me to remind you when it's time for dinner. They're going in now. And William, would you mind stepping into my office before you leave?"

The tall young man with the short stylish beard clicked the door behind him and stood beside the Director's desk.

"These hallucinations are progressing pretty rapidly, as I'm sure you've noticed since your last visit."

"He can't be making it all up, can he, doctor?"

"It's so hard to tell. But we have a post-doc working with several of our patients, including your grandfather. She's been all over the country, interviewing people, tracking down leads. There'll be a paper out soon. Bottom line is, we can't document the existence of any of the folks Dr. Wing talks about. There are no records over at State of any of them! No basketball player. No New Yorker writer. No dentist. And no Tanya Piriak. No Piriak family in Monessen, Pennsylvania, and no MIA from Vietnam named Piriak. As for Miles Swoboda, well…"

"So what do we do?"

"I wish we had more options. There are some new drugs in the pipeline. Nothing ready now, though. Keep him safe and happy. Your visits really help. The hell of it is, these hallucinations are a sign of worsening Alzheimer's. It may get very bad. Soon. It's hard to watch. I love the guy. Did you know he was my Professor?"

Mickey Wing, M.D., former Chairman of Neurology at the Neuropsychiatric Institute of Illinois, looked in the mirror and straightened his bow tie. He ran his comb through his thin white hair and buttoned the middle button of his well-tailored blue blazer. He opened the small left-hand drawer of his dresser, removed a plaid pocket silk, folded it and placed it in his upper left jacket pocket, with just the top of the triangle showing. Reaching all the way to the back of the drawer, he withdrew a rolled-up black sock. From the toe of the sock he took a worn yellow envelope, addressed to him, but also, if one could read it, printed in a foreign alphabet. He opened the little package and shook a bright object into the open palm of his hand. It was a ring.

An oval ruby-red birthstone set in 14K yellow gold encircled by the words, "UNITED STATES MARINES," comprised the face of the man's ring. On one side he read, "TUN TAVERN, 1775." On the other was, "IWO JIMA 1945." Inside the band, around the full circumference, in capital letters: "SEMPER FI...M. SWOBODA...1963."

He kissed the ring, placed it back in the envelope, folded it neatly and returned it to the toe of the sock, which he rolled and pushed to the back of the drawer. Then he walked out of his room to join the others at the dinner table, but when he sat down he no longer remembered what he was doing there or who they were.

List of Materials Contained

John Barbee

Six years ago, I attempted to record a few stories about the adventure of raising our eight children. The attempt was a total failure so I took a class, read a few books on the subject, and tried again. Still not satisfied, I joined a writers' group, made some great new friends, and with their help started to make some progress. As my work got better, storytelling became fun, I became more interested, and then writing became a fulltime hobby. Writing became a bigger and bigger part of my life, until I became addicted.

Over the following years I have written about three hundred stories… some of which have even started to show a little promise. No one will ever ask for my autograph or pay me any money for my work, and there are no writing awards in my future. But I am happy to muddle along the way things are. My friends have helped a lot with grammar, punctuation, and the many other parts of good writing. There is, however, one problem I have yet to overcome, and neither my friends nor books have been able to help me with it: the dreaded fiction or nonfiction category choice.

At first glance it seems simple: it's the truth, or it's not. Fiction stories entertain and are 100% made up…right? But they are not; everyone knows you write best about things you know. We model our characters on people we have known, and then use places we've been and the experiences in our lives. How many true parts can we add to a fiction story before it becomes nonfiction?

On the other hand, when writing a nonfiction tale, we leave out things that do not help the story, and we add half-truths. We rearrange events, polish facts, then add a few odds and ends to make a good story. How much can we change a nonfiction narrative before it becomes fiction?

I have given this a lot of thought and think I may have come up with the answer. Referencing the clothing business, I suggest we steal our idea from the tags they sew in shirts, and change them to suit our needs. It would go something like this:

Contains
83% untruths
15% facts
2% unknown material

Made in Nuevo
Dry clean only
Do not wash

No writer was permanently injured in the creation of this story!

A Lesson Learned

Rosemary Bennett

After all these years, I wouldn't call myself a spring chicken anymore. Indeed, I have come to anticipate and relish a good night's sleep. However, the other evening I found myself wide awake, deep in thought, and feeling just a tad dreary. It was nearly midnight, and I had just realized that I've had more than one experience of being on the wrong side of a half truth.

Looking back, I wish I had been smarter and more critical. I wish I had been quite saintly and practically perfect. But, as we know, those wishes fly past us, and we are stuck with the reality of our own shortcomings. Without divulging the downright dumb and really ridiculous details, I will say that, many years ago, I was conned. I believed what I should not have believed, and I did not do a complete check of a particular story. The consequences of my actions were just as the con artist planned: I lost a lot of money, which led to losing my house, my confidence, my self-esteem, and (so I thought) the love and support of my sister and brothers. Yet there were also unintended consequences: through the love and support of my sister and brothers, I learned to forgive myself, to fight for myself legally, and to downsize a lot of the extra baggage in my life. I learned to appreciate each new day, and I began to believe in myself once more. The bad guy is just a bad guy—nothing more. And I am determined to keep moving forward.

Having discovered this new knowledge, I am much more careful now. Would I let this happen again? "No! Nevermore!"

Questions for Juan Gonzales

Maurice Hirsch

"Call this number immediately,
ask for Miss Miller. You have outstanding
debt. Your call may be monitored and recorded,"
then the mobile phone message
gives an 866 number. I call.
A recorded voice says: "This call will
be monitored and recorded
for compliance reasons," then "Your call
is important to us, please stay on the line
for the next…" interrupted
by a woman who asks: "Juan Gonzales?
You aren't Juan Gonzales?
But this is his number.
Oh, I'm sorry. We'll correct our records."

Juan, where are you and what have you done?
I've gotten a dozen calls
since inheriting your phone number.
Are you a victim or a perpetrator?
Are you legal? Are you still around?
What trail of bills
leads to all these messages?
Juan, who the hell are you?
Call me. You know the number.

Honorable Mention

Ode to a Kerosene Lamp

Una Nichols Hynum

Your globe, soot black
from the last burning,
gleams when we wash
off layers of dust.
Your wick still soaked
in oil catches fire casually
doesn't leap from the wooden
match. Old reliable, your steady
flame is not romantic
like a candle shivering,
it's more like a cat purring.
One yellow eye unlocks
the dark but leaves corners
in shadow inviting ghost stories.
You are the lamp of my childhood
the one we read by. Our whole life
was reflected in your light repeated
on our faces, in our eyes.
You were not just for storms.
When we got electricity
Dad turned the switch on only
long enough to find a match.

Chili-pepper Hot

David Braun

The sky was crystal-clear blue. It was hot, a searing, dry hot, one of the hottest days in recent memory, maybe the hottest. The town of Manuel Ojinaga, Mexico is across the Rio Bravo from Presidio, Texas, which is north of the river, the Rio Grande, as it's called in America. The people of this region were accustomed to hot summers, but not like this one.

Juan was sitting in an old rocking chair on the wooden porch of a dilapidated old adobe building that had been built in several stages and styles. In earlier days, the building had had more than one use. A "Cantina" sign still hung above the entrance. Another sign over a door said "Tienda"—rough translation, "General Store." An ancient, rusty hitching post stood unattended next to the warped wooden steps.

For decades, the place had been the only drinking spot for several kilometers in any direction on that side of the border. Over the years the area had developed more modern structures, not so modern, however, that some of the buildings weren't painted the various standard pastels or earth tones typical of Mexico. There were other stores and cantinas now, but some of the older citizens—mostly grizzly old men—still came here for their cerveza (beer) out of habit.

Until about ten or so years ago, the street had been sand and rock and dirt. Now it was paved with asphalt, but still very dusty. Juan was now the sole owner of the place, so he was the one who muttered to himself about how hot it was. Juan was old, his skin dark, scaly, and leathery, what was left of his long hair stiff and gray. He was almost as dilapidated as the building. He looked as if he had been through many trials, but he also wore a slyly cheerful mien.

Juan was having an imaginary conversation in Spanish. He seemed to be talking to the air. He said, "Its hotter than a chili-pepper…hotter than quince habaneros. If I were to stick my tongue out into the air, it would sizzle;

it would shrivel up and turn to sand. I myself am becoming well cooked... all my juices are leaving me...rack of cabrito turning on an open fire...that's what I am...." He mumbled on and on, occasionally taking a long drink from the Carta Blanca in his hand.

Pete came up on his blind side and said, "Crazy old man...esta loco en la cabeza," meaning "crazy in the head." Pete was a tan young man in shorts, wearing a light blue cotton sports shirt. On his head was a blue baseball cap with the white outline of a Dallas Cowboy star. Pete wiped his forehead with a damp hand towel. He lived in San Antonio, but was visiting his great uncle, Juan, before the beginning of the fall semester at the University of Texas. Pete's Spanish was rudimentary and certainly limited, so Juan, who was more bilingual, talked in a sort of patois called "Tex-Mex" when he conversed with Pete, speaking first in Spanish, then translating himself to English.

Juan didn't miss a beat. "This reminds me of that day, when was it...I was just quarenta y quatro, forty-four. I am now setenta y quatro: seventy four...it must have been sesenta y quatro años hace: twenty-four years ago. Mi abuelo, my uncle, he built this con su hermano with his brother. My grandfather, he ran the cantina, and my great uncle, he ran the store. Now what was I telling you? Oh, si, that was when Jesus got himself killed and almost got Magdalena killed with him." Juan fell silent, as if considering what he was saying, then said, "Sientarse, sit." He gestured to another rocking chair, reached into an ice chest, and handed Pete a beer.

"Tome una cerveza (drink a beer)," he ordered.

Pete accepted the beer and said, "Yeah, I remember someone telling me something about that story...maybe my mom. I don't remember much about it, though. I wish she were still alive."

Juan looked at Pete quizzically. "So you could ask her?"

Pete withdrew into himself for a minute, then said, "Well, yes, but also, I still miss her after all these years. She was like a mother to me."

Juan took a deep breath and glanced quickly at Pete. "Well, I've got nothing but time on my hands. Sit down, mi hijo, and listen. Ahora, Jesus was a 'chico molestada'...how do they say that...he was abused, had many problemas. His father was a borracho; he drank the beer and the tequila all the time. Que mas, worse, he was a mean drunk. He hit the mother and Jesus and anyone else around. He finally died when Jesus was young...

quando crecio sus primeras barbas…when he grew his first, how you say…beard whiskers. His mother, Maria, ella era muy pobre, they were very poor, so Jesus, él debe trabajar, he had to work. He did not like the school anyway, so he went off with the vaqueros, cowboys, to the North for the cattle drive. He could ride, so he could make some dinero for him and his mother. And she did todas las clases de cosas…you know, all kinds of things…to feed her family.

"The second time Jesus came back from the drive, he came here to the cantina and started drinking. He know Magdalena all her life. She was helping at the cantina for dinero. He always love her and want to marry her. She was…well, she like him…pero…tenía miedo, he was wild and she was afraid. So they talk at the cantina, but she did not go with him.

"One night, he got into a fight with some other vaqueros borrachos, you know, drunk cowboys. They fight, Jesus pulled a cuchillo, a knife, and killed one of them. He rode over to the casa of a friend and hid out. But he missed Magdalena and sneaked out one night to the cantina to see her. One of the other vaqueros saw him, and a posse was organized. Jesus found out and he and Magdalena rode out of town into el desierto de Chihuahua, the desert. I do not know why she would go with him, but they found an old shack, and that night they sleep on the floor. Then they ride far the next day, but the posse was fast.

"They caught them that night just as the sun go down. Jesus shot at them, and they saw the flash of his pistola and shot back. Before he die, pero tell Magdalena to shoot them. She made one shot, and they shot her in her hand, but she don't die. She scream and cry like a girl and lay her pistola down. She tell them Jesus is dead. So they take her to the Presidio, and they help her find a doctor.

"Then they take her back to Ojinaga. Then she grow up…fast. Later, she tell me the story. Todos. How I say this? I just tell you. That night in the shack, Jesus made you with your mother. They make the love. Magdalena was not your sister; she was your mother. The one you call 'Mama,' she is your grandmother. Jesus esta tu papa…"

Juan fell into a long silence. After a while he asked, "Quieres otra cerveza? Aqui." Juan took two more bottles from his ice chest. "Aqui." They both took long swallows and the silence continued for a while as they studied the boards under them.

Pete looked up. "Juan, did she say anything else. What all happened? I can't understand why she would have gone off with him like that. I mean, her knowing what kind of guy he was and she had to figure they'd be shooting at him and all…." He trailed off, a bewildered look on his face. He took another swallow of his beer.

Juan drank, too. He looked up with a gentle smile. "Yes, I asked her the same questions. She told me a lot. I told you she knew him from when she was young. He was always in trouble. I guess that is one thing she liked about him. She was very proper, and Jesus let her be a little wild. She said he was mostly nice to her. When they were younger, he said to her they should run away together. When she be adolescente, una niña bonita…she grow up pretty…he was romantic with her. There were not many other young men her age in the area so he was almost all she had. When he talked to her that night about running with him, she was feeling low; she was bored. She went with him without she think about it.

"I ask her once, and she say when they were sleeping in that shack, he say many things to her like, 'Tú eres mi corazón' y 'Dios nos vigila' and 'God is watching over us'…I do not know; she think he romantic; maybe she wants to love him or something. I think he wild-crazy. You not like him, not the same…" Juan was quiet for a while, trying to remember what Magdalena had told him.

Pete also remained silent, then asked, "What else did she say? She never told me anything about this, and now she's gone…I don't know…I have so many questions only she could answer. Nobody else has…they sound sort of like Bonnie and Clyde."

Juan looked up, a puzzled expression on his face. "Who? Never mind. She said he talked about robbing for money, but she say she not ride with him if he did. Jesus didn't rob, so she had to stay with him. Then they catch up to them. That was the end him…of them. But look at you now, you a good man, a student, a good son. She was a good mother; she would be proud of you now."

Folklore at Its Best

Jack Campbell

It was the mid-1930s and the great depression was in full stride. Many folks were dirt poor in a day to day struggle. Most of them hung in by planting big back yard vegetable gardens, fruit trees, and maintaining a yard full of chickens. They would can and preserve fruits and vegetables to sustain themselves during the long winter months, a dire necessity back then, a mere page in *Arts and Crafts* today. The fruit harvest would find the womenfolk boiling huge pots of apples or plums on outdoor fires to be sealed in jars as plum butter and jams. A lost art, to say the least! A home-grown oven-roasted or fried chicken would pretty much serve as Sunday's dinner.

As a pre-teen, I was able to navigate the whole town, keeping an eye out for any chance of earning a buck doing chores for the needy. Any tidbits of town gossip I might gather on those travels were unwittingly gleaned from me by my mother, an expert at interrogation. Looking back, it became apparent how the gossip chain worked. I would tell my mom what I had seen or heard that day. If it was juicy enough, she in turn would put it in the pipeline for further distribution. With each family unit in town privy to that same pipeline…well, you get the gist!

I must have been about ten years old when I first became aware of the existence of the mysterious "Fast Annie." She was rumored to walk the town in the wee hours for equally mysterious reasons. I don't remember ever having an encounter with her, but there were plenty of folks who had and were more than happy to enlighten any and all with their harrowing experiences.

Some thirty years after I left that small town, I returned to bury my widowed mother. I had difficulty recognizing some people, while others were seemingly unchanged. At the home reception after the funeral, while chatting with my old school chum, Mel White, I made a tongue-in-cheek inquiry about the current status of the mythical Fast Annie. I was astounded when he assured me she was still up to her old tricks. I was almost fifty years old and estimated that Fast Annie had to be in her seventies or eighties by now, maybe more.

He went on to explain how Arnold Heil saw her disappear down the alley behind Werner's Bakery just last week with Al Dyke's rake. Arnold admitted to the sighting as he turned around to face us both. He was nodding his head in agreement, proclaiming that he damn well would have caught her, too, if it hadn't been for his game leg from WWII. I smiled and suppressed the urge to pursue the subject any further, patting Mel and Arnold on the shoulder and thanking them for coming. I melted into the crowd and proceeded to the kitchen, making myself a whiskey-water from bottles I had provided for those so inclined.

Drink in hand, I walked into my mother's bedroom and quietly closed the door. I sat on the foot of her bed, looking up at a picture of her on her wedding day.

It had hung in that same spot ever since I could remember. She always said, it was the best picture ever taken of her, and I agreed. I raised my glass to her with a smile, and then let the whiskey and memories of this fine woman warm me through. My last real contact with this town was now gone forever, and I knew I would never return.

I freshened my drink and headed for the porch swing, a likely place to ponder the myth of Fast Annie, who apparently was still as much a part of this town as the bell on top of the old Baptist church. Recalling Annie's history, you might discover you were missing those first ripe tomatoes of the season, the ones you intended to pick the next day. You could be missing a hoe, a rake, or your morning milk delivery might be one bottle short. All petty items to be sure, but annoying and mystifying enough to maintain a myth that has lasted through the years.

It would appear as if my hometown had created its own folklore and continued to cling to it rather than believe any of its neighbors capable of pilfering from one another. The description of this phantom relied entirely on fleeting eyewitness accounts from various townsfolk. And, like all good folklore, the tale was embellished as it passed from mouth to ear. So, basically, we're dealing with a woman (hopefully mortal), ageless and always dressed in a black hood and cape, with a rap sheet that reads like a pack rat. She pilfers whatever strikes her fancy, while existing in the same town for most of the years of my life and possibly beyond.

Doctor Harry Davis, who had taken care of my mother, joined me on the porch swing with a smile and a final condolence. He had heard me quizzing Mel White about the latest deeds of Fast Annie and felt, since I was leaving town anyway, he would make me privy to a secret he had kept, lo, these many years.

It seems that Sheriff Luther Dunbar, on his death bed, had indeed confessed to the good doctor that he invented the myth of Fast Annie out of necessity. After jailing a couple of neighbors overnight for quarreling over a petty theft, he got the idea while getting a haircut and started it right there and then.

"It was easy," the sheriff told the doc. "I would go on about chasing a shadowy figure late at night down various alleys around town, but never quite catching up." At any gabfest, be it lunchroom, church, or play, he would yak it up about this mysterious night thief. The town took it from there. A name, description, and gender soon evolved with sightings most nights in some part of town.

Doc Davis appeared slightly relieved after his confession, and I thanked him for his confidence, promising to take his secret to my grave.

Driving out of town the next day, nothing but pleasant memories followed in my wake. Haunting flashbacks occurred as I passed by streets and places that, indeed, had been my childhood. As the pièce de résistance, it somehow pleased me to know my hometown will be no worse off pursuing Fast Annie into a few more generations.

What the hell, isn't that what folklore is all about?

Not What They Seem

Maurice Hirsch

Like a field of shriveled, discarded pumpkins,
large gray stones lie on the rich brown loam,
basketball to hardball size, strewn
as if rained from the sky,
or scattered by some errant seeding.
Amidst lush Wisconsin corn and pasture,
the field seems
like a giant art installation, one part
natural, one part out of place.
I feel a cold sweat on the back of my neck,
sense the *Invasion of the Body Snatchers*,
wonder if I have just seen
the first set of pods,
and will be dead by morning.

Moxon's Masterpiece: An Alternate History

Neal Wilgus

> *Can such things be?*
> —Ambrose Bierce

I

Yes, I am Herbert Haley, the one accused of leading the rebellion against Dr. Moxon's malevolent machines. I am also charged with the actual murder of Moxon on that stormy night in 1870, but I proclaim my innocence. My only role in that unfortunate incident was that of a rescuer, for I was the one who entered Moxon's burning house and pulled Professor Clive Denneker from the flamss.

To my knowledge Prof. Denneker was the only person other than Moxon and myself to enter the machine-shop where Moxon's analytical engine was kept. I was a metal worker and handyman, a local laborer whose family had once worked at the Moxon estate in its heyday several decades before. I was hired as his assistant by Moxon when he learned of my extensive knowledge of Babbage's mechanical calculator in England. Because of my work with boilers and steam engines, I was more Moxon's partner than a mere workman, but this was never acknowledged.

Yes, I did feel some resentment because of Moxon's lack of appreciation for my contributions, but I did have a genuine respect and affection for the old man and even fancied myself something of a bodyguard or watchdog for the poor fellow. So, when the eccentric Prof. Denneker began his visits and the two spent hours sitting before the fireplace discussing philosophical issues, I began to linger around the grounds instead of returning to my lonely rooms in the village. At times, it is true, I managed to listen at the window and eavesdrop on their conversations, but this was only to assure myself that Moxon was safe.

Curiously, Moxon said nothing in their talks about the mechanical calulator on which we were working. Instead, they debated endlessly about the nature and meaning of life, and I must confess there were times when I drifted off or left the window and returned to my abode. I rather resented that Moxon never introduced me to Denneker, and it didn't help that the philosophy professor rarely acknowledged my existence.

Something else Moxon never mentioned to Denneker, as far as I know, were the various writing projects that Moxon called his "scribblings." He kept notes on all his experiments and inventions, as well as a personal diary and a manuscript of something he called DEAD LETTERS. This last he allowed me to look at from time to time, saying it was akin to the mysterious Roger Bacon Cipher Script and was perhaps a record of the Great Old Ones of ancient myth. I understood nothing of the LETTERS, but did enjoy his ramblings about unexplained disappearances and his theory of Rhythm.

Even before the advent of Prof. Denneker, I had begun having doubts about Moxon's thinking machine, as he called it, for it seemed an impossible dream that, should it come true, would surely lead to disaster. Suppose that machine-brain were placed into some sort of mechanical man that could walk and talk and perform all the actions now done by we mere mortals? Such creatures, if I may call them such, would not need food or drink or sleep or, most importantly, money. What, then, would we do for jobs to bring us the worldly goods that never come free?

Not long before that fateful night when Moxon met his end, I fell asleep at my place beside the window where the two learned thinkers sat by the fire bloviating. And soon I had ths first of the dreams that have haunted me ever since. Yes, that cursed dream of a steam-driven world where the Automen, as I came to call them, ran everything while those of us who still survived lived in the shadows and fought an endless war against our metallic twins.

In the dream I led the underground forces that secretly raided the command centers of the Automen, and in desperation used explosives to destroy their factories and fortresses. At first I was startled and repelled by what was becoming a recurring nightmare, but the more we worked on the Thinking Man during the day and entertained Denneker each night, the more real those dreams seemed. It was then I began to accumulate weapons and ammunition in preparation for a future I feared might be on us sooner than any could imagine.

Yes, I was preparing for war against Moxon's masterpiece, but I bore no ill will against him, and even Prof. Denneker could be amusing from time to time. Moxon carelessly left his copy of Denneker's MEDITATIONS in a place where I could read parts of it from time to time, but its strange ramblings meant little to me and had no real impact an my thoughts of rebellion. Some considered Denneker's book, which had just been published,

MOXON'S MASTERPIECE 335

to be subversive, even dangerous, but I came away from it only with the impression that he thought a person could somehow be in two places at the same time: "...their bodies go fore-appointed ways, unknowing..." was his remarkable conclusion.

What Denneker could not know, of course, was that the Thinking Man that Moxon was constructing was not a war machine at all, but merely a mechanical chess player with decidedly human characteristics. It was this last unexpected development, this human dimension, as he called it, that gave Moxon pause and moved him to stare silently into the fire each night, much to Denneker's frustration. At the window I often had to chuckle quietly as I observed the two supposed allies on such totally different tracks.

On that final stormy night Moxon hinted that he was close to perfecting a cognizant machine, and it was then that Denneker shouted, "Do you really believe that a machine thinks?"

Moxon rambled on with speculations about everything being somehow alive, saying, "Every atom is a living, feeling, conscious being." And to Denneker's outrage he concludad with the thought that, "Consciousness is the creature of Rhythm."

At this, Denneker stormed out, and I too wondered what Moxon might mean.

Yes, Denneker issued a statement about the night in question, but my memory differs. Denneker claims that, as he walked through the raging storm, he came to the conclusion that Moxon's observation that consciousness is rhythm was "infinitely alluring," as he put it, and that he turned back to discuss the matter at greater depth. From my point of view at my wet and windy perch by the window, I saw that Denneker only left the house for a moment, then turned back and re-entered with hardly time to reconsider the rhythm of consciousness.

In his statement Denneker claims that he entered the machine-shop just in time to witness Moxon declaring checkmate, at which point the Automan supposedly attacked its creator and began strangling him with iron hands. Denneker then states that, as he tried to intervene, there was a blinding light, followed by total darkness, at which point he passed out, only to learn later that I had come to his rescue.

What I saw when I climbed through the window and followed Denneker into the room was totally differant. Rather than attacking Moxon, the

Automan merely nodded its acceptance of the checkmate and waved its hand. Denneker, however, pushed the machine aside and rushed forward to grasp Moxon by the throat and strangle him. The blinding light he reported was eventually found to be caused by the boiler exploding beneath the shop, and in that aspect alone was I indirectly responsible for the destruction of the Moxon manor.

At the end of his statement Denneker recalls that, from his hospital bed, he asked me if I'd also rescued the mechanical chessplayer that murdered its inventor. When I asked him, "Do you know that?" he stated, "I saw it done." But he goes on to conclude: "If asked today I would answer less confidently." Yes, this is no confession of guilt, but is it not cause to wonder?

II

What followed that tragic incident has become our modern history, and indeed our second Civil War. It began when Clive Denneker took possession of Moxon's business affairs and of his estate, something he found easy to do given Moxon's strange and isolated lifestyle and Denneker's own legal connections and business genius. At first, it was proposed that the old estate with the remains of the machine-shop and the chess-playing Automan be made into the Moxon Museum to honor the eccentric inventor. But it wasn't long before it became clear that Denneker had much more in mind—the Moxon Calculating Machine Enterprise, later known as the MCME Corporation.

Soon after the museum opened, I decided to make a quiet visit to see how Denneker chose to honor his old friend. The displays and exhibits were rather bland, I thought, but for the most part presented an accurate portrait of the Great Man. Satisfied, I was about to leave when, to my surprise, I noticed Denneker himself talking to a group of distinguished looking men, shaking hands and slapping backs. At first, I thought he would not notice me or ignore me as he had in the past, but as I was heading for the exit he looked directly at me and nodded. Soon my nightmares began again, as I saw Denneker's business enterprises booming.

My experience with Moxon's Automan had convinced me that a revolution was coming, and those of us opposed to it must move quickly. At first I attempted to make it a Union issue and tried to enlighten the working class as to the threat posed by the Automen. But of course the Unions were small and weak, and their members had not the imagination to understand the threat we faced, so all my organizing efforts failed.

Denneker's efforts, however, were now in high gear. In the first three years after Moxon's death, MCME Corp established several research labs to develop the Moxon Thinking Machine, labs that soon turned into large manufacturing facilities. The new machines were being turned out by the hundreds, then thousands, and it became commonplace for manual labor and mathematical calculations to be done by what I came to think of as Moxon's ghosts. Some were disturbed by the development, but the major newspapers and magazines praised it. Only a few of us remained disgruntled.

So I turned to politics, trying to convince members of state legislatures and the Congress in Washington that we would be facing economic disaster if the Automan industry continued to grow and cause unthinkable changes in the workplace. I was naive enough that I didn't realize the members of these powerful bodies were the very ones who would profit from the Thinking Machines, at least in the short run, and so they turned a deaf ear to my proposals. I wasted precious time trying to bring the issue before the public and establish some kind of control of what I had come to call the Automan Empire, but it was all in vain. Six states even passed laws banning the movement as "subversive of the State and its Economic Destiny."

Meanwhile, Denneker had become a public figure approaching the status of Mark Twain or Randy Hearst. He was given swords, degrees, and honorary titles, his picture often seen smiling at us from the periodicals as he held high his champagne glass. His marriage to the beautiful daughter of a Wall Steet tycoon was celebrated widely and followed by a world tour, during which he founded numerous branches of his manufacturing enterprise. Two decades after Moxon's murder, Clive Denneker was seriously being suggested as a presidential candidate.

In desperation I turned to the religious community, recalling how it was the church that was most active in abolishing slavery, establishing women's rights, and supporting other social issues. At first I did find a few likeminded members of the clergy and their followers, and I began to hope that here at last was a way to seriously oppose the rise of Dennekerism, which was beginning to make important inroads in business and financial institutions. Alas, when the church higher-ups learned of our movement, they did all they could to turn their congregations against us, which wasn't hard, for most of their members were so easily led into whatever schemes their masters proposed. It was no coincidence that Denneker's MEDITATIONS became required reading in many churches.

Despite my failures at organising a mass movement against Denneker's evil work, I had made friends here and there—workers displaced by the infernal machines, rebels searching for a cause, religious fanatics, rogue adventurers, men who could only be called out of their minds. And I had kept up my efforts to stockpile weapons for use against Denneker's forces, should that become necessary. In abandoned warehouses, empty schools and churches, ranch houses left to rot, even mines and caves in the mountains, we secretly stored our guns and cannons and ammunition in preperation for the uprising to come.

It came in early 1909, when we attacked Denneker's main manufacturing facility, the Sledge Assembly Plant near Selma, Alabama. We struck hard, our little band surrounding the plant at midnight and launching our attack at one o'clock. By three in ths morning the plant had burned to the ground and twelve of the workers there were dead. We lost ten of our own, but gloried in our victory.

Of course, it was not to last—we had less than a million in our army, even when the rebellion grew strong, with perhaps another million sympathizers who gave us whatever support they could without taking part in the fighting. It just wasn't enough. By Spring of 1911 Denneker had risen to the position of Secretary of War in the Root administration and had personally led the battle against us in Hoboken, Dallas, Salt Lake City, and San Francisco. His propaganda campaign called us the Luddleys and turned many would-be sympathizers against us through economic manipulation.

We might yet have won, but Denneker reinforced his armies with mechanical soldiers from his own factories—marching machines that we were unable to stand against. We still might have prevailed had the metal soldiers been subject to some sort of laws respecting human life, but alas, it was not to be. By the end of that year the war was over, and Denneker was on his way to the White House in 1912.

III

Yes, I was captured, tried by Denneker's Extraordinary Legal Proceedings Commission, and sentenced to death by hanging. No doubt the execution would have been at the hands of one of his Automen, but there were still Luddleys secretly devoted to my cause, and through great sacrifices on their part I was able to escape and flee to Brazil. There I sought out Moxon's old friend, Count Szolnok, late of Pragus, only to find all human life long since eradicated by the so-called mechanical Golems the count had invented.

I next sought refuge in Cuba, but Denneker's Secretary of War, Theo Roosevelt, had just launched the invasion that would lead to annexation of the island and eventually to statehood. I thought of Moxon's correspondence with the inventor R. U. Rossum, also of Prague, but learned in time that he was developing automated workers of his own. Yes, I thought of fleeing to Japan, India, the Philippines, but such a long journey was beyond my supporters' means and involved too many unknowns, too many chances of betrayal.

Then I got word from Mexico that one of the revolutionary leaders there, General Tomás Arroyo, was seeking help from farmers, laborers, rebels, anarchists, and even Luddleys. General Arroyo was part of Pancho Villa's army, and I vaguely recalled he had said something about Moxon's work in a rabble-rousing speech in Mexico City. I wrote Arroyo a long letter expressing interest in his cause, little expecting a reply, let alone an agreement to meet and discuss possible collaboration. To my great surprise and relief he agreed to meet in Ciudad Juarez in early 1914.

I arrived at our meeting place on the outskirts of the city a day early, full of hope and optimism, but found delays and frustration instead. General Arroyo was a gruff, impatient man who askad many questions but ignored my answers, being too busy consulting with his staff to listen. When he finally focused on me after a sparse meal and too much tequila, his single question was about how many troops I could supply. When I said I had only a rag-tag band of volunteers, he turned away in contempt and joined his men in a noisy card game.

As I turned away, wondering what to do next, an elderly American gentleman I'd seen in the crowd earlier stopped me and asked if I was the leader of the Luddleys. He was wearing a gunbelt and a twisted smile, and I feared my past was catching up with me. But he held out his hand and said, "Don't worry, I'm just an old gringo like you. Perhaps we can throw in together." We shook hands and I somehow felt I could trust him.

Taking me aside, he introduced himself as Jack Robinson and explained that he'd come down from San Francisco to find out what the excitement was all about and to see if the Mexican soldiers had discovered anything new about fighting and dying. He assured me he was free to move about and that despite General Arroyo's rudeness I would be treated the same way. "Just stay out of the way," Robinson warned sternly. He invited me to join him at the nearby Ysleta del Sur Pueblo, where he was staying with a family he knew. I gladly accepted.

I was anxious to hear Robinson's thoughts about the possibility of spreading the revolution across the border to overthrow Denneker, but the old adventurer was in a philosophical mood and loved to make sarcastic comments without providing any useful information. Somehow, he got talking on Indian history and pondered the fate of the tribe that inhabited the Chaco Canyon Pueblo in New Mexico, but which mysteriously disappeared over eight hundred years ago. When I showed little interest, he asked if I was perhaps more familiar with the disappearance of the Salem witch, Kaziah Mason, in 1692, or the famous Benjamin Bathurst, who walked around the horses in 1809 and was never seen again. I lamely admitted I knew a little about these disappearances, but commented that Moxon had been fascinated by the subject.

"You knew Moxon?" he asked, a bit startled.

"I saw him murdered by the assassin, Denneker," I said. "I'm surprised you aren't familiar with my account of what happened."

"Ah, the memory plays tricks without treats," he said. "Yes, now I recall your accusation, but you were never able to prove your case. Even if you'd had an honest judge, it was your word against Denneker's. But tell me what Moxon had to say about those strange disappearances."

"One I recall," I said, "is the planter, Williamson, who disappeared while crossing a field near Selma before the war. Another was the so-called Spook House in Kentucky, where a whole family disappeared around 1858 or so, and where a judge also went missing several years later. Moxon collected such stories."

Robinson seemed to find this quite amusing and his grin was frightening. "He died before two more famous examples occurred—the English athlete, Worsen, I believe in 1873, and young Charles Ashmore near Quincy, Illinois, a few years later." He smiled and licked his lips.

We were silent for a while and, perhaps to relieve the tension, Robinson began asking more about Moxon—how did he live, how did he work, did he really believe machines could think?

I tried to avoid saying too much, but mentioned that the great inventor kept copious notes, as well as a diary, and a strange manuscript he called DEAD LETTERS.

Robinson perked up at this and asked what had happened to the old man's scrlbblings.

"I rescued them from the burning house," I told him, even as I wondered if it was a good idea. "I stored them in a shed that escaped the fire. They might still be there."

Robinson was silent for a while, and the sardonic smile faded from his lips. "Do you know if Moxon was familiar with the work of the German scientist, Dr. Hern of Leipzig, or with Hern's book, VERSCHWINDEN UND SEINE THEORIE?"

"Yes, he told me about Dr. Hern's theories having to do with non-Euclidean holes in space and time where unknown forces hold sway. I can't say I followed it all. I worked more with my hands than my brain."

Robinson fell silent again, and I thought he might be asleep, but after a long pause he smiled coldly and asked if I had ever read Denneker's MEDITATIONS. I was almost asleep myself and tried to brush him off by saying I'd tried but it made no sense to me. Robinson nodded and suggested it was time to get some rest.

I was exhausted and should have nodded off quickly, but somehow our conversation echoed through my head and I couldn't stop thinking, trying somehow to make sense of it all. After an hour of turning and tossing, I finally drifted into an uneasy sleep. That was when the dreams began. A face appeared in a shadowy room and somehow I knew it was Dr. Hern telling me, "We are Hyperboreans." Then I remembered it was some other philosopher or poet who had said that—Zoroaster perhaps.

I suppose it was dream logic that led me next to a performance by the stage magician who called himself Sing Loo, who moved effortlessly from "Swing Low" to the mechanical nightingale that puzzled a Chinese Emperor…then to London quoting Schopenhauer's absurd definition of life...the good ship Lolliprague and Harford's missing marrow...animals thinking perpetual emotion...The Red One...a clockwork puppet in the Wilde Harlot's House...Diablo Rivera's Manchinery Mural...Doyle's shipwreck puts Watson in jeopardy...the machine breakers and the Iron Heal...Salem Salami/stomotans do their best/confusing chess chests...Poetic hungary gray barron Kempelensmen...Tik-Tok, a fine wind-up man always does best that he can...frankly flexible time termination...the magic mace of mad machination...

Then I dreamed myself back at my perch outside Moxon's window, but this time the guest was not Dennecker, but Dr. Hern and an ancient crone I somehow knew was the witch, Kaziah. Dr. Hern was saying, "There are void places in the luminiferous ether which I call *vacua*, where our cloying measurers no longer matter and we can travel at the speed of thought wherever we wish. But there are dangers here—if one is not careful, he may become trapped and lost forever."

Moxon pondered a moment, puffing on his pipe, then asked, "But you say one can learn how to move between these angles to other cosmos or far places in an instant?"

At this the crone, Kaziah, cackled and made mysterious motions. Then she stood and moved toward the place where wall meets ceiling, which briefly opened, allowing her to step up and through, and she disappeared.

The dream scene faded but was far from over, for I seemed to be accompanying the old witch through unimaginable passageways to a cold empty plain that might have been the Moon, another where winds blew the sands of Mars, and yet another cold hell she called Yuggoth. Then she made a strange turn toward the royal star, Aldebaran, and I was left alone.

Dr. Hern spoke in my ear. "Be glad she didn't leave you in Carcosa!"

Then Dr. Hern walked around the horses and out of my dream, and I was back at Moxon's window. Now Denneker was there again, just as before on that fateful night in 1870. Moxon was speaking and Denneker's frustration was evident on his face. Moxon had just quoted Herbert's definition of life in support of his belief that everything in the cosmos, even atoms, was alive, and thus it was possible, even certain, that machines do think.

The mechanical chess player in the next room laughed, and Denneker seemed even more outraged. Moxon raved on, insisting Conciousness is the creature of Rhythm.

Now everything began to move at top speed. Denneker bolted from his chair and left the house, while Moxon returned to his workroom and resumed his chess game. Then Denneker was back, interrupting the game and shouting, "Yes, damn you, we're all creatures of Rhythm—even in death!" The murder was over in a flash, and then the dream was interrupted by the explosion that brought down the house.

I almost woke at this point, thinking the dream was over, but then I saw the dark figure of Moxon in the library with all his "scribblings" laid out on the table. "Here are the answers," he told me, "and all is told in the DEAD LETTERS, if you can translate them." He faded to a ghostly shadow, but the book of answers had an eldritch glow that captured my attention. I had tried to read the book before, but it was in no alphabet I could discover until now.

And now I did wake and woke poor Robinson as well, shouting, "It's the A-Rhythm, Jack! The secret is in what Moxon called Null-R. Consciousness is the creation of Rhythm, but pan-consciousness is found in anti-Rhythm. That's how old Kaziah could walk through walls, how Bathurst walked around the horses, how Williamson and others disappeared."

Robinson did his best to quiet me down, but I had disturbed the whole Yiron family, and it was nearly an hour before things calmed down and we were able to try again to get some sleep. In the morning, with Robinson's help I was able to explain to General Arroyo that I would instruct my followers to help in his efforts. He was unimpressed, but was about to join Pancho Villa in the raid on Columbus, New Mexico, so he allowed us to join his followers.

And now at last I have proof that Denneker stole Moxon's ideas without really understanding them. In his MEDITATIONS, Denneker writes of being "drawn away...and apart from the body for a season," and that there are "certain of kin whose paths intersecting...while their bodies go foreappointed ways, unknowing." Thus his claim one could be in two places at once, and with this poorly understood tool of Rhythm he could accomplish much. But he had set the world on the wrong path, and the struggle to return to normalcy must now begin again.

Yes, there is still a long way to go, but with the newly launched invasion of the United States and the defeat of General Jack Pershing at Las Cruces, there is a new spirit through the land. Denneker has perished at the hands of his own Automen and has been replaced by President Winthrop of the Yellow Party. The so-called Luddleys have been accepted by the new majority around the world. There is much yet to do, but at last we're on the right track, and I have a profound feeling that old man Moxon would be pleased.

IV

Jack Robinson grinned and tapped his forehead when we discussed all this in Yaleta. He understood that a new world was unfolding, but he'd had enough of thinking machines, of being in two places at once, of Rhythm and Null-R. He wished me luck as he saddled up his horse and shook my hand one final time. Then he rode off alone and disappeared into the dark desert.

Honorable Mention

Outsmarting the Technology

Judy Ray

The house that Jack built is a sensitive wonder.
It lights up at the approach of humans,
checks passwords in the form of codes.
When the sun rises, the kitchen wakes, grinds coffee,
fills the pot. The high-alert alarm mode of night
settles down for daytime doze.
It warms or cools itself to an average habitat.

The heart of the house that Jack built
lies concealed behind a *2001 Space Odyssey* poster,
relaying messages to lock and unlock,
open and close, humidify, dehumidify,
select the classical station, make the Jacuzzi hum.

On his personal computer "Fatal Error"
memos startle the screen. His house
doesn't have a screen. But it has a Fatal Error.
The day the circuits blow there is no coffee aroma
in the morning, but there is extended quiet and dark.

With an override power fix, things begin to hum anew
but codes are crossed. Things won't turn off,
won't shut down, the switch for the garage door—
too heavy to raise by hand—starts
the waste compactor. Jack creeps on all fours
around his house trying to avoid the invisible beam—
which finds him anyway, videos and broadcasts
his foolishness, and locks all the doors, codeless.

The Perks

Carol Christian

A tree pruning
Wind blew in from the northeast
This morning
Winnows of
Birch branches whipped from the supple trees
Now clad the yard
Over the morning news
We see pictures of large branches
Swept from firs and oaks and maples
Power lines are down
In large parts of east county
Angry swirling dark clouds skitter scatter
Across the winter morning's sky
We are warm and dry
We agree, husband and I
It is a good morning to be inside
And be retired
With the power on
And no need for travel
On backed up freeways

Power

Sarah Traister Moskovitz

My husband who cannot walk twenty feet without pain and uses a wheelchair or two canes can still sit himself down on the ground to pull out a heavy broken kitchen drawer with two strong arms from below the stovetop cabinet and lay himself into that cabinet where all the wires congregate to make things right and then paint it all.

He wields a vacuum hose to clean out old crud, lifts a heavy iron drill to replace the screws and rollers of the broken drawer. The arm and upper body strength needed to do all this, the power to use these tools requires that he lift himself into an unpleasant position to get it done and he does it because he loves to fix and build and hammer and work.

He can still draw on a mystic magic source of will and energy that he has always owned in the marrow of his bones from the time I met him 68 years ago. I recall him with his brother then working on our jalopy to muscle out and lift its heavy failing motor to make it run again. He became a lineman and climbed the great four hundred foot towers to bring power from the Owens Gorge to Los Angeles station C and food to our young family's table, before he got his engineering degree.

With soldering iron, wire cutters, pliers, drills, chisel, vacuum tubes, and schematics he built us our own first television set…so we wouldn't have to go to Cousin Libby's to see Sid Caesar and Imogene Coca on Saturday nights.

Out in the coastal Redwood wilderness when we were there among the ancient redwood sentinels camping with the children in the trailer he had built, he made the most wonderful gift for me with just a hammer and nails and a small hand saw; he built for me a special Adirondack chair out of fallen wood found on the forest floor so I could sit and read beneath the trees…

Once after we'd been married for twenty years we sat in our living room and noticed that the couch was looking shabby. He said, "I'm going to re-upholster it but you choose the material." I trusted him to use the old Singer sewing machine we inherited from Aunt Riva and *Wow!* That couch of blue, beautiful tapestry, stuffed well and smartly seamed—that couch was great to see and sit on for many, many years. I think he got his golden hands from Lena, his mother, who was a brilliant seamstress.

He has always loved to make things work right, to make something better, and best of all to make something out of nothing.

My competition to make him happy has always been tools: tools to build us another room for when the adult children come to visit; tools to create, fix maintain, improve, embellish, remake; tools to actualize his need for taking care of people by making gifts for them with his imagination and know-how and, most important, with the generous hard labor of his loving hands.

Losing Someone Close

Keith Trammell

I never thought of my relationship with her as being intimate—just that she was a friend, an old family friend. She always arrived at my house early every morning while my wife was still asleep upstairs. We would have breakfast together at the kitchen table, then move to the couch in the living room, perhaps with a second cup of coffee. It was more comfortable there. I enjoyed the quiet time alone with her. She was knowledgeable, witty, and sometimes funny. I do have to admit, though, she usually did end up on my lap. Perhaps you knew her too. She was the old daily print edition of our local newspaper.

Those who take care of her declared she was getting too old and needed to slow down, so last fall she started coming to my house only four times a week, and from her physical appearance it was obvious she was declining. A scrawny little thing now, she is hardly recognizable, actually being held together by staples. The changes in her I find hard to accept.

In addition to the sad loss of old-fashioned, daily news coverage, the loss of her large robust pages means we now have less packaging material around the house whenever needed, less protection for our dining room table from the grandkids' art projects, and less paper for starting fires in the fireplace in winter. Her usefulness in all of these matters will be sorely missed.

Her caretakers, recognizing that many others besides myself are saddened and upset by their actions, have tried to appease us with a substitute: a daily online digital version of our new, scrawny little friend. There are a number of difficulties with her new persona. You can't just read the front page anymore and pass another section on to someone else to read when it only exists on your computer screen. If you can figure out a way of printing specific items, you may be able to get by. But, if not, have you ever tried doing a Sudoku or crossword puzzle on your monitor? And how do you "clip out" a piece you want to save for a friend?

Losing someone close is always difficult, but we may as well have our feelings about it and get on with whatever changes we need to make.

This is called progress. Like our beloved old daily, our new scrawny little paper someday won't be making it to our homes, either. We'll be reading her obituary…online, of course.

Give me a newspaper

William Killian

My ninety-one year old friend
lost her husband when he was forty-six.
I had a dream about him, she said—
he was on a slab, sat up, said,
"*Give me a newspaper.*"
He read it, threw it down, said,
"*I'd rather be dead*" *and fell backwards.*

She had another dream about him—
He was on one side of a river,
and I was on the other. A small girl
was with him, and he said,
"*I'm here to help you cross over.*"
(His younger sister had died years before.)
I awakened immediately,
 thinking out loud, "I'm not ready yet."

She told me some other stories,
like when her husband
was about to be sent overseas—
she appeared at the military base
and announced, *I'm here to get pregnant.*

She really loved this man—
she was *in love* with him,
and it was her grandmother
who helped her through her grief—
"*Do something physical,*" grandma said,
so she said to the children,
"*Let's paint the house.*"

My ninety-one year old friend
quit driving last year.
Hearing is a problem, but she loves to read
and tell stories from her life.
She is proud of her three daughters

and their families,
she is proud of getting her college degree
as a single mother,
she is a proud professional woman,
full of joy and laughter—
she is prepared to die and ready to live,
and when she crosses over
she will be home again.

CONTRIBUTOR'S NOTES

NANCY ALAUZEN resides in Bridgeville, Pennsylvania. She works full-time for a non-profit in Pittsburgh. Desiring to help jobseekers, she published a self-help booklet titled "66 Power Tips To Help You Land the Job You Want" and articles on Workforce Development. Recycling is Nancy's passion! She has published articles on recycling and was even nicknamed Nancy "Green" by her co-workers. A short story on Nancy's life is included in a book titled *My Dirty Little Secret Before Success*, 2013, by James Tudor. Nancy believes she hit the "parent lottery" and recently starting writing articles to capture stories about her family. [121]

BILL ALEWYN lives in Arizona with his wife and cats. Over the years his essays and short fiction have appeared in several publications. His play, "An American Execution," was awarded first place in the 2012 Beverly Hills Guild/Julie Harris competition. In 2013 his short play, "The Faulkner/Hemingway Letters," was featured at the WIT Kauai Shorts festival and, in 2014, was awarded first place in the League for Innovation national competition. [279]

MARY MARGARET BAKER started to write poetry at the age of fourteen. As she got older, she wrote stories. She completed a writing course with the Institute of Childrens' Literature. Her articles have been in bulletins. Writing, beading, painting, and going out with friends keep her busy. Her article, "Terrifying Moments," was published in *OASIS Journal 2012*. This senior realizes that, no matter what your age, you can keep busy writing and doing something worthwhile. Her two nieces, who lead exciting lives as flight attendants, inspired her to write "The Adventures of Flight Attendants." [273]

JOHN BARBEE: After losing my wife, I searched for something to fill the empty hours of my life; then friends sent in a story I had written and you published it. Thus encouraged, I started to write on a regular schedule. This has helped fill some of the emptiness in my life. I have been playing around with writing for the last five years and am a complete amateur. Seeing my stories printed in *OASIS Journal* has given me both pleasure and encouragement. [320]

TABINDA BASHIR, a medical doctor, immigrated from Pakistan in 1998 and took up creative writing. Her stories have been published in Pakistani magazines, "Moon Journal," and a chapbook, "Turning Point." In the U.S. she won Daily Herald's "Citizens' Competition" award twice. "Bound" and

"Odyssey" were published in *OASIS Journal 2010* and *2011* respectively. "Sheru Goes To School" received an honorable mention in *OASIS Journal 2012*. A short autobiography, "My Journey," was published in Jane's Stories Press Foundation's chapbook, "Bridges and Borders." "Odyssey" was also published in Jane's Stories Press Foundation's anthology in 2012. [1]

KEVEN BELLOWS, a student of poetry and a poet herself, has published two books of poems: *Taking Your Own True Name* (2004) and *The Blue Darter* (2010), which chronicled her husband's long battle with Alzheimer's and its impact on their marriage. She teaches poetry appreciation and writing in the Osher Program of UCLA Extension and volunteers as a writing teacher at the VA Hospital in West Los Angeles. In addition she has collaborated and/or edited books with other authors, including her husband's memoir, *The Last Editor*. Her latest collaboration is *The Board Game: How Smart Women Become Corporate Directors* (2014). [161]

ROSEMARY BENNETT: I am retired from many years of working in and managing a nursing home kitchen. I'm taking the "Your Story" memoir class at the Milwaukie Center. "A Lesson Learned" was in response to a writing assignment about believing in a half-truth, and how it affected my life. Putting it on paper helped me quite a bit with continuing my positive recovery from that experience. [322]

HELEN BENSON: Of all the holidays, the one I treasure most is my birthday. I know of no better way to acknowledge it than to celebrate the entire day. Morning is my favorite time, so it is easy for me to start early to appreciate that another year is given to me. Poetry is always a proper way of saying "thank you." [87]

BETTY BIRKEMARK: "The General" was just part of the rich fodder for stories I found on my '67 trip to Europe; the facts were in my journal and only put together after I joined a writer's group, seven years ago. "White Sands, N.M. 1953" was written fifty-five years ago, but to submit it in this day and age, I felt the last two lines had to be updated...so I changed them. Who would have dreamed that one day we would see "Old Glory" flying on the moon? *I* didn't. [56, 173]

BOBBIE JEAN BISHOP: My poems have been published in a variety of small journals since 1974 and were included in two Doubleday anthologies. I've won contests in poetry, first prizes from the University of Texas, *Tidepools Journal* (Miracosta College), and *OASIS Journal* (2005, 2011, 2012). I've been a student in an OASIS poetry class (San Diego) for ten years taught by Mary Harker. [42, 206]

BERNADETTE BLUE discovered poetry writing with a fifth-grade class assignment. While she has explored many forms of expression over the years – from painting and crafting to short story writing and journaling – poetry remains closest to her heart. She writes from her home in southern Arizona and is pleased to have "A Study of Small Days" included in this year's *OASIS Journal*. It is her fifth poem with the publication. [276]

DAVID BRAUN: I am a retired, 73-year-old psychologist/psychotherapist, 2nd of 5 sibs, divorced father of three, and grandfather of three. I graduated from the University of Texas at Austin in 1973 and also attended Corpus Christi State University and Texas Tech Universities, and have lived and practiced in various capacities all over the state of Texas, ending in San Antonio. Writing is a recreation for me, as is engaging in a writers' critique group (special thanks to Joanne Johnson, Ruth Mallory, and Don Moye). [325]

FRED BRIDGES: My education includes a BS from Utah State and a MED from the University of Oregon. I am retired from the military, having served in both the navy and army. I was leafing through some old photo albums and this true story unfolded. Barbasol shaving signs and the wonders of penicillin seemed to mesh among memories of long ago. [38, 67]

JACK CAMPBELL: I held services for my Underwood typewriter the day I got my first computer, leading to a fun retirement with spellcheck and printout at my beck and call. Memoirs, fiction, and poetry have been spewing from a bottomless well to the delight of family and friends, who now know where I come from, but, more importantly, where they came from. That computer is now my wife's only rival. I have published a book of my Army/Navy service for family and friends, and a book of 70 short stories. At 87, the end is not yet in sight. [329]

TERESA CIVELLO describes herself as an undisciplined writer who takes to the keyboard by assignment deadline only. Apparently, the nuns are still in her head. Her work has been published in *OASIS Journal 2010* and *2011*, as well as the *SouthWest Writers SAGE*. Teresa acknowledges Maralie BeLonge, Program Supervisor of the Albuquerque Osher Lifelong Learning Institute, for creating an extraordinary writing program, and thanks Osher Instructor Connie Josefs, MFA, for her insightful writing classes. Teresa's Unibrow story is based on an actual event. And no, she hasn't had her eyebrows tattooed yet. [299]

DAVID P. CRESAP: I have been writing poetry since 1961. Over the years I have discovered that, when I might be having a life challenge, a poem will come as an impression to ease my soul or teach and clarify my understanding. This poem came to me recounting when I helped Dad make cookies. It was always like a ritual experience to be a participant. I had been thinking about our time together. My poetry seems to be universally appealing. I have had a couple of poems published, but many requests to publish. I am currently organizing anthologies for publication. [111]

ARIS DENIGRIS: The creative non-fiction piece, "It Takes Two To Tango," was inspired by our 2014 winter vacation in Florida. And there really was a beautiful older couple who danced the tango, and he really did stop and kiss the top of her head. It was beautiful! And my imagination took off from there. It was lots of fun to write. I am in my 84th year, and my husband and I will be celebrating our 65th anniversary in September. I really don't know where the "music" went—all I know is that I have to keep writing. [213]

ALAN DENNIS uses prose and poetry to explore contemporary issues, like aging and changes in cognition. A member of OASIS and the Osher Lifelong Learning Institute. he lives with his wife in San Diego. Characters and events in his story are based on newspaper articles from different sources, collected over several years, that seemed to fit together. Or perhaps there were suppressed memories. How do your memories fade in and out, creating images that become more real than reality itself? What exactly is reality? To quote the late, great Robin Williams, "If you remember the sixties, you weren't there." [305]

BUCK DOPP retired from a 27-year career in business management in 2009 to pursue his lifelong dream of writing full-time. His first novel, *Kingpin and Eli*, was published in 2013 and is available on Amazon.com and Kindle. Dopp works as a freelance writer for the *Today's News-Herald* in Lake Havasu City, Arizona. His short stories have appeared in *OASIS Journal 2010, 2011* and *2012*. He is the past president of the Lake Havasu City Writers Group, which has published his stories in its anthology, *Offerings from the Oasis*. Visit the author's website at www.buckdopp.com. [141]

After a poetry-saturated childhood, JOAN T. DORAN taught school, enjoyed a career as a psychotherapist and executive of a family service organization, and, with her husband, raised three sons and one daughter. With the recent publishing by Imago Press of her first book of poetry, *Herding Mice at Three A.M.*, she has returned full circle to poetry. [236]

ELISA DRACHENBERG: I actually do own a beautiful tan leather camel, found at a local Goodwill store. And the wildlife scene that starts "What's Luck Got To Do with It?" is equally based on numerous encounters with deer in my back yard. A camel, deer, an unbearable hot summer, and musing about the element of luck inspired this story about a relationship between two people who eventually learn to commit to each other. All could have ended well, if only the husband had not taken his good fortune for granted. [221]

MARY ROSE DURFEE: In 2010, my family created the Mary Rose Clinic, a free clinic for the uninsured, in my honor because, as a child growing up on a hop farm, we had no money to pay a doctor when we got sick. Instead, he gladly accepted a dozen eggs or a gallon of homemade cider as payment. Today, doctors don't work that way! My story, "A Sack of Potatoes," is about my past. Now, at 98-years-old, I am eternally grateful for my good health and to be accepted into *OASIS Journal* for my seventh time. [239]

RUTH FEATHERSTONE: Born in Massachusetts. My family and I have been residents of St. Louis since 1965. I'm 87 years old and retired in 1991 from Maritz Inc. as a Division Vice President. I was an OASIS tutor for 12 years and a member of an OASIS Creative Writing group for many years. My stories have been published in *The Storyteller* and in two genealogy magazines, *The Argus* from Novia Scotia and *Featherstone Family News* from England. I am currently working on two books containing my memoirs for my family. I believe this is going to be an ongoing endeavor. [157]

SHELLY LYNN FLETCHER is a native Californian. She grew up on the fringe of show business, participating in a variety of local television shows and theatre productions. As an adult, she taught English and Drama to middle school and high school teens, writing original scripts for her Youth Theatre productions. Throughout her teaching career, her students were treated to "Mrs. Fletcher's Stories," the oral-retelling of silly escapades. Now, with more than 35 years of teaching under her belt, Shelly has decided to put those stories on paper. Shelly lives in Southern California with her husband, Mark. They both enjoy writing. [191]

HELEN MURIEL GANAPOLE: I'm happy to have three successive years of *OASIS Journal* acceptances. You have offered a wonderful venue for later life memoirs! My happy and active piano playing years were the inspiration for "The Perfect Pitch." Like many of my surprising memories, it erupted onto my computer page, and seemed to write itself. Thanks for a chance to be encouraged to write forever and ever. I have been fortunate to have a lifetime of opportunity; study, teaching, travel, and clusters of inspirational friends and family. Now, I am most grateful for a friend named "Oasis." Thank you. [39]

MARIE THÉRÈSE GASS loves to capture stories growing out of true stranger-than-fiction experiences. Though officially retired from teaching and editing, Marie frequently finds herself in discussions of others' writings. She and her TBI husband jot down little childhood memories, personal sports stories, anecdotes about relatives of the olden days, etc., add photos, then have them printed and bound for Christmas gifts – an exciting continuing project! [123]

KATHLEEN ELLIOTT GILROY: I am an artist, write poetry, essays, short stories, and am currently collaborating with my adult daughter, Erin Gilroy Thomas, on a series of stories for young adult readers. Erin is also an artist and writer. I am a retired Special needs Educator, an Animal Advocate, parent, grandmother, great grandmother. I live in Chula Vista, California. [233]

NORMA GLICKMAN: The lump in my throat caught me completely by surprise as I casually riffled through the remnants of an unknown person's life. [112]

LOIS GODEL has worked as an artist, mother, family law attorney, mediator, and writer. Her strong interest in family issues and a desire to make a positive difference for families, especially children, is the thread that runs through these endeavors. She currently lives in Maryland, a short distance from Washington, D.C., and divides her time between family mediation and writing. She has had poems published in Writer's Journal and OASIS Journals 2011, 2012, and 2013. An adapted chapter from her memoir about adoption and her successful search for her biological families was also published in OASIS Journal 2013. [48]

MARGARET GOLDEN: I have lived in Oregon all my life – graduated from Rainier High School and Portland Community College. I was a dancer, and taught tap dancing and ballet for 35 years. I was a Local Pastor for four United Methodist Churches for about 10 years and was sometimes able to bring sacred dancing into the worship services. Now I live in a retirement community with my husband (we have been married for 57 years!). We have five children and four grandsons who live from Florida to Washington. I enjoy water aerobics, tone chimes, and writer's corner! [144]

DIANA GRIGGS wrote "Wielding your machete" while watching her grandson clear a wild area of her garden and feeling how quickly time had gone from when his imagination created a living jungle in this space. "Welsh Cakes" reaches further back to her own childhood in England. [65, 70]

San Diego resident ANITA CURRAN GUENIN grew up in Providence, Rhode Island. Her poems and essays have been published in *OASIS Journal, San Diego Poetry Annual, Magee Park Poets Anthology* and numerous haiku publications. She was a third place winner in the Haiku Society of America

Haibun Contest in 2013 and received an Honorable Mention in the Harold Henderson Haiku Contest in 2012. [140, 271]

TILYA GALLAY HELFIELD's short stories and essays have appeared in *TV Guide, The Fiddlehead, Viewpoints, OASIS Journals 2010* (Best Nonfiction Award), *2011, 2012, 2013* (First Runner-up: Best Nonfiction Award), on CBC Radio One and online. A collection of her stories will soon be published by *Imago Press*. A multi-media artist, she has participated in 16 solo and more than 76 juried group exhibitions in Canada, the U.S., Spain, Brazil, Japan, and Korea, and has won several awards. Her work can be found in 27 public collections and in numerous private collections in Canada, the U.S., and Europe (http://www.tilyahelfield.com/). [269]

MAURICE HIRSCH has four poetry collections: *Taking Stock, Stares to Other Places, Roots and Paths,* and *Rails and Ties.* His work is in *Switched-on Gutenberg, Lake City Lights, OASIS Journal 2013, 2012, 2011,* and *2010, Winter Harvest: Jewish Writing in St. Louis, 2006-11, New Harvest: Jewish Writing in St. Louis, 1998-2005.* "Questions for Juan Gonzales" comes from getting a new mobile phone number; "Nevermore" is about actual experiences, but also about getting old, and we have moved – I no longer have horses after 42 years. "Not What They Seem" was prompted by a creepy visual experience driving in rural Wisconsin. [260, 323, 332]

ANDREW HOGAN received his doctorate in development studies from the University of Wisconsin-Madison. Before retirement, he was a faculty member at the State University of New York at Stony Brook, the University of Michigan, and Michigan State University, where he taught medical ethics, health policy, and the social organization of medicine in the College of Human Medicine. He has published twenty-six works of fiction in *OASIS Journal, Hobo Pancakes, Twisted Dreams, Thick Jam, Grim Corps, Long Story Short, Defenestration, Foliate Oak Literary Magazine, The Blue Guitar Magazine, Fabula Argentea, Mobius, Thrice, The Lorelei Signal, Colliers, SANDSCRIPT,* and *Copperfield Review.* [177]

JENNIFER HOLLINGSHEAD: I was 13 when my family went to live in Nairobi, half a world away from Rancocas, the small town in New Jersey where I grew up. It was 1966, Kenya was newly independent, and former colonists were reluctantly giving up their privileges. As an adolescent, I struggled to negotiate the shifting social norms and outright racism I encountered during our two-year stay in East Africa. I often fell short, caught between my desire to fit in and the egalitarian ideals I had absorbed from a family of social justice activists. Those memories inspired this personal essay. [7]

BELLA HOLLINGWORTH is a watercolor artist and collagist. She was born in Madeira, Portugal and now lives in San Diego, California with her husband, Stanley, a short fiction writer and pianist. She earned a bachelor's degree from the Massachusetts College of Art and a graduate degree in counseling from the University of Bridgeport in Connecticut. She has exhibited her award winning artwork in California for the past thirty years. [18, 101]

SANDRA SHAW HOMER has lived in Costa Rica for 24 years, where she has taught languages and worked as a translator and environmental activist. For several years she wrote a regular column, Local Color, for the English-language weekly *The Tico Times*. She became a Costa Rican citizen in 2002. Her writing has appeared on a few blogs, notably http://www.allysonlatta.ca/2013/12/04/travelling-to-write-reflections-aboard-a-cargo-ship-an-essay-by-sandra-shaw-homer/ and http://www.livingabroadincostarica.com. Her first travel memoir, *Letters from the Pacific*, is available in paperback and as an e-book. [129]

UNA NICHOLS HYNUM: At the age where I don't get out much, so I'm writing from memory and hoping others will connect to some of the fun of looking back...most of what I remember had a least some elements of fun mixed with all the other things life throws at us. I hope I have captured that. [41, 298, 324]

BARBARA NUXALL ISOM: Let's see – a wonderful 75th Birthday party; a Viking River Cruise in Russia; recognition of a specific quilt; and now another story to be published in *OASIS Journal*. If only I could repeat this year! The first 20 years of my life were spent on the other side of the state in the Wallowa Mountains and so much of my writing is a recollection of that time. "The Kick Is Up and It's Good" is a more recent experience. Yes, the first home football game was last Friday night, and yes, we were there. [295]

TERRIE JACKS has taught school, substituted and currently volunteers as a tutor. When her two sons were young, she made up stories to tell them. Now her grandchildren give her inspirations for stories and poems. Several of her poems have been published in Missouri Baptist University's literary magazine, *Cantos, Fireflies Light*, and *OASIS Journal 2012*; several stories have appeared in the Missouri Baptist University chapbooks, *Right Word* and *Flash*. Recently, she has been published in *Cattails*, and she has been illustrating stories published in the *Korean-American Journal*. [218]

JOANNE JOHNSON holds a multi-disciplinary M.A. in Special Education, Adult Education, Gerontology, and a B.A. in Art/English from the University of the Incarnate Word, San Antonio, Texas. She has published three children's books, one Sci-fi novel, *Nephilim Awakened*, and recently finished a mystery novel, *The Voice*. Her love of New Mexico continues to inspire her quirky short stories that always include at least one native-American Indian as a main character. [97]

LEONA JONES: I was thrilled to learn that "Gone Too Soon" and "Twelve Days of Christmas" were accepted for *OASIS Journal 2014*. In my 82 years I have written just for fun until I enrolled a year ago in a creative writing course at Clackamas Community College with Pat Arnold. She encourages her students to send their best work for possible publication in *OASIS Journal*. When I told Pat my good news, she sounded as joyful as I felt. I've been recovering from a severe illness the past 6 weeks, so this news gave me a much needed lift. [32, 85]

HELEN JONES-SHEPHERD, born in New York, received her B.A. and M.A. in English Composition & Literature in California, where she taught English Composition, Literature, and Children's Literature for many years at Cal State, San Bernardino, Riverside Community College, and others through 2013. Several of her stories and poems have been published in other editions of *OASIS Journal*. A vacation trip to the mountains prompted these intriguing memories of fishing and bear encounters in "A Beary, Scary Mountain Visit." [43]

CAROLE KALIHER, born in New Orleans, Louisiana, the fifth of six children, always loved to read and write. Transplanted to California in 1946, she worked for Pacific Bell Telephone until marrying Jim Kaliher in 1959. Attended college while rearing six sons, and currently enjoys her fourteen grandchildren. After losing her husband in 1997, followed his advice: "Get back to your writing." Published in local papers, magazines, and *OASIS Journal*, she facilitates a writing class in California, where she receives inspiration, support, and friendship from her fellow writers. This is a true story of her time in Ireland. [163]

YASUE AOKI KIDD was born and raised in Japan. Now living in California, she finds creative outlet in writing, both in Japanese and English. Since 1995, she has been a publishing member of a Tanka group in Japan. (Tanka is the oldest form of poetry in Japan, predating even haiku.) She enjoys writing tanka, and also contributes essays and critiques to the tanka magazine. She has been writing a memoir in English for her children and grandchildren. "Our First Valentine's Day" is an excerpt from her memoir. [23]

WILLIAM KILLIAN: The reason I write is because I like reading what I write. These three poems, "Give me a newspaper," "Mark's Chair," and "Going home to kill," are no exception. A small percentage of my Zip Code responds well to my poetry. All my poems start with photography. I have no camera, but I see them, and they write me into a corner. Then I paint some images on paper to help me get on with life. [68, 291, 351]

LINDA KLEIN: I have been writing poetry since the age of 15. I am now a senior citizen and in my second year of an OASIS poetry workshop. In 1996 I had a poem published by the National Library of Poetry. It was my first attempt at publication. This submission was my second. I am so pleased that it has been accepted. The poem is about my brother Michael's death at the age of 17 from Hodgkin's Lymphoma. Michael was my only sibling. He died at home in my arms. [238]

JANET KREITZ: I have been taking writing classes through OASIS for about five years. I hope soon to finish a book about a family that purchased my house in 1922. [196]

RICHARD LAMPL: This is the (alliterative) sixth successful short story submission to *OASIS Journal* for this author. Mr. Lampl turned to writing fiction as a hobby to relieve the boredom of his paying job – writing trade books on aerospace facts and figures for a book publishing company. He shares this year's entry with four others from a Bethesda, Maryland writing group that has been in continuous existence for more than 30 years. Look for entries from the others in this no-name writing group: Lois Godel, Helen Moriarty, Judith O'Neill, and Barbara Scheiber. [197]

MARLENE C. LITTLE lives in Arizona. Her first poem was published in a 1960 national anthology. Subsequent works have been published in newsletters, bulletins, newspapers, websites, *OASIS Journal 2013*, and *Avocet*, a journal of nature poetry. In 2012, two of her poems were featured in *Arizona: 100 Years, 100 Poems, 100 Poets*. A business education instructor for many years in Arizona, she is currently retired from 20 years of Federal service. "My Father Used To…" was the result of a recent writing class assignment. After receiving an old wedding photo from a relative, "Faceless Bride" revisited a childhood memory. [119, 212]

JEAN BRIER LUSK: Born and raised in Honolulu, Hawaii, December 7, 1941, held special meaning for me. "December Brunch" tells how I first heard of that event. I have always enjoyed writing poetry and was first published at eight years old in a national children's magazine. I have published a book of poems, *Patterns on Parquet*, been published in Portland Community College newspaper and *The Oregonian*, and in three volumes of *Poetry From the Heart*. Memoir writing is now my passion, and these are combined in a volume, *Prose From the Heart*. At this publication I will be 93 years old. [59, 195, 243]

SERETTA MARTIN serves as a regional editor for *San Diego Poetry Annual*, an associate editor for *Poetry International, Synesthesia Literary Journal*, and *Blue VorText Publishers Journal*. She teaches poetry at San Diego Writers Ink and in schools. A Philip Levine Prize (2012) and Washington Prize (2014) semi-finalist, her second book, *The Art of Climbing Shadows*, is forthcoming. Published credits include: *Serving House Journal, Web del Sol, Poetry International, California Quarterly, Margie, City Works, A Year in Ink, Modern Haiku, Weave, San Diego Poetry Annual, OASIS Journal* and others. She has an MFA in Creative Writing from San Diego State University. [128]

MARILYN L. KISH MASON: My "farm girl" life ages behind me, my thoughts often journey back to a slower pace of life. Although I would not change much about my life since then, the memories of those days on the farm are not far from my mind. My father was a joy, and I still miss him. I enjoy penning stories about him to give to my children and grandchildren, so he may live on as I remember him. Mary Harker's OASIS poetry class gives me the venue and support to make each poem better. [83, 118]

MARGARET S. MCKERROW: We hear so much about elder abuse these days that I was inspired to write "Golden Ties" after observing the beautiful generosity of spirit and loving way the woman in my poem cared for her mother. I am grateful that I can continue to share my poetry with Mary Harker's OASIS class and the San Diego Poetry Annual. [170]

WYNN MELTON is 83 years of age and resides in St. Clair, Missouri. He was always been interested in writing, but he only began taking OASIS writing classes about seven years ago. He is currently involved with a peer-led group and is entertaining his fellow writers with a series of stories about a priest named Father Bill McHeck. [207]

Award-winning Tucson author SUSAN CUMMINS MILLER, a research affiliate of the University of Arizona's Southwest Institute for Research on Women, writes the Frankie MacFarlane, Geologist, mysteries. *Fracture*, fifth in the series, was a Finalist for the WILLA Award in Contemporary Fiction. Her latest novel, *Chasm*, set in Grand Canyon National Park, will be released in 2015. In addition to writing fiction, Miller edited *A Sweet, Separate Intimacy: Women*

Writers of the American Frontier, 1800-1922. Her award-winning poems, essays, and short stories have been published in regional journals and anthologies. Her Website/Blog is at www.susancumminsmiller.com. [247]

SARAH TRAISTER MOSKOVITZ: Both poems included in this book come from the same creative place, one of very deep appreciation of my mother and my husband. The older I get, the more I recognize how fortunate I have been to have lived long with the love of these two wonderful people. "Swan" is about Clara Rubenstein Traister, who was orphaned very young, but miraculously became a very giving mother without having had that model. "Power" is about my husband, Itzik (Isaac) Moskovitz, also loving and generous, whose love has been tried and true for the past 68 years. Lucky me. [156, 347]

MICHAEL B. MOSSMAN was born in Alton, Illinois, graduated from Southern Illinois University in Edwardsville, and received a Masters from the University of Oklahoma at Norman. Michael spent thirty-three years in the fields of Elementary and Special Education. Now retired, he spends his time making art and writing stories. Michael's story, "The Last Letter," appeared in *OASIS Journal 2008*. "A Date to Remember" appeared in *OASIS Journal 2010*. His current story, "I Would Have Been a Hero If..." is a fictionalized story about being a football hero. Michael and his wife, Barbara, live in Edwardsville, Illinois. [293]

WILFRED F. MOSSMAN was born in Calhoun County, Illinois. He attended school in Grafton, Illinois and graduated from Jersey Township High School. While in high school, Wilfred was a leading actor in school plays and was interested in creative writing. Because he lived close to the river bluffs, his poems were often about nature. After high school, Wilfred was employed by Shell Oil Company in Wood River, Illinois until the time of his death. He is Michael Mossman's father. [235]

ELEANOR WHITNEY NELSON has spent most of her professional career as an exploration geologist working abroad, often in remote, primitive areas. Although she has experienced many breath-holding adventures in those places, one of the most harrowing events took place right at home in the U.S., the subject for this year's *OASIS Journal* entry. Retired and living in Arizona, Nelson devotes her time to writing. Her short stories, memoirs, and poems can be read in several anthologies, including: *The Story Teller, A Way with Murder, Chicken Soup for the Soul (Dog Lover's; Loving Our Dogs)* and nine previous *OASIS Journals*. [49]

KATHLEEN A. O'BRIEN began writing two years after the death of her husband in 2000. "In High Gear" was written for a class assignment: "re-purpose cliches." "Breakfast in Bed" is a recent event with a grandson. Hobbies include: reading, writing poetry, dancing, attending plays and workshops, gardening, volunteering for hospice, travel, tent camping with family. Kathleen writes that she has become addicted to the iPod game, "Bookworm." A former teacher and LPN, she is now retired and loving it. She looks forward to a sleepover in one grandson's new treehouse and visiting her oldest grandson, a freshman at Ithaca College. [58, 288]

JUDITH O'NEILL, a former Peace Corps Volunteer (Dominican Republic, 1963-65), retired teacher, and technical writer now living in Virginia, has published short stories in *Ellery Queen's* and *Alfred Hitchcock's Mystery Magazines* and in numerous short story anthologies. "High Noon in the Garden of Good and Evil" is fiction, but was inspired by events and spoken family narratives from her childhood in the Midwest of the 1940s. [149]

BARBARA OSTREM: It is a pleasant encouragement to be accepted for *OASIS Journal* a fourth time. I am retired, a widow, and have a group of friends who share creative writing pursuits, our own book club, and gardening interests. My two married daughters and their husbands, five grandchildren, plus two great-granddaughters delight and enrich my life. Soon to be eighty, I look forward to continuing to live independently – and writing! [219]

BONNIE PAPENFUSS: In addition to writing book reviews for her local newspaper, Bonnie enjoys writing poetry about nature and the perils of growing older. She is a member of the Santa Cruz Chapter of the Society of Southwestern Authors. Bonnie has had poems published in three separate anthologies: Stuart Watkins' book, *Arizona: 100 Years, 100 Poems, 100 Poets*; OASIS Journal 2013; and *Mother Nature's Trail*, an anthology published by Wolf Creek Habitat, Brookville, Indiana. [81, 268]

DOROTHY PARCEL: I have been writing since I learned many years ago, and lately, because I'm too old to go to other planets to notice all the little things that make my life so much fun, I spend all my time in this one. I belong to a weekly writer's club and write a Message each meeting. I am only 86 years old, and hope to continue this for many more years. *OASIS Journal* has been a blessing for so many of us, and I wish you and your staff all the best for many years to come. [263]

ROBERT POURIEA: I started writing a couple years ago at the retirement home where I was living and never thought that anything I wrote would ever be published. The first thing I wrote, "The Broken Limb," was in *OASIS Journal 2013*. I was so proud, I bought books for everyone in the family. I'm 84 years old. I can't say I had a good education, but I did serve 20 years in the Navy, married, we had two girls, and lost my wife after 52 years of marriage. Writing has been a blessing for me. [303]

JEAN MARIE PURCELL: I posit most writers are loners. We play at gregariousness to get along and fool most people. I love rhyme and hope to live a few more years to push it. I'm eighty-seven. [287]

SABINE RAMAGE was inspired to write this poem by hiking at Point Reyes National Seashore over time and exploring coastal Northern California with her friend, Greer. Its peaceful spaciousness and breathtaking scenery provided a stark contrast to the overwhelming stimuli of modern life. Sabine lives in the Portland, Oregon area, where she pursues adventures in cooking, gardening, photography, studying foreign languages, travel, and reading. She joined a writing class a year ago, with the encouragement of her husband and her friend, Misty. [122]

DAVID RAY is author of 23 books, including *Hemingway: A Desperate Life* (Whirlybird Press), *When* (Howling Dog Press), and *After Tagore: Poems Inspired by Rabindranath Tagore* (Nirala Editions). *Music of Time: Selected & New Poems* (Backwaters Press) offers selections from fifteen previous volumes, several of which received national awards. *The Endless Search* (Soft Skull Press) is a memoir. David is an emeritus professor of the University of Missouri-Kansas City's English department, where he was founding editor of *New Letters* magazine and *New Letters on the Air*. He now lives in Tucson and continues to write poetry, fiction, and essays (www.davidraypoet.com). [176]

JUDY RAY's most recent poetry book is *To Fly Without Wings* (Helicon Nine Editions), about which Richard Wilbur wrote: "The poems of *To Fly Without Wings* see with a fine descriptive eye, but also and always…with compassion or joy." Earlier books include *Pigeons in the Chandeliers* and chapbooks *Fishing in Green Waters* and *Judy Ray: Greatest Hits*. A collection of personal essays is forthcoming from Whirlybird Press. More information at (www.davidraypoet.com/JudyRay). [345]

A native southern Californian, LYNDA RIESE lives in San Diego with her husband of thirty years and her two rescue dogs. She began writing seriously twenty years ago and has published poems in *Calyx, Onthebus, Poet Lore*, and other small press literary magazines in print and on the net. When she's not writing or taking endless photographs of her dogs, she works as an antique dealer specializing in vintage and Victorian jewelry. She'd like to thank Mary Harker and the San Diego OASIS poetry group for their generous support and invaluable critiques. [135, 237]

MURIEL SANDY: Journalistic-style travel writing has been an integral part of my life for 20 years, with publication in San Jose Mercury News, Chicago Tribune, Toronto Sun, and South China Morning Post. Personal narrative writing is very different, so for the last two years I have been a member of San Diego OASIS Creative Writing Class under Caroline McCullagh, a published author in her own right. I also attend San Diego Writers and Editors Guild, and volunteer in the travel section of San Diego OASIS, as an usher for Old Globe Theatre, and am Usher Captain for San Diego Symphony. [19]

NANCY SANDWEISS has been a life-long observer of the people and world around her, finding inspiration at every turn. She tries to capture life's ironies and complexities, pointing to connections in seemingly unrelated events and humor in our shared human follies. Her poetry has been published in previous volumes of *OASIS Journal* and in *San Diego Poetry Annual* and *A Year in Ink*. She is grateful to Mary Harker, her classmates at OASIS San Diego, and Bluestocking Poets for their helpful critiques and ongoing support and encouragement. [22, 220]

PHYLLIS SELTZER wrote "Onion Eggs" as part of a journey down memory lane, her process of discovering herself as a child, teenager, young bride, new mother, divorcee, new wife, full-time mother of three inherited children before birthing their fifth child. Morphing into mother-in-law, granny, world traveler, senior citizen, business owner, writer, artist, potter, poet, daughter of an aging parent, caregiver. Now regrettably a widow, living alone and, for the first time, reflecting on her Journey. [145]

Critics describe BARBARA SCHEIBER's novel, *We'll Go to Coney Island* (Sowilo Press, 2014), as "exquisitely written and remarkable for its detail and insights into family life" (for information about obtaining the book, see http://amzn.to/1giw24b). She includes several stories from *OASIS Journal* – including "Sycamore Farm," 2005 Fiction Winner. Retired from journalism, Barbara began writing fiction, publishing stories and personal essays in literary journals and anthologies, including *Antietam Review*, *Fine Print*, *OASIS Journal*, and *Whetstone*. Her novella, *The Queen of Sheba*, received an Individual Artist Award from Maryland Arts Council. She lives in Gaithersburg, Maryland with her husband of 66 years. [137]

SHIRLEY SHATSKY: I have been a member of Deborah Clayton's poetry class at OASIS for a good number of years. Through her inspiring teaching I have grown as a poet. I also belong to a critique group where the women are both helpful and supportive in their comments. I work with sick children and their parents as a volunteer at a large children's hospital in Los Angeles. This work is an inspiration to me. I've had a number of poems published in journals. [266]

MITZI SKRBIN: An 80-year-old widow, mother, grandmother, and busy retiree, I am active in my church, AARP chapter, and Silver Sneakers. I joined OASIS Scribes, a writing group, in 2006. We stayed together after our OASIS Chapter closed, and now meet in the back room of our public library. I love to write (especially poetry) and have been published in OASIS Journal in 2006, 2007, 2008, 2010, and 2013. Thank you for this opportunity to share our work. [261]

SHERRY STONEBACK: A nurse for 30 years, I just this week retired and hope to volunteer in the future. "The Garden" was started in a workshop with Alice Carney in Texas when I was on vacation three years ago. I love my garden; it gives me a positive start in the morning, no matter what I face for the day. Pat Arnold, my Creative Writing teacher at Clackamas Community College, has kindly encouraged me to finish some of my work. Most of them are memoirs, but Pat has encouraged creativity I never thought I had! [245]

IRENE THOMAS: Thanks to Pat Arnold and her Creative Writing Class for encouraging me. Yesterday, for the first time, I read a copy of *OASIS Journal* and found it to be amazing. My peers are a very talented group and, if I had read it sooner, I probably would have been afraid to send "Mississippi Memoirs." I have been an avid reader from the age of four to the present, and have enjoyed writing all my life. Now I am in the process of adding to the story of my life facts that my children have never known. [35, 148]

KEITH TRAMMELL: I am thrilled once again to be published in *Oasis Journal 2014*, the first time being "A Perfect Match," *Oasis Journal 2013*. I appreciate the encouragement I receive from Pat Arnold in her creative writing and memoir writing classes and from all of my wonderfully creative classmates in Milwaukie, Oregon. Although "Losing Someone Close" is specifically about the frustrations over the demise of our traditional print media, it relates perhaps more broadly to our aging population's struggles to learn, understand, and keep pace with what seems to be an ever-accelerating use of new means of communication of all types. [349]

PHYLIS WARADY: Her award-winning short fiction, essays, and light verse frequently appear in anthologies, quarterlies, reviews, and journals in the U.S. and Canada. This past April, her short story, "God Bless Marilyn," was published for the 4th time in the current edition of *Fresh Ink Literary Journal*. As for the prestigious *OASIS Journal*, 2006, 2009 and 2012 editions feature one of her short stories. Even more gratifying, 2014 contains her essay, "A Moveable Feast," written in praise of the public library system. [277]

MO WEATHERS is a native Oregonian who grew up roaming through the forests and plains of Oregon, trying unsuccessfully at times to stay out of trouble. Following a hitch in the Navy, he attended the University of Oregon, graduated with a degree in Mathematics, then served 22 years in the Air Force, retiring in 1987. Lois, his wife of 55 years, is a retired social worker that he met on a blind date. Their son is an aerospace engineer and their daughter is a pastor. "Thrown Rod" details one of Mo's early lessons in the importance of car maintenance. [289]

In the past, ANNE WHITLOCK has enjoyed studying French, Russian, Swedish, and Spanish. Language has always delighted her – its sounds, rhythms, and imagery. That is why she chose in 1978 to get her Masters in Linguistics and why she continues to teach a French reading class at San Diego OASIS. A recent trip to Norway rekindled her interest in the Scandinavian branch of Indo-European, and she is currently reading a series of Norwegian novels set against the background of World War II. Other interests are present day politics and animal rights. [6, 16]

JEFFREY WIDEN was raised in Los Angeles. He became a sports medicine doctor who practiced in Ashland, Oregon. He has journaled for thirty-five years. He wrote a column on sports injuries for a local paper and has written both prose and poetry in many classes he's taken over the years. He's been published anonymously in the national magazine of AA and in other periodicals. He now lives in Portland, Oregon with his wife, Lois, who edits most of his work. He is currently writing a memoir that will reflect his varied, interesting, and ofttimes exciting life. [153]

NEAL WILGUS has had poems and/or short stories in every *OASIS Journal* since 2006; he won the Best Fiction Contest in 2006 and 2012. His short story this time is a sort-of-a-sequel to "Moxon's Master" (1909) by Ambrose Bierce, and incorporates material from two other Bierce tales. It reflects Neal's feelings about the high tech world that is emerging. He has been writing poetry, fiction reviews, and satire for over fifty years and is published in print publications in the US, UK, and Canada. He is retired and lives in Corrales, New Mexico with his pet typewriter. [333]

ILA WINSLOW: 77 RAH's and 3 WOW's for my third publication with *OASIS Journal*. Thank you, Leila, for creating a niche for the 'Over 50' gang. Further honors go to my classmates in dubbing my play-on-words style as Ila-isms. "How Many" is a lighthearted example of me. Thank you, Pat Arnold, my creative writing instructor, for releasing my imagination to Paper. [155]

KEN YAROS is an alumnus of Albright College. He received his DDS degree from Temple University. Having spent six years as a dentist with the Air Force and seven years of service with the Connecticut Air National Guard, he has had the opportunity to serve in numerous locations around the world. Now retired after thirty-five years of teaching and private practice, he has turned his hand to writing human interest stories and fables. He is an active member and contributing author for the San Diego Writers/Editors Guild. Currently he is penning a movie script and a TV series. [89]

JOAN ZEKAS: Political pins have long been used to trumpet political candidates. But Madeleine Albright was a game changer when she used her lapel pins to focus high level political talks. It tickled me to see that, in the midst of military men dripping with medals and various insignia, she found this way to insert herself and to compete. Our Pittsburgh Scribes will again have our *OASIS Journal* Book Celebration, in April 2015. This is my 7th acceptance in the *Journal*, and I am thankful for these wonderful writing opportunities. [285]

ORDER INFORMATION

Copies of *OASIS Journal 2008* through *2014* are available for $14 at:

www.amazon.com
www.barnesandnoble.com

Copies of *OASIS Journal* from previous years (2002-2007) may be ordered at a discount from the publisher at the address below as availability allows. Please enclose $10.00 for each book ordered, plus $3.00 shipping & handling for the total order to be sent to one address.

Please make checks payable to Imago Press. Arizona residents add $0.81 sales tax for each book ordered.

Proceeds from the sale of this book go toward the production of next year's *OASIS Journal*. Your purchase will help us further the creative efforts of older adults. Thank you for your support.

To view submission forms, information about *OASIS Journal*, and winning selections from the current anthology, go to: www.oasisjournal.org

Imago Press
3710 East Edison
Tucson AZ 85716

CPSIA information can be obtained at www.ICGtesting.com
Printed in the USA
BVOW07s1630091014

370111BV00002B/4/P